REPORT OF THE STATES
REORGANISATION COMMISSION

REPORT OF THE STATES REORGANISATION COMMISSION

1955

MANOHAR
2021

First published 1955
Reprinted 2021

ISBN 978-93-90729-89-0

Published by
Ajay Kumar Jain *for*
Manohar Publishers & Distributors
4753/23 Ansari Road, Daryaganj
New Delhi 110 002

Printed at
Replika Press Pvt. Ltd.

CONTENTS

Part IV. Administrative and Allied Matters

Notes and Summary

Appendices

INTRODUCTION

On 22nd December, 1953, the Prime Minister made a statement in Parliament to the effect that a Commission would be appointed to examine "objectively and dispassionately" the question of the reorganisation of the States of the Indian Union "so that the welfare of the people of each constituent unit as well as the nation as a whole is promoted". This was followed by the appointment of this Commission under the Resolution of the Government of India in the Ministry of Home Affairs, No. 53/69/53-Public, dated 29th December, 1953 (Appendix A).

2. The task before the Commission has been set out in paragraph 7 of this Resolution in the following terms:

> "The Commission will investigate the conditions of the problem, the historical background, the existing situation and the bearing of all important and relevant factors thereon. They will be free to consider any proposal relating to such reorganisation. The Government expect that the Commission would, in the first instance, not go into the details, but make recommendations in regard to the broad principles which should govern the solution of this problem and, if they so choose, the broad lines on which particular States should be reorganised, and submit interim reports for the consideration of Government."

3. Under this Resolution the Commission were required to make recommendations to the Government of India not later than 30th June, 1955. This period was subsequently extended to 30th September, 1955.

4. According to their terms of reference, the Commission were at liberty to devise their own procedure for collecting information and for ascertaining public opinion. After giving careful thought to the procedure to be followed, the Commission issued a Press Note on 23rd February, 1954 (Appendix B), inviting written memoranda from members of the public as well as public associations interested in the problem of the reorganisation of States. The relevant portion of this Press Note is given below:

> "The States Reorganisation Commission, after giving due consideration to the procedure that would be most suitable for the expeditious execution of the task entrusted to them, have decided to dispense with a questionnaire.

> They invite members of the public as well as public associations interested in the problem of the reorganisation of States to put their views and suggestions before the Commission by submitting written memoranda on matters on which they feel they can assist them. The Commission expect that wherever any concrete suggestions are made they will be supported by historical and statistical data and, if any proposal regarding the formation of any new State or States is made, it will, if possible, be accompanied by one or more maps, as the case may be."

5. It was announced in this Press Note that all memoranda should reach the Commission by 24th April, 1954. However, on account of the keen interest evinced by public organisations as well as the people in general in various aspects of reorganisation, and the nature of our enquiries, we did not adhere to this time limit, and communications ranging from simple telegrams indicating the wishes of particular localities to well-considered memoranda dealing with the problem as a whole continued to come almost to the very end of our appointed task. The total number of such documents received by us reached the figure of 1,52,250. The bulk of these communications is accounted for by simple telegrams, printed resolutions etc., denoting the wishes of particular localities to be included within one or the other unit. The number of well-considered memoranda does not exceed about 2,000.

6. Side by side with the study of these memoranda, we commenced interviewing people from all walks of life. These interviews were held in private to enable the persons interviewed to express their views freely and frankly. The interviews started in New Delhi from 1st March, 1954, and were continued till about the end of July, 1955. We started on 8th April, 1954, on our all-India tour during the course of which we covered virtually the entire country and visited 104 places which involved travelling over thirty eight thousand miles. We have interviewed over nine thousand persons.

7. We made every effort to get a complete cross-section of public opinion. Care was taken to see that all those who represent public opinion were heard unless they were themselves averse to expressing any views. The people interviewed included members of political parties, public associations, social workers, journalists, municipal and district board representatives and other people representing cultural, educational, linguistic and local interests. The purpose of the all-India tour was not only to ascertain public opinion

but also to make on-the-spot studies at different places and to understand the background of the problem and the popular sentiment on various aspects of reorganisation.

8. Under our terms of reference, it was open to us to submit an interim report, but at a fairly early stage we came to the conclusion that the submission of any interim report would not be feasible. The problems in peninsular India and some parts of the country outside it are inter-connected and we, therefore, did not consider it desirable to formulate our views on any question in isolation. We accordingly decided to study the various problems over the entire country before coming to any final conclusions about any particular region. This excluded the possibility of our submitting an interim report.

9. In our examination of the various proposals for reorganisation we have mainly relied on statistical figures as given in the Censuses of various years. The Census figures for 1951 have been compiled according to what are known as "Census tracts". It has, therefore, been difficult to estimate the mother-tongue figures on a taluk or tehsil-wise basis. We were given to understand that it might be possible to make estimates of taluk or tehsil-wise figures on the basis of certain statistical assumptions. Having regard, however, to the controversies which surround such assumptions, we took into consideration only the figures as printed in different Census reports in reaching our conclusions.

10. We have been cautious also with our financial estimates. We have studied in some detail the possible financial position and the economic potentialities of each of the proposed units. We have been reluctant, however, to lay undue emphasis on these estimates as figures of revenue and expenditure depend, to some extent, on imponderable factors. It may be theoretically possible to raise revenue in a particular unit according to a phased taxation programme, but whether such taxation will be imposed depends, at least to some extent, on political considerations. Control of expenditure in the broadest sense is also influenced by non-economic considerations. We did not consider it safe, therefore, to project present figures of revenue and expenditure into the future.

11. On the other hand, these financial estimates have some validity, because no unit will really start from scratch. It will have a certain financial heritage and a pattern of revenue and expenditure to begin with, and the picture of its financial position, at least in the near future, is not likely to be strikingly different from the present

pattern. We have given some weight, moreover, to a study of the potentialities of economic development in the proposed units. Our financial estimates, therefore, represent only broad judgments of what is probable.

12. Our report is divided into four Parts. Part I deals with the conditions of the problem of reorganisation of States and its historical background. Part II deals with the factors bearing on reorganisation. Part III contains our proposals for the reorganisation of the existing units. In Part IV we have discussed briefly the administrative and other implications of reorganisation and measures which might be adopted to minimise the stress of transition.

13. Before we conclude this introductory Chapter we wish to place on record our deep appreciation of the invaluable assistance we have received from the Secretariat of the Commission and all members of the staff. Had it not been for their ungrudging help and devoted work, cheerfully and efficiently rendered, it would not have been possible for us to complete our difficult task within the period at our disposal. We should also like to express our thanks to members of the public and representatives of political organisations and public associations who responded to our Press Note by submitting written memoranda containing much useful information and statistical and other material.

PART I

THE CONDITIONS OF THE PROBLEM

CHAPTER I

STATES OF THE INDIAN UNION

14. The existing structure of the States of the Indian Union is partly the result of accident and the circumstances attending the growth of the British power in India and partly a by-product of the historic process of the integration of former Indian States. The division of India during the British period into British provinces and Indian States was itself fortuitous and had no basis in Indian history. It was a mere accident that, as a result of the abandonment, after the upheaval of 1857, of the objective of extending the British dominion by absorbing princely territories, the surviving States escaped annexation. The map of the territories annexed and directly administered by the British was also not shaped by any rational or scientific planning but "by the military, political or administrative exigencies or conveniences of the moment".[1]

15. The provincial organisation of British India was meant to serve a two-fold purpose: to uphold the direct authority of the supreme power in areas of vital economic and strategic importance and to fill the political vacuum arising from the destruction or collapse of the former principalities. Of these two, the first was obviously the primary objective, and it required the suppression of the traditional regional and dynastic loyalties. This was sought to be achieved by erasing old frontiers and by creating new provinces which ignored natural affinities and common economic interests. The administrative organisation of these provinces was intended to secure their subordination to the Central Government, which was the agent and instrument of imperial control exercised from London. This process inevitably led to the formation of units with no natural affinity.

16. During the early phase of the rise of the British power in India, moreover, the accretion of territories was gradual and the need for the rationalisation of administrative units was not seriously felt. British dominion in India started with small settlements in the coastal regions established at different times during the seventeenth century. From the middle of the eighteenth century they

---

1. Report on Indian Constitutional Reforms, 1918, para. 39.

provided the bases from which British authority expanded inwards by the acquisition of further territories which were attached to one or the other of the three presidencies.

17. The Presidencies of Madras and Bombay had practically acquired their final shape by 1801 and 1827 respectively. Accretion of fresh territories to the Bengal Presidency, however, continued up to the year 1865.

18. The Charter Act of 1833 had provided for the creation of a fourth presidency out of the overgrown Presidency of Bengal, to be called the Agra Presidency. It was, however, considered expedient later to set up a less expensive form of government for the new province, and accordingly the North-West Provinces were set up under a Lt.-Governor in 1836 by detaching from Bengal all British territories west of Bihar. The Punjab, annexed in 1849, was the next province to be formed. It extended at that time up to the then north-west frontier of India. Placed first under a Board of Administration and later, in 1853, under a Chief Commissioner, the Punjab was made a Lt.-Governor's province on the transfer of Delhi to it in 1859.

19. Oudh, annexed in 1856, constituted a Chief Commissionership until it was joined to the North-West Provinces in 1877. The Central Provinces were formed in 1861 by taking the Saugor and Narbada districts out of the North-West Provinces and joining them with the territories of the Raja of Nagpur that had been acquired in 1854. Assam, attached to the Bengal Presidency on its acquisition in 1826, was made a separate Chief Commissioner's province in 1874. In 1901 the strategically important north-west frontier regions were detached from the Punjab and constituted into a separate Chief Commissioner's province. This also resulted in the North-West Provinces and Oudh being renamed the United Provinces of Agra and Oudh.

20. Thus far the formation of provinces had been mainly governed by considerations of administrative convenience and economy and by reasons of military strategy and security. To the extent, therefore, there was a conscious or deliberate design behind the demarcation of the territories of administrative units, it was grounded in imperial interests or the exigencies of a foreign government and not in the actual needs, wishes or affinities of the people. Administrative convenience itself required compact units with some measure of homogeneity. In some cases, therefore, various factors

conducive to the growth of natural units operated in the background. They were, however, subordinate to the prime considerations of administrative and military exigencies.

21. With the emergence of nationalism as a new factor in the last quarter of the nineteenth century, the policy of balance and counterpoise began to override purely administrative considerations in making territorial changes, though on such occasions arguments based on administrative needs and other principles were also put forward. Thus, Bengal, undoubtedly unwieldy as it included at that time also Bihar and Orissa, was divided with a view at least as much to dispersing revolutionary elements as to securing more manageable administrative units.

22. In 1905 Bengal was divided to form, along with Assam, the provinces of (a) East Bengal and Assam and (b) Bengal, which included the western part of Bengal, Bihar, Orissa and Chota Nagpur. The change in the outlook regarding provincial boundaries was reflected in the famous Resolution of Lord Curzon, dated 19th July, 1905, which, while providing for the partition of Bengal, also commented on the proposed territorial realignment of areas between Madras, the Central Provinces and Bengal. Thus, "reasons of administrative expediency, arising out of the peculiar linguistic and racial conditions and the geographical conformation of Ganjam and the Agency tracts of Vizagapatam" were cited against the transfer of these areas from the Government of Madras. "Commercial considerations" were relied upon for the continued retention of the districts of Chota Nagpur under the Bengal Government. The linguistic principle was mentioned in support of the transfer of certain Oriya-speaking tracts from the Central Provinces to Bengal; and the principle of close contact between the governors and the governed was put forward to justify the concentration of the "typical Muhammadan population" of Bengal in a separate province of East Bengal and Assam.

23. Six years later the partition of Bengal was annulled, though it was considered impossible both on "political and on administrative grounds" to revert to the *status quo ante*. In 1912 Assam was reconstituted into a Chief Commissioner's province and the eastern and western parts of Bengal were rejoined to form the province of Bengal. At the same time, Bihar, with Orissa and Chota Nagpur, was constituted into a separate province of Bihar and Orissa.

24. These changes were made in order to provide convenient administrative units and to satisfy the legitimate aspirations of the

expediency as to negative any presumption that it has been exacted by clamour or agitation".

25. The shape of the provinces and the principles underlying their formation, before and after 1905, continued, however, to be very far from satisfactory. As late as 1930 British statesmen themselves admitted that there were in India "only a number of administrative areas" which had "grown up almost haphazard as the result of conquest, supersession of former rulers or administrative convenience".[1] The desirability of a reorganisation of provinces on a rational basis was pointed out earlier by the authors of the Report on Indian Constitutional Reforms, 1918, who had observed: "We are impressed with the artificial, and often inconvenient character of existing administrative units".[2] The Indian Statutory Commission, 1930, endorsed this view and observed: "Although we are well aware of the difficulties encountered in all attempts to alter boundaries and of the administrative and financial complications that arise, we are making a definite recommendation for reviewing, and if possible resettling, the provincial boundaries of India at as early a date as possible".[3] The Commission recommended the examination of the question by a Boundaries Commission under a neutral chairman.[4]

26. The Commission made a special mention of Orissa. "An urgent case for consideration and treatment", it observed, "is that of the Oriya-speaking peoples, most, but not all, of whom are now included in Orissa, because we consider that so close a union as now exists between Orissa and Bihar is a glaring example of the artificial connection of areas which are not naturally related".[5]

27. The province of Orissa was created in 1936 by joining together the Oriya-speaking areas of the provinces of Bihar and Orissa, the Central Provinces and Madras.

1. Report of the Indian Statutory Commission, Vol. II, para. 25

2. Report on Indian Constitutional Reforms, 1918, para. 246.

3. Report of the Indian Statutory Commission, Vol. II, para. 25.

4. *Ibid*, para. 38.

5. *Ibid.*

Integration of the Indian States

28. The administrative units of British India have remained virtually intact after the achievement of Indian Independence. The only changes which have been made so far as these units are concerned are the formation of a separate Andhra State and the merger in these units of some of the territories of the former Indian States.

29. So far, however, as the former Indian States are concerned, the period immediately following the transfer of power to India saw a revolutionary change come over them with dramatic speed. Of about six hundred units known as Indian or princely States,

(a) 216 States having a population of a little over 19 millions were merged in the provinces;

(b) 61 States having a population of about 7 millions were constituted into new Centrally-administered units; and

(c) 275 States with a population of about 35 millions were integrated to create new administrative units, namely, Rajasthan, Madhya Bharat, Travancore-Cochin, Saurashtra and PEPSU.[1]

Only three States, namely, Hyderabad, Mysore and Jammu & Kashmir, survived these processes of integration, but the internal structure of these States as also their relationship with the Centre were cast into a new mould so as to fit them into the constitutional structure of India.

30. While factors such as linguistic and ethnic homogeneity or historical tradition were taken into consideration to the extent practicable in the process of integrating these diverse units with adjoining provinces or constituting them into separate administrative units, the compulsion of the dynamic urges of the time necessitated prompt decisions. A number of settlements, therefore, made in respect of these States had to be in the nature of transitional expedients.

31. The princely States, as they existed at the time of the transfer of power, were themselves in varying phases of development. Their integration into the new democratic Constitution of India involved many problems, both administrative and political. So far as the political structure was concerned, in most States it was a form of direct personal rule; and even in the States which had introduced some of the forms of democratic government, the personal authority of the Ruler was hardly affected. So far as administration was

---

1. White Paper on Indian States, 1950, para. 147.

concerned, while some of the larger States had developed a fairly efficient machinery, in most cases it was of a rudimentary character.

32. It was, therefore, inevitable that some of the features of the old order should be found in the Indian Constitution and leave an impress on the administrative and political structure of the units comprising territories of the erstwhile princely States.

Disparate status of the constituent units

33. A peculiar feature of the Indian Constitution is the disparate status of the constituent units of the Union. The Constitution recognises three categories of States and gives each category a pattern and status of its own. The status of the first two categories of States, *i.e.*, those specified in Parts A and B of Schedule I of the Constitution, is based on the concept of federalism. Apart from the institution of Rajpramukh, the main feature that distinguishes Part B States from Part A States is the provision contained in Article 371, which vests in the central executive supervisory authority over the governments of these States for a specified period. This provision is, no doubt, un-federal in character, but it does not alter the basic relationship between these States and the Centre, which essentially rests on the principle of a clear division of powers between the Centre and the States. Part C States, which rank lowest in the hierarchy, are, however, administered by the Centre on a unitary basis. The devolution of powers to the legislatures and governments of some of these States under the Government of Part C States Act, 1951, does not detract from the legislative authority of Parliament over these States or from the responsibility of the Union Government to Parliament for their administration.

34. Apart from the States of the Union, there are also territories specified in Part D of Schedule I, which form part of India. In respect of such territories as also of any territory comprised within the territory of India but not specified in this Schedule, the Central Government has not only full executive authority but also regulation-making power.[1]

Historical background of the classification of States

35. If the present alignment of the boundaries of States has been largely determined by the vicissitudes of British rule in India and the integration of the former Indian States, the same holds true also of their existing constitutional classification into different categories.

1. Constitution of India, Article 243.

36. Even before the Act of 1935 introduced, to a limited extent, the federal principle in the governance of this country, the relative status of administrative units *vis-a-vis* the Central Government had varied from one category to another. This was to a certain extent due to the historical reason that different parts of the country were acquired and their administration organised by the British at different times, so that they could not be patterned as units of an administrative structure constituted on a systematic and rational basis. Considerations of economy and administrative expediency also led the British rulers to give to newly-organised and smaller provinces less expensive and simpler government than that of the older, more settled, and developed provinces.

37. By the close of the nineteenth century, there were in existence three different forms of provincial governments, namely, those under a Governor and Executive Council, those administered by a Lieutenant Governor and those administered by a Chief Commissioner. Many of the British Indian provinces, such as Assam, Bihar and Orissa, the Central Provinces, the North-West Frontier Province, the Punjab and the United Provinces, passed through one or both of the earlier stages before acquiring the Governor-and-Council form of government.

38. The difference in the form of government of a province carried with it a difference in status. It is, no doubt, true in a sense that, after 1833, all the provincial governments became agents of the Central Government. Still the different categories were clearly distinguishable in their status. A broad distinction was made between territories which were under the immediate authority and management of the Central Government and those which were not. To the former category belonged all territories not included in Governorships or Lt.-Governorships, *i.e.*, the provinces administered through Chief Commissioners.

39. A distinction was also made between "major provinces" and "minor administrations". In the first category were included the Governors' provinces, Lt.-Governors' provinces and the two largest Chief Commissionerships, *i.e.*, Assam and the Central Provinces, whose Chief Commissioners were, in practice, entrusted with powers nearly as wide as those of a Lt.-Governor. All the other Chief Commissionerships were called "minor administrations" and were administered under the direct control of the Central Government acting, except in the case of Ajmer-Merwara, British Baluchistan and

the North-West Frontier Province, mainly through the Home Department. The North-West Frontier Province and British Baluchistan constituted a special class because of their strategic importance and special political problems. Central control over these, as well as over Ajmer-Merwara, was exercised through the Foreign and Political Department of the Government of India.[1] It was these "minor administrations" which, on account of their geographical position and other special characteristics, continued to be centrally-administered, while the territories which were initially placed under a Chief Commissioner mainly because of administrative expediency, acquired more advanced forms of government in course of time.

40. The Government of India Act, 1935, recognised, in the circumstances in which it was formulated, three categories of component units, namely, Governors' provinces, federating Indian States and Chief Commissioners' provinces. This classification is reflected in the grouping of the States of the Indian Union as Parts A, B and C States, except that not all the former Indian States are now represented by Part B States, a number of them having been merged in the provinces or consolidated into centrally-administered areas. A departure, however, from the old classification is the recognition under the Constitution of two categories of centrally-administered areas, namely, Part C States and Part D territories, as against only one such category recognised under the Act of 1935.

States not pre-existing sovereign units

41. Another important feature of the States of the Indian Union is that none of them represents a pre-existing sovereign unit. The units corresponding to the Part A States, namely, Governors' provinces, were administered until 1937 on a unitary basis, although from 1919 there was a certain measure of devolution of powers to the provinces. With the enforcement of the provincial part of the federal scheme embodied in the Act of 1935, certain subjects were assigned to the provinces on a federal basis, but the federal principle was heavily circumscribed by the special powers of the Governors, in the exercise of which they were answerable to the Governor-General. The Chief Commissioners' provinces, although recognised as constituent units of the federation, continued to be administered on a unitary basis. It was only in the case of the former Indian States that the right of accession on a negotiated basis was conceded. Rulers of these States, no doubt, claimed a measure of sovereignty, but this sovereignty was severely overborne by the paramountcy of the British Crown, not only in the field of external affairs but also in

1. Report on Indian Constitutional Reforms, paras. 43 and 44.

respect of internal administration. Whatever the content of the sovereignty of the rulers, it was surrendered by them to the national Government of India before the commencement of the Constitution.

42. Thus, none of the constituent units of India was sovereign and independent in the sense the American colonies or the Swiss Cantons were before they decided to pool their sovereignty to form federal unions. Accordingly, the Constituent Assembly of India, deriving its power from the sovereign people, was entirely unfettered by any previous commitment in evolving a constitutional pattern suitable to the genius and requirements of the Indian people as a whole. Consequently, unlike most other federal legislatures, Parliament, representing the people of India as a whole, has been vested with the exclusive power of admitting or establishing new States, increasing or diminishing the area of an existing State or altering its boundaries, the legislature or legislatures of the States concerned having only the right to an expression of views on the proposals.[1] It is significant that for making such territorial adjustments it is not necessary even to invoke the provisions governing constitutional amendments. Unlike the United States of America, therefore, the Indian Union is not an "indestructible Union composed of the indestructible States" in that the Union alone is indestructible but the individual States are not.[2]

Changes since the adoption of the Constitution

43. At the time of the commencement of the Constitution, there were nine Part A States, eight Part B States and ten Part C States. Since then, Parliament has, by law, established a new Part A State, namely, Andhra, and merged one Part C State, namely, Bilaspur, in another such State—Himachal Pradesh.

1. Constitution of India, Articles 2, 3 and 4.
2. Munro: The Government of the United States, 5th edition, p. 591.

CHAPTER II

Rationale of Reorganisation

44. The demand for the reorganisation of States is often equated with the demand for the formation of linguistic provinces. This is because the movement for redistribution of British Indian provinces was, in a large measure, a direct outcome of the phenomenal development of regional languages in the nineteenth century which led to an emotional integration of different language groups and the development amongst them of a consciousness of being distinct cultural units. When progressive public opinion in India, therefore, crystallised in favour of rationalisation of administrative units, the objective was conceived and sought in terms of linguistically homogeneous units.

45. Recent years have, however, seen some shift in emphasis on the linguistic principle and a growing realisation of the need to balance it with other factors relevant to the reshaping of the political geography of India, such as national unity and administrative, economic and other considerations. In the paragraphs which follow, we shall trace the evolution of thought on the rationale and objectives of the reorganisation of States with particular reference to the concept of linguistic States.

The British approach

46. As we have observed earlier, during the British period, territorial changes were governed mainly by imperial interests. However, as an ostensible factor the linguistic principle figured, for the first time, in a letter from Sir Herbert Risley, Home Secretary, Government of India, to the Government of Bengal, dated 3rd December, 1903, in which the proposal for the partition of Bengal was first mooted. Later, in the partition Resolution of 1905, and in the despatch of Lord Hardinge's government to the Secretary of State, dated 25th August, 1911, proposing the annulment of partition, language was again prominently mentioned. The linguistic principle was, however, pressed into service on these occasions only as a measure of administrative convenience, and to the extent it fitted into a general pattern which was determined by political exigencies. In actual effect, the partition of Bengal involved a flagrant violation of linguistic affinities. The settlement of 1912 also showed little respect

for the linguistic principle, in that it drew a clear line of distinction between the Bengali Muslims and Bengali Hindus. Both these partitions thus ran counter to the assumption that different linguistic groups constituted distinct units of social feeling with common political and economic interests.

47. The authors of the Montagu-Chelmsford Report, 1918, not burdened with the task of finding *a posteriori* reasoning for decisions taken on political grounds, approached the problem with greater objectivity. They examined the suggestion for the formation, within the existing provinces, of sub-provinces on a linguistic and racial basis, with a view mainly to providing suitable units for experiment in responsible government. Although they rejected the idea as impracticable, they commended the objective of smaller and more homogeneous units. "We cannot doubt", they observed, "that the business of government would be simplified if administrative units were both smaller and more homogeneous; and when we bear in mind the prospect of the immense burdens of government in India being transferred to comparatively inexperienced hands, such considerations acquire additional weight. It is also a strong argument in favour of linguistic or racial units of government that, by making it possible to conduct the business of legislation in the vernacular, they would contribute to draw into the arena of public affairs men who were not acquainted with English".[1]

48. Twelve years later, the question of redistribution of provinces was considered by the Indian Statutory Commission, who recognised that the provincial boundaries, as they then existed, embraced, in more than one case, areas and population of no natural affinity and separated those who might under a different scheme be more naturally united. Speaking of the factors which should govern redistribution, the Commission stated:

> "If those who speak the same language form a compact and self-contained area, so situated and endowed as to be able to support its existence as a separate province, there is no doubt that the use of a common speech is a strong and natural basis for provincial individuality. But it is not the only test—race, religion, economic interest, geographical contiguity, a due balance between country and town and between coast line and interior, may all be relevant factors. Most important of all perhaps, for practical purposes, is the largest possible measure of general agreement on the

---

1. Report on Indian Constitutional Reforms, 1918, para. 246.

changes proposed, both on the side of the area that is gaining, and on the side of the area that is losing, territory".[1]

The Commission thus gave only qualified support to the linguistic principle. It attached great importance to agreement amongst the people affected by the changes.

49. The Indian Statutory Commission's view that the question could not be settled by any single test received support from the O'Donnell Committee, which was appointed in September, 1931, to examine and report on the administrative, financial and other consequences of setting up a separate administration for "the Oriya-speaking peoples" and to make recommendations regarding its boundaries in the event of separation. In framing their proposals, the Committee took into account all relevant factors, such as language, race, the attitude of the people, geographical position, economic interests and administrative convenience. But more than all these factors, the Committee claimed to attach "great, indeed, primary importance to the wishes of the inhabitants where they can be clearly ascertained."[2]

50. Sind came into existence, along with Orissa, in April, 1936, but the demand for this province was conceded mainly to placate Muslim opinion. The Indian Statutory Commission, while expressing sympathy with the claim for the separation of Sind, had taken the view that there were grave administrative objections to isolating Sind and depriving it of the powerful backing of Bombay before the future of the Sukkur Barrage was assured and the major adjustments which it would entail had been effected.[3] However, the Joint Committee on Indian Constitutional Reforms, 1933-34, took note of the fact that separation of Sind had been pressed not merely by the Sindhi Muslims but also by Muhammadan leaders elsewhere in India and recommended it on the ground that "apart from other considerations, the communal difficulties that would arise from attempting to administer Sind from Bombay would be no less great than those which may face a separate Sind administration."[4]

The approach of the Indian National Congress

51. The Indian National Congress lent indirect support to the linguistic principle as early as 1905 when it backed the demand for annulling the partition of Bengal which had resulted in the division

1. Report of the Indian Statutory Commission, Vol. II, para. 38.
2. Report of the Orissa Committee (O'Donnell Committee), Vol. I, para. 6.
3. Report of the Indian Statutory Commission, Vol. II, para. 38.
4. Report of the Committee on Indian Constitutional Reforms, Vol. I, para. 57.

of the Bengali-speaking people into two units. Yet another concession to the linguistic principle was the formation of a separate Congress province of Bihar in 1908[1], and of the Congress provinces of Sind and Andhra in 1917. This involved a deliberate departure from the normal organisational pattern which had so far followed the boundaries of the existing administrative provinces. However, at this stage, Congress opinion had not clearly crystallised in favour of linguistic provinces and at the session of 1917 the principle was strongly opposed by the group led by Dr. Annie Besant.

52. It was only some thirty-five years ago that the Indian National Congress was converted officially to the view that linguistic provinces were desirable. It was at its 1920 session at Nagpur that the Congress accepted the linguistic redistribution of provinces as a clear political objective and in the following year the principle was adopted for the purposes of its own organisation.

53. In 1927, following the appointment of the Indian Statutory Commission, the Congress adopted a resolution expressing the opinion that "the time has come for the redistribution of provinces on a linguistic basis" and that a beginning could be made by constituting Andhra, Utkal, Sind and Karnataka into separate provinces. Those supporting the resolution spoke of the right of self-determination of the people speaking the same language and following the same tradition and culture.

54. The question of redistribution of provinces was also examined by the Nehru Committee of the All Parties Conference, 1928. The Committee lent its powerful support to the linguistic principle in the following terms:

> "If a province has to educate itself and do its daily work through the medium of its own language, it must necessarily be a linguistic area. If it happens to be a polyglot area difficulties will continually arise and the media of instruction and work will be two or even more languages. Hence it becomes most desirable for provinces to be regrouped on a linguistic basis. Language as a rule corresponds with a special variety of culture, of traditions and literature. In a linguistic area all these factors will help in the general progress of the province".[2]

55. The Nehru Committee recommended that the redistribution of provinces should take place on the basis of the wishes of the

---

1. B. Pattabhi Sitaramayya—History of the Indian National Congress, Vol. I., p. 147.
2. Report of the Nehru Committee, All Parties Conference, 1928, p. 62.

population, language and geographical, economic and financial principles. Of all these factors, however, in the opinion of the Committee, "the main considerations must necessarily be the wishes of the people and the linguistic unity of the area concerned".[1] It will be of interest, however, to note that the Committee, while recognising that the argument for the separation of Sind was very strong on the grounds that it was a definite linguistic area and that the great majority of the people demanded separation, regretted that they could not take the declaration of the Sind National League to "cut their coat according to their cloth", as a final solution of the financial problem.[2]

56. Between the years 1928 and 1947, the Congress reaffirmed its adherence to the linguistic principle on three occasions:

(i) at its Calcutta session held in October, 1937, it reiterated its policy regarding linguistic provinces and recommended the formation of the Andhra and Karnataka provinces;

(ii) by a resolution passed at Wardha in July, 1938, the Working Committee gave an assurance to the deputations from Andhra, Karnataka and Kerala that linguistic redistribution of the provinces would be undertaken as soon as the Congress had the power to do so; and

(iii) in its election manifesto of 1945-46, it repeated the view that administrative units should be constituted as far as possible on a linguistic and cultural basis.

57. The Congress election manifesto of 1945-46, which assured the people that provinces would be constituted on a linguistic and cultural basis, not in every case but as far as it was possible in the circumstances of each case, would appear to be the first attempt to qualify the linguistic principle. There was a perceptible change, however, in the outlook of the Congress leaders on the subject with the Partition and the achievement of Independence. These brought in their wake unthought-of problems, giving rise to serious doubts as to whether the old pledges could be redeemed in the new conditions.

58. Speaking before the Constituent Assembly (Legislative) on 27th November, 1947, soon after Partition, the Prime Minister, while conceding the linguistic principle, remarked: "First things must come first and the first thing is the security and stability of India".

---

1. Report of the Nehru Committee, All Parties Conference, 1928, p. 61.

2. *Ibid*, pp. 68-69.

This was followed by the appointment, on the recommendation of the Drafting Committee of the Constituent Assembly, of a Linguistic Provinces Commission, known as the Dar Commission, for the purpose of enquiring into and reporting on the desirability or otherwise of the creation of any of the proposed provinces of Andhra, Karnataka, Kerala and Maharashtra and fixing their boundaries and assessing the financial, economic, administrative and other consequences in those provinces and the adjoining territories of India. It follows from the terms of reference of this Commission that reconstitution of provinces solely on a linguistic basis was no longer taken for granted.

59. The Dar Commission reported to the Constituent Assembly in December, 1948. It not only expressed itself strongly against any reorganisation being undertaken in the prevailing circumstances but also held that the formation of provinces exclusively or even mainly on linguistic considerations would be inadvisable. The Commission felt that in forming provinces the emphasis should be primarily on administrative convenience. The homogeneity of language should enter into consideration only as a matter of administrative convenience.[1] The Commission emphasised that everything which helped the growth of nationalism had to go forward and everything which impeded it had to be rejected or should stand over.[2] Among many other factors which should be given due weight the Commission mentioned history, geography, economy and culture.[3]

60. In the opinion of the Commission, if new States, formed after taking into consideration all these factors, possessed linguistic homogeneity also, that would be an additional advantage.[4]

61. The Dar Commission listed certain "generally recognised" tests which a linguistic area must satisfy before it could be formed into a province. These were:

(i) geographical contiguity and absence of pockets and corridors;

(ii) financial self-sufficiency;

(iii) administrative convenience;

(iv) capacity for future development; and

(v) a large measure of agreement within its borders and amongst the people speaking the same language in regard

1. Report of the Linguistic Provinces Commission, para. 131.

2. *Ibid*, para. 147.

3. *Ibid*, para. 131.

4. *Ibid*, paras. 151 and 152(4).

to its formation, care being taken that the new province should not be forced by a majority upon a substantial minority of people speaking the same language.[1]

62. Soon after the Dar Commission had submitted its report, the Indian National Congress appointed at its Jaipur Session in December, 1948, a Committee to consider the question of linguistic provinces and to review the position in the light of the report of the Dar Commission and the new problems that had arisen since Independence. The Committee, known as the J.V.P. Committee, which consisted of Shri Jawaharlal Nehru, Sardar Vallabhbhai Patel and Dr. Pattabhi Sitaramayya, was the first Congress body to sound a note of warning against the linguistic principle. It stated that:

(a) when the Congress had given the seal of its approval to the general principle of linguistic provinces it was not faced with the practical application of the principle and hence it had not considered all the implications and consequences that arose from this practical application;[2]

(b) the primary consideration must be the security, unity and economic prosperity of India and every separatist and disruptive tendency should be rigorously discouraged;[3]

(c) language was not only a binding force but also a separating one;[4] and

(d) the old Congress policy of having linguistic provinces could only be applied after careful thought had been given to each separate case and without creating serious administrative dislocation or mutual conflicts which would jeopardise the political and economic stability of the country.[5]

The Committee admitted that if public sentiment was insistent and overwhelming the practicability of satisfying public demand with its implications and consequences must be examined. However, it imposed two limitations on the possible satisfaction of such a demand:

(i) that, at least in the beginning, the principle might be applied only to well-defined areas about which there was mutual agreement; and

---

1. Report of the Linguistic Provinces Commission, para. 10.
2. Report of the Linguistic Provinces Committee, Congress, p. 2.
3. *Ibid*, pp. 4, 5 and 15.
4. *Ibid*, p. 7.
5. *Ibid*, p. 15.

(ii) that all the proposals which had merit behind them could not be implemented simultaneously.

The report stated that a beginning could be made with the creation of Andhra.[1]

63. The J.V.P. Committee's report was adopted by the Congress Working Committee in April, 1949. Since then, the Congress has broadly adhered to the views expressed in this report. This would be clear from the election manifesto issued by the Congress in 1951 and the resolutions passed by it since 1949.

64. The manifesto declared that the decision about the reorganisation of States would ultimately depend on the wishes of the people concerned but expressed the opinion that, while linguistic reasons were important, there were other factors also, such as economic, administrative and financial considerations, which had to be taken into account. As a practical example, the Congress agreed to the formation of the Andhra State because the Andhra Provincial Congress, the Tamilnad Congress and the Madras Government had agreed to it, but withheld support to the proposal for the formation of a Karnataka State for want of agreement of the great majority of the people including the people of Mysore State.

65. A question which has become important since 1951 is the implementation of the five-year plan. This found a specific mention in the All-India Congress Committee resolution adopted at Hyderabad in January, 1953.

66. The latest Congress stand on the subject as announced at the Hyderabad Session in January, 1953, and reiterated in the Working Committee resolution adopted in May, 1953, and further reaffirmed at Kalyani in January, 1954, is that in considering the reorganisation of States all relevant factors should be borne in mind, such as the unity of India, national security and defence, cultural and linguistic affinities, administrative convenience, financial considerations and economic progress both of the States and of the nation as a whole. It may be noted that there was emphasis both at Hyderabad and at Kalyani on the unity of India and national security which, as the Kalyani resolution says, "must be given first priority".

Views of other Parties

67. The linguistic redistribution of States also figured prominently in the election manifestos of other political parties. The Socialist

1. Report of the Linguistic Provinces Committee, Congress, pp. 15-16.

Party expressed itself in favour of the redistribution of States on a linguistic basis consistently with geographical contiguity and economic viability. The Communist Party stood for national States enjoying wide powers including the right of self-determination. The Kisan Mazdoor Praja Party advocated the appointment of a high-power committee to go into the whole question of the redistribution of States including the question of bilingual border areas. The Hindu Maha Sabha believed in the policy of formation of provinces on a linguistic basis but was of the opinion that due regard should be paid to the problem of defence and to other factors like area and economic stability.

The creation of Andhra

68. The post-1947 period also witnessed the formation of the Andhra State. The J.V.P. Committee had suggested that a beginning could be made with Andhra. The Committee had, however, suggested in its report certain general principles, one of which required that disputed areas should not be included in the new provinces. Accordingly, Madras city, which was a disputed area, was not to form part of Andhra. The Prime Minister made it clear in his statements in Parliament in December, 1952, that Government could proceed with the formation of the Andhra State only according to the principles of the J.V.P. Committee. After the death of Shri Potti Sriramulu, the Government of India announced their decision to establish the State of Andhra "consisting of the Telugu-speaking areas of the present Madras State but not including the City of Madras". Shri Justice Wanchoo was appointed to report on the financial and other implications of the decision.

69. In his report submitted in February, 1953, Shri Justice Wanchoo recommended the transfer of the Bellary district to Andhra with the provision that, if and when a Karnataka State was formed, the Kannada-speaking areas of the district should go to that State. However, the Government of India decided to include in Andhra only the three taluks of the district which had a Telugu majority, and to transfer the other taluks, excepting Bellary, to Mysore State. The decision of the Government of India in respect of Bellary taluk was deferred because it was felt that "in view of its very mixed population not only its linguistic composition but certain other matters would also need examination before a final decision is reached".[1]

70. Following this decision, Shri Justice Misra was asked to examine and report on the future of the Bellary taluk after taking into

---

[1] Shri Justice Misra's Report, para. 2, p. 2.

consideration all relevant factors which were to include "linguistic composition and cultural affinity, administrative convenience and economic well-being". On the basis of the recommendations made in Shri Justice Misra's report, the Government of India decided to transfer the whole of Bellary taluk to the State of Mysore.

71. On August 10, 1953, a Bill was introduced in the House of the People "to provide for the formation of the Andhra State". The State of Andhra, which, according to the statement made by the Deputy Home Minister in Parliament on 17th August, 1953, was a province which approximated as much as possible to a linguistic province, came into existence on 1st October, 1953.

CHAPTER III

TIME FOR REORGANISATION

72. As we have stated earlier, the desirability of the redistribution of provincial territories was recognised from time to time even by British statesmen. As early as May, 1903, Lord Curzon, the then Governor-General, considered the time to be appropriate for such an undertaking, because of

(i) absence of political passions on the subject;

(ii) preparedness of educated public opinion for redistribution; and

(iii) availability of experienced administrators with special knowledge of the areas involved.

However, the only result of Lord Curzon's initiative in the matter was the first partition of Bengal.

73. The Montagu-Chelmsford Report, 1918, recognised the need of a general redistribution, but did not consider the time opportune for such changes, because they considered it unwise to undertake simultaneously the revision of the Constitution and of the political geography of the country. It expressed the view that redistribution "ought in any case to follow, and neither to precede nor accompany, constitutional reform" and suggested "that it should be recognised as one of the earliest duties incumbent upon all the reformed provincial Governments to test provincial opinion upon schemes directed to this end".[1]

74. The Indian Statutory Commission also recommended a readjustment of provincial boundaries, particularly in view of the change in the status of provinces consequent on a substantial decentralisation of powers, and the ultimate establishment of a federation of which the provinces would form units. The Commission was conscious of the very great difficulties in the way of redistribution, but urged that the main cases in which provincial readjustment seemed called for, be investigated by a Boundaries Commission to be set up by the Government of India.[2] No such Commission was, however, set up, the only changes introduced following this recommendation being those relating to the creation in April, 1936, of Sind and Orissa as separate provinces.

1. Report on Indian Consitutional Reforms, 1918, para 246.

2. Report of the Indian Statutory Commission, Vol. II, para. 38. p 26.

75. During the period between 1936 and 1947, major political and constitutional issues and the prosecution of the war engaged the attention of the government and nothing further was heard about the reorganisation of provinces.

76. After the transfer of power to India, the question was examined by the Linguistic Provinces Commission of the Constituent Assembly in July—December 1948, and the J.V.P. Committee, appointed by the Congress; which reported in April, 1949. Both these bodies were concerned with the limited question of the formation of certain linguistic provinces. However, they suggested the postponement of the formation of new provinces on grounds which could be applied to a large extent to the general question of the reorganisation of States.

77. The Dar Commission recommended that no new provinces should be formed for the time being and that the question could be taken up when India had been physically and emotionally integrated, the Indian States problem solved, the national sentiment strengthened and other conditions were favourable[1], on the grounds that

(i) India was burdened with problems more urgent than the problem of the redistribution of provinces, such as those of defence, food, refugees, inflation and production;

(ii) it could not afford to add to its anxieties the heat, controversy and bitterness which the demarcation of boundaries and the allotment of capital cities of Bombay and Madras would involve;

(iii) the economic consequences of splitting up of existing provinces into several new provinces required a great deal of study, preparation and planning; and

(iv) the administrative personnel available at the time was inadequate to bear the additional burden of running new governments.[2]

78. The J.V.P. Committee generally concurred in this view and did not consider the time opportune for reorganisation, because it was likely to

(i) divert attention from more vital matters;

(ii) retard the process of consolidation of the nation's gains;

---

1. Report of the Linguistic Provinces Commission, paras. 138 and 152 (3).

2. *Ibid.* para. 132

(iii) dislocate the administrative, economic and financial structure of the country and seriously interfere with the "progressive solution of our economic and political difficulties"; and

(iv) let loose, while we were still in the formative stage, forces of disruption and disintegration.[1]

79. The Committee, however, admitted that if public sentiment was "insistent and overwhelming" they would have to submit to it, subject to certain limitations in regard to the "good of India as a whole" and other conditions specified by them.[2]

80. A similar view was taken by the Prime Minister when he spoke on 7th July, 1952, in the House of the People on the resolution for the reorganisation of States on a linguistic basis. He emphasised that "we must give the topmost priority to developing a sense of unity in India and anything that might come in the way of that unity might perhaps be delayed a little," and added that at a time when the world was hanging on the verge of a crisis it was extraordinarily unwise to unsettle and uproot the whole of India for a theoretical approach or a linguistic division.

81. With the appointment of this Commission, the problem is now again before the country, with opinion divided on the appropriateness of the time for undertaking large-scale changes in the existing set-up.

82. Those opposed to reorganisation argue that:

(a) there has been no marked change in the situation, internally or externally, which would justify the view that factors which made the consideration of any proposal for the reorganisation of States inadvisable in 1948 and 1952 have now disappeared;

(b) problems created by the Partition, including the complicated problem of Kashmir, have still to be settled;

(c) the international situation and developments across the borders do not admit of any dissipation of national energies and resources;

(d) the economic development of the country continues to demand the highest priority; and

(e) any large-scale changes in the existing set-up are bound to generate provincial feelings and impair national solidarity.

---

1. Report of the Linguistic Provinces Committee, Congress, p.9.

2. *Ibid*, pp. 15-16.

83. The opponents of reorganisation have accordingly suggested the postponement of the whole issue for a period of at least twenty or twenty-five years to allow for the creation of a proper atmosphere in the country so that we might concentrate during this period on other matters of vital national importance.

84. These arguments are not without substance. While internally as well as externally the situation is, no doubt, easier than it was immediately after the attainment of Independence, neither the international scene nor the economic and other problems facing the country would justify a complacent attitude. It is also true that any large scale reorganisation of States is likely to involve a heavy financial and administratve burden on the resources of the country. But this logic must yield now to the realities of the situation which render further postponement of the question impracticable.

85. The problem of reorganisation has become emergent, because India, with her programme of large scale planning, has to think in terms of enduring political units. A direct and regrettable outcome of the present state of uncertainty is that there has been a general reluctance to invest funds in the disputed areas.

86. One of the main impediments in the way of reorganisation was that a certain measure of territorial inviolability was enjoyed by the former Indian States, both under the British rule and during the period immediately following the transfer of power. The integration of these states has, however, removed this impediment and has paved the way for a rational approach to the problem.

87. It may be recalled in this connection that the Indian Statutory Commission had considered it extremely important "that the adjustment of provincial boundaries and the creation of proper provincial areas should take place before the new process has gone too far. Once the mould has set, any maldistribution will be still more difficult to correct".[1] This applies in a greater measure to the ill-assorted units representing territories of some of the former Indian States whose future should be considered, before vested interests get too strongly entrenched and reasonable settlement becomes difficult.

88. The appointment of this Commission itself has given rise to expectations and prepared the country psychologically for the readjustment of state territories. The Commission has had the benefit of the views of prominent leaders of public opinion and has received

---

Report of the Idian Statutory Commission, Vol. II, para. 38.

valuable material on the various aspects of reorganisation. Unless a constructive approach is now recommended, it will cause a sense of frustration with all its attendant evils.

89. A good deal of reasoning against the reorganisation of States has also been coloured by the presumption that reorganisation must lead to a linguistic redistribution of States. But for this tendency to equate reorganisation with the formation of linguistic States, there would be a fair measure of agreement on the desirability of rationalising the existing units. Thus, for instance, informed public opinion is agreed on the point that the present classification of States into three categories can no longer be defended, and that of the two alternatives of equalising the status of the existing small units with that of Part A States or their merger in adjoining larger units, the latter is more practicable.

90. It would, perhaps, have been possible to defer the process for some time, but the decision to create the State of Andhra and the events leading to it have precipitated matters. Even without this decision, so long as the political parties stand committed to the policy of reorganisation, further deferment of a general reorganisation might lead to more dissatisfaction.

91. The task of redrawing the political map of India must, therefore, be now undertaken and accomplished without avoidable delay, in the hope that the changes which are brought about will give satisfaction to a substantial majority of the Indian people.

PART II

FACTORS BEARING ON REORGANISATION

CHAPTER I

COST OF CHANGE

92. Although the Resolution appointing this Commission vests in this body full discretion to consider any proposal or principle bearing on reorganisation, the Government of India have indicated some broad principles which should govern the consideration of the problem. The relevant portion of this Resolution is quoted below:

> "The language and culture of an area have an undoubted importance as they represent a pattern of living which is common in that area. In considering a reorganisation of States, however, there are other important factors which have also to be borne in mind. The first essential consideration is the preservation and strengthening of the unity and security of India. Financial, economic and administrative considerations are almost equally important, not only from the point of view of each State, but for the whole nation. India has embarked upon a great ordered plan for her economic, cultural and moral progress. Changes which interfere with the successful prosecution of such a national plan would be harmful to the national interest."

93. The principles that emerge may be enumerated as follows:

(i) preservation and strengthening of the unity and security of India;

(ii) linguistic and cultural homogeneity;

(iii) financial, economic and administrative considerations; and

(iv) successful working of the national plan.

94. Before we go into these and other principles relevant to the task with which we are charged, it would be well to take note of the unsettling consequences of reorganisation. The pace of change in recent years has been such and the changes themselves have been so far-reaching that there has been a general tendency to assume that the administrative and financial consequences of reorganisation

cannot be serious. This is an unrealistic view. Changes in the existing set-up resulting in the breaking up of old ties and the creation of new associations must involve, at least during the transitory phase, a large scale dislocation of the administrative machinery, no less than of the life of the people. As the J.V.P. Committee has pointed out, whatever the origin of the existing units, and however artificial they might have been, a century or so of political, administrative and, to some extent, economic unity in each of the existing State areas, has produced a certain stability and a certain tradition. Any change would naturally have an upsetting effect.

95. To begin with, parliamentary legislation in terms of Articles 3 and 4 of the Constitution, in order to give effect to any scheme of reorganisation, must itself entail a great deal of effort and time. If one were to judge by existing tensions, the proceedings in State Assemblies, preceding parliamentary legislation, may be protracted and may give rise to strong feelings. Reorganisation of States on a rational basis may also necessitate a number of constitutional amendments which will add considerably to the burden of piloting legislation concerning reorganisation proposals.

96. The problems of transition will, by no means, be over with the passage of enabling legislation. In the first instance, there is the difficult question of the unification of the laws in force in the areas which might be grouped together. The laws extant in the existing administrative units, including those governing such vital matters as land tenure, agrarian reforms and prohibition, are not the same even in the geographically contiguous States. There has been no uniform attempt in the recent past, when mergers have taken place, to apply straightaway the laws and regulations of one predominant area to the whole State. Some States have had to depart from this principle because of the prevalence of social and economic conditions in those areas justifying disparity in laws. In some States old laws are still operative because of the delay in completing the process of unification of laws.

97. The initial phase of transition during which two or more sets of laws are applicable in one State cannot, however, last for any length of time. Apart from *prima facie* objections on general grounds and the administrative inconvenience which it will involve,

lack of uniformity in the application of tax laws will make budgeting difficult, and the lack of uniformity, in so far as it involves discrimination without justification, may even prove to be bad in law. For these reasons every reorganised State will have to undertake, in the initial years, a laborious and exhaustive review of its existing legislation.

98. The process of disintegration and re-integration of the existing administrative units must also entail serious dislocation of the administration. It involves a difficult process of integrating the service personnel belonging to one State with the personnel of another State; retrenchment of surplus and unsuitable personnel, if necessary; introduction of unified pay scales; refixation of cadres; re-determination of relative seniority in the different services, etc. It may also be necessary in consequence of reorganisation to devote attention in the initial years to the basic structure of the administration in some of the States, that is to say, the system of district administration, the number of districts and other administrative units and sub-units.

99. In the case of the Part B and Part C States this administrative integration has proved to be a complex problem. In spite of the fact that the utmost importance was attached at the highest level to the early completion of this process, there are some States where it is still to be completed. In the light of this experience it cannot be anticipated that the transition will be easy.

100. In the case of Andhra it was possible, to some extent, to hasten separation. But for various reasons (such as that *inter se* seniority was not disturbed, that surplus staff was retained by the residuary State, and that no great changes in the number or the constitution of the districts were involved), Andhra cannot be regarded as a good precedent. Moreover, the Andhra administration has itself had to face such difficulties as the dispersal of its offices, absence of duplicate records, and lack of experienced staff. It cannot, on the whole, be anticipated that reorganised administrative machinery will start functioning smoothly in the new States within a short period.

101. This must be regarded as the indirect cost of change; to the extent that revision of salaries after reorganisation becomes inevitable (and such a revision, it must be remembered, can only be upwards), there will also be a direct recurring cost. It is not possible or necessary to attempt a forecast of this cost except to indicate

broadly the magnitude of the problem. One estimate which has been made on certain assumptions is that the lump sum provisions which will be needed in order to introduce uniform scales of pay may run into ten or eleven crores per annum. Without necessarily accepting this estimate, it may be assumed that one of the consequences of reorganisation will be the intensification of the existing demands for salary revision to such an extent as to render an increase in State Governments' expenditure unavoidable.

102. Whether there is or there is not a case for salary revision is not a question on which it is necessary for this Commission to express an opinion. In the event of a revision being ultimately decided upon, the State Governments may be able to meet the extra cost involved in the introduction of uniform scales of pay by retrenchment and administrative rationalisation to some extent, but too much reliance cannot be placed on these possibilities in the initial years after reorganisation. In the light of the experience of the working of some of the Part B States, a reduction in the number of districts and other administrative units or large-scale retrenchment, even if justified on administrative grounds, would appear to be a remote possibility. Retrenchment and rationalisation will have to be spread, in all probability, over a number of years; the extra cost of salary revisions will, therefore, be fairly heavy.

103. One other major consequence of reorganisation will probably be the upsetting of the work of the Delimitation Commission. Much of the work of the delimitation of constituencies will have to be done all over again, and major amendments will clearly be needed in the Representation of the People Act, 1950.

104. This discussion is not, and cannot be, exhaustive. It does not take into account, for example, what may be called the human factor, which should be a relevant consideration in breaking up old associations and alignments, or the fact that the service personnel allotted to a State may be inadequately equipped to deal with the needs of that State. There will also be many other minor difficulties with which the new States may be faced. The division of assets and liabilities has never proved to be easy. What are known as unique institutions, that is to say, institutions which serve the needs of the State as a whole, may not be equitably divided on partition; arrangements may have to be made to duplicate them or to ensure that they serve the separated units. Separation of records would involve a process of sifting, collating and large-scale copying. Some changes in the judicial organisation of the States will

also be necessary, and considerable volume of accounts work will be created at a time when the Comptroller and Auditor-General is planning an experiment in the separation of accounts and audit, which will itself add greatly to the responsibility of State Governments.

105. The integration of princely States involved administrative changes in an area of about 360,000 square miles inhabited by about 59 million people—not counting the major and minor units the boundaries of which were not changed. Impressive as the scale and swiftness of these changes were, it can now be seen in retrospect that the process of rationalising the administrative system in these areas has been spread over seven or eight years and, as has been stated already, it is still not complete. If the reorganisation of States at the present time is to be on a comparable scale, the effects of the change are bound to be considerable.

106. A preliminary but essential consideration to bear in mind, therefore, is that no change should be made unless it is a distinct improvement in the existing position and unless the advantages which result from it, in terms of the promotion of "the welfare of the people of each constituent unit, as well as the nation as a whole"—the objectives set before the Commission by the Government of India—are such as to compensate for the heavy burden on the administrative and financial resources of the country which reorganisation of the existing units must entail. The reorganisation of States has to be regarded as a means to an end and not an end in itself; that being the case, it is quite legitimate to consider whether there is on the whole a balance of advantage in any change.

CHAPTER II

Unity and Security of India

107. The first essential objective of any scheme of reorganisation must be the unity and security of India. Any movement which may tend to impair the unity of the country must ultimately affect the welfare of all sections of the Indian people. Any measure of reorganisation which is likely to create tensions and disharmony must weaken the sense of unity among the people of India and should not, therefore, be countenanced.

108. While it is generally agreed that the unity of India must be regarded as the prime factor in readjusting territories, there has been considerable difference of opinion as to how this objective is to be realised. Basically, the difference of approach arises from the measure of emphasis put on the relative suitability, in the conditions prevailing in the country of federal and unitary concepts, not merely as the basic postulates underlying the constitutional structure of India, but as embracing concepts covering the political as well as the social and cultural life of the people. The problem is essentially one of determining how far the free play of provincial sentiment deriving from a consciousness of cultural and linguistic distinctiveness is a factor making for unity or disunity.

109. One view is that:

(a) it will be unrealistic to disregard the patent fact that there are in India distinct cultural units; the unity of the country, therefore, should not be sought in terms of an imposed external unity but a fundamental unity recognising diversity of language, culture and tradition of the Indian people;

(b) the strength of the Indian Union must be the strength which it derives from its constituent units; and

(c) since the unity and strength within the constituent units is a condition precedent to a healthy feeling of unity at the national level, any attempt to eliminate tensions and contradictions and to make units more homogeneous and internally cohesive is bound to strengthen the unity of the whole nation.

110. The other view is that:

(a) in the past India did not achieve a real measure of political unification or develop into a living body, social or political, constituting an integrated whole; if, therefore, we have to create a united India, it must be based on a new concept of unity which cannot be achieved by reaffirmation or re-enunciation of old values such as religion, community, culture and language, which operate more to separate than to unite;

(b) regional consciousness never contributed to India's oneness in the past. In fact, it is inherent in narrower loyalties, whether based on communal, provincial or linguistic considerations, that they ally themselves with centrifugal forces and become instruments of inter-state discord and other disruptive trends. The idea of sub-nations or nationalities, which must foment resistance to the growth of national unity, is implicit in the demand for a reorganisation of States or a rectification of their boundaries, on the basis of exclusivist factors such as linguistic and cultural homogeneity; and

(c) if, therefore, the unity of India has to develop into a dynamic concept capable of welding the nation together, it must transcend community and language and recognise the entire nation as one integrated unit.

111. In the Chapter dealing with the implications of the linguistic principle we have examined at some length the question of finding an equilibrium between the regional sentiment and the national spirit. Here we shall briefly indicate the basic considerations which should govern our approach to the problem:

(i) an essential feature of our social fabric is undoubtedly a wide variation in our life within the framework of a broadly united culture. This, however, does not mean that diversity is a pre-requisite of unity or that over-emphasis on diversity will not hamper the growth of the national sentiment;

(ii) in a vast country like ours, governed by a federal Constitution, centrifugal forces are not an unnatural phenomenon, but what is important is not that they should be eliminated, but that such forces must not be allowed to impede the achievement of our national unity; and

(iii) the strength of the nation is undoubtedly the sum total of the combined strength of the people of the component States. But while the building of contented units, strong enough to bear their share of the burden, is an important objective, it is no less necessary that the links between the units and the nation should be equally strong so that under the stress of regional loyalties, the Union does not fall apart.

112. It follows that, while internal adjustments at State level are to be desired, it is imperative to ensure that these do not lead to maladjustments at the inter-state and national level. From the point of view of national unity, therefore, reorganisation has to aim at a two-fold objective:

(a) firm discouragement of disruptive sentiments such as provincialism or linguistic fanaticism; and

(b) consistent with national solidarity, provision of full scope for the unhampered growth of the genius of each group of people.

This requires that we must build the administrative and political structure of the country on the basic concept of the primacy of the nation, conceding to lesser units an autonomous existence and an intrinsic life and purpose of their own, but only within the harmoniously integrated organism of Indian nationhood.

National Security

113. A fundamental pre-requisite of national security is the unity of the country. What promotes unity, therefore, also strengthens security. Other considerations which we have to keep in mind from the point of view of national security are:

(i) it is of great importance that the composition of administrative units should not assume a form which might foster regional, communal or other narrower loyalties in any section of the armed forces of India and thereby undermine their undivided allegiance to the Union of India;

(ii) in strategic areas where effective or direct central control is necessary, the administrative structure as also the measure of autonomy given to the people, should be governed by considerations of national security; and

(iii) another factor relevant from the point of view of national security is the size and resources of the border States.

While the primary responsibility for defence arrangements must be that of the Central Government, a considerable burden relating to security arrangements must be borne by the State. It is, therefore, important that a border State should be a well-administered, stable and resourceful unit, capable of meeting the emergent problems arising out of military exigencies. This means that normally it would be safer to have on our borders relatively larger and resourceful States rather than small and less resilient units.

114. It may be desirable to elaborate the last-mentioned point a little further. It has been argued in some important memoranda that the formation of the separate North-West Frontier Province in 1901 involved the recognition of the principle that, for defence purposes, a small province on the border is preferable to a large one. This view is based on an incorrect appreciation of the reasons for the detachment of the frontier districts from the Punjab to form a separate Chief Commissioner's province.

115. The main consideration underlying the detachment of the frontier region in 1901 was the establishment of direct central control over it in preference to control through the medium of "a Local Government of the first class". In fact, when the proposal to establish the North-West Frontier Province was approved, the Secretary of State for India recounted the advantages of a strong administration on the frontier and pointed out that the existing arrangements had been found unsatisfactory and that the assumption of direct central control over the frontier areas had become essential. He said:

> "In remarking that the need of a strong administration equipped with all the resources of Government would be felt on the frontier, I did not refer to the political administration. I referred to the advantages that must accrue to the frontier districts of British India from the application to them of the ways and means at the command of a first-class administrative unit. The construction of roads, bridges, rest houses, and hospitals, and generally the assignment of provincial resources to a particular district, may be of the utmost value, and are best secured if the district is an integral part of a large province. In times of disturbance or threatened danger a larger province can draft in additional police, procure transport, change local

officers, and do much to prepare for troubles before they arise or assume the form of military operations".

116. This puts succinctly the case for larger States on the frontier. It seems clear to us that, when a border area is not under the direct control of the Centre, small units and multiplicity of jurisdictions would be an obvious handicap from the point of view of national security.

CHAPTER III

Language and Culture

117. The question that has caused the greatest controversy is the position to be accorded to language in the reorganisation of the States of the Indian Union. One of the major facts of India's political evolution during the last hundred years has been the growth of our regional languages. They have during this period developed into rich and powerful vehicles of expression creating a sense of unity among the peoples speaking them. In view of the fact that these languages are spoken in well-defined areas, often with a historic background, the demand for the unification of such areas to form separate States has gathered momentum and has, in some cases, assumed the form of an immediate political programme. The Resolution appointing this Commission makes a specific reference to the importance of language. A careful examination of the pros and cons of this problem is, therefore, necessary as an essential preliminary to the consideration of the question of the reorganisation of States.

The case for Linguistic States

118. The advocates of a rigid and uniform application of the linguistic principle in determining the boundaries of States advance important arguments in support of their claim which may be briefly stated and examined here.

119. A federal union, such as ours, presupposes that the units are something more than mere creatures of administrative convenience. The constituent States in a federal republic must each possess a minimum degree of homogeneity to ensure the emotional response which is necessary for the working of democratic institutions. The States of the Indian Union can achieve this internal cohesiveness only if they are constituted on a unilingual basis, because language being the vehicle for the communion of thought and feeling, provides the most effective single bond for uniting the people. Linguistic homogeneity, therefore, provides the only rational basis for reconstructing the States, for it reflects the social and cultural pattern of living obtaining in well-defined regions of the country.

120. In a democracy such as we have in India, based on universal adult franchise, the political and administrative work of a State has

of necessity to be conducted in the regional language. A multiplicity of such languages would lead to weakness and inefficiency in administration and rivalry and jealousy in politics. It is pointed out that already in some of the States a large percentage of members in the legislature know only one language and this trend is likely to become more and more emphasised. In some States even ministers know only one regional language. Discussions in legislatures would become difficult, if a considerable number of members are unable to follow the proceedings.

121. Under an alien rule the basic need of unity of outlook between the people and those governing them could be subordinated to imperial and other considerations. But under a democratic form of government based on adult franchise, it is imperative that there should be a real consciousness of identity of interests between the people and the government, and that both should work in an atmosphere of co-ordination and mutual understanding. The success of a welfare state depends essentially on broad-based popular support, which cannot be secured if the processes of government are not brought home to the people. If the Legislature of a State is not to develop into a babel of tongues, it must conduct its work in one language, the language of the people. The various devices adopted in multilingual States to meet the communicational needs of the people have led only to a dissipation of energy and national resources.

122. Educational activity can be stimulated only by giving the regional languages their due place. If the educated few are not to be isolated from the masses, the education of the people must necessarily be through the medium of the mother-tongue.

123. The demand for linguistic States does not represent mere cultural revivalism. It has a wider purpose in that it seeks to secure for different linguistic groups political and economic justice. In multilingual States political leadership and administrative authority remain the monopoly of the dominant language groups, and linguistic minorities are denied an effective voice in the governance of their States. Even where there are substantial minorities having adequate representation in the cabinet, the representatives of linguistic minority groups find it impossible, owing to party discipline and other factors, to do anything effective to safeguard the interests of minorities.

124. Similarly, in multilingual States welfare activity as well as development plans are unequally and unfairly distributed, the areas inhabited by the dominant language groups developing at the expense

of other areas. The demand for unilingual States, therefore, aims at securing for minorities a fair deal not only in the social and cultural spheres but also in the political and economic fields.

125. Conflict and discord are inherent in administrations in which diverse elements are forcibly held together. Where the requisite sense of unity is absent, an unwilling association or co-existence, however long, would not succeed in producing that atmosphere of mutual goodwill and understanding which is essential for the working of democratic institutions.

126. Under foreign domination, when opportunities for self-development were denied to all alike, different linguistic groups could live together without apparent conflict. Now that the people of India have to shape their own destinies, consciousness of the lack of a community of interests between different language groups tends to become deeper and deeper with the progressive realisation of their divergent economic and other needs.

127. With the limited resources at the disposal of States, plans for the economic development of different areas have inevitably to be based on a system of priorities and it is difficult to reconcile the rival claims of different regions. It is a peculiar feature of multilingual States that in each one of them suspicion of favouritism and charges of partiality have centred round the linguistic division, each language group considering that it is being unfairly treated. Only the removal of minority consciousness by reorganising the States on a unilingual basis can eliminate this widespread sense of distrust.

128. The argument that composite States provide a common meeting place for different linguistic groups and help them to accustom themselves to living together in a spirit of tolerance and understanding would have had some validity if different linguistic groups were interspersed in these States. Far from this being so, there is, generally speaking, a clear-cut integration of different regions in composite States on the basis of linguistic homogeneity. The argument, therefore, that different linguistic groups in these areas are living together in close amity is unreal.

129. The political atmosphere, vitiated by linguistic differences, has now permeated into the administrative structure as a whole. Important administrative posts tend to become the monopoly of the members of dominant language groups and appointments and promotions are no longer governed by considerations of administrative purity, efficiency and fairness.

130. A majority of the States in the Indian Republic are already predominantly unilingual. The States of West Bengal, Orissa, Bihar, the U.P., Rajasthan, Madhya Bharat, Saurashtra, Mysore and Travancore-Cochin are all either completely unilingual or could be made so with only minor adjustments of boundaries. The creation of Andhra as a new unilingual State has left residuary Madras mainly a Tamil State. In these circumstances, the apprehension that the linguistic redistribution of the remaining multilingual states will create new problems or constitute a threat to national unity seems to have little justification.

131. Linguistic redistribution of provinces has been an integral part of the Indian national movement. Having sponsored the linguistic principle for nearly forty years, it is impossible for the leaders of political thought now to reverse the current.

132. The national movement which achieved India's independence was built up by harnessing the forces of regionalism. It is only when the Congress was reorganised on the basis of language units that it was able to develop into a national movement. The Congress under Mahatma Gandhi realised that the same forces which worked for our national unity had also helped to develop the regional languages, which led to the integration of language areas. It is this alliance between regional integration and national feeling that helped us to recover our freedom.

133. With the achievement of freedom, a tendency has developed to overlook the claims of different regions, by denying to them the right to internal integration, on the plea that this will weaken the unity of the nation. This, however, is a false cry, for true development will be possible, only if we are able to utilise genuine loyalties which have grown up around historic areas united by a common language.

134. Finally, it is contended that the urge for linguistic States has now gone deep down into the minds of the masses and a refusal to create such States at this stage would lead to a widespread sense of frustration which might have very grave consequences.

The case against Linguistic States

135. While there is undoubtedly much that is valid in the arguments briefly stated above, there are also weighty considerations which have been urged against accepting language as the determining principle in the creation of States. The more important of these may now be stated.

136. The idea of a federating unit, organised as the political expression of a single language group, would inevitably encourage exclusivism. It may even tend to blur, if not to obliterate, the feeling of national unity, by the emphasis it places on local culture, language and history. The self-image that any such language group creates is necessarily one of superiority as compared to others, and this will inevitably be reflected in its educational and cultural institutions. In fact, experience everywhere has shown that States based on languages are intolerant, aggressive and expansionist in character. Already a sense of irredentism is noticeable in the existing unilingual States of India, which claim neighbouring territories on the basis of language statistics.

137. In view of the uneven development of India's languages, education as a whole is moreover bound to suffer and will lose its national character. If the different States pursue policies of their own without regard to the interests of the nation as a whole, there will be no co-ordination and unity of purpose in education. In fact, this tendency might lead to education itself being used as a vehicle of regional particularism and revivalism, resulting in inter-state conflicts and the weakening of the national tie.

138. Already in the schools of some of the States, songs exalting the regional idea have been introduced into text books. History books taught in lower classes have disclosed a marked tendency to exaggerate the past achievements of the dominant linguistic groups. These inevitable tendencies in language-based States will unavoidably weaken our sense of national unity.

139. Grievances and a sense of frustration in the political and economic field are not the inevitable or necessary features of multilingual States. Even after a State is reconstituted on a linguistic basis, there is no reason to suppose that all areas will receive equal attention and that there will not develop an equally strong sense of frustration and neglect in areas which feel that their claims are not receiving adequate attention. The remedy for redressing such grievances lies in the fulfilment of the aspirations of the various groups by positive measures based on the merits of each case, and not in the wholesale reorganisation of States on the basis of language.

140. Planning on a national scale also cuts across linguistic affiliations. Economic development should obviously proceed on such considerations as the capital-income ratio, the more remunerative projects being preferred to the less remunerative ones, the employment possibilities of various projects, the requirements of river valley projects, the optimum utilisation of natural resources etc.

141. The formation of linguistic States would not only not accelerate but may retard the pace of planned economic development of the country, for local sentiment may resent the utilisation of the resources of one area for the benefit of another. Besides any large-scale reorganisation of States may result in the diversion of national energies into unproductive channels, and, to that extent, impair the economic advancement of the people and the execution of various development projects.

Importance of language for administrative and other purposes

142. It is obviously an advantage that constituent units of a federation should have a minimum measure of internal cohesion. Likewise, a regional consciousness, not merely in the sense of a negative awareness of absence of repression or exploitation but also in the sense of scope for positive expression of the collective personality of a people inhabiting a State or a region may be conducive to the contentment and well-being of the community. Common language may not only promote the growth of such regional consciousness, but also make for administrative convenience and for a proper understanding of governmental measures by the people. Indeed, in a democracy the people can legitimately claim and the government have a duty to ensure that the administration is conducted in a language which the people can understand.

143. The objective, therefore, of community of language between the people and the government is not only wholly unexceptionable but also highly commendable. The essential point to remember, however, is that if we pursue it as an abstract proposition and not as a practical administrative issue, we are apt to lose a sense of perspective and proportion.

144. The problem of linguistic groups within a state is not unknown outside India, but precedents elsewhere, which are often cited, provide but little guidance. Except in Yugoslavia and the Soviet Union, there are in the States of Europe no language groups large enough to claim separate political organisation. Linguistic minorities continue to exist in many States even though the political settlement following the First Great War had demarcated the boundaries of Central Europe broadly on a language basis. In view of the intermingling of languages and peoples in Central Europe, this settlement, however, left large minority groups within the new States, for example, over three million Germans in Czechoslovakia and several considerable minorities in Poland. The problem in these countries, however, was one of the protection of linguistic minorities in

sovereign States erected on a linguistic basis. The problem of minorities exists in India also but the character of the problem is different, as the States of the Indian Union are not sovereign independent units, but parts of a national whole.

145. European history, however, clearly shows that language is one of the fundamental elements of social life and influences to a large extent national psychology, so much so that speaking of Central and Eastern Europe, Professor Toynbee has been led to observe that "the growing consciousness of Nationality had attached itself neither to traditional frontiers nor to new geographical associations but almost exclusively to the mother-tongues.."[1] It is to be noted that most bilingual or multilingual States have had to face separatist movements. Belgium and Spain are notable examples. Catalan separatism has been one of the most persistent strands of Spanish history. In Switzerland divided sympathy for Germany and France severely strained Swiss neutrality during the war of 1914—18.

146. Only in the U.S.S.R. and Yugoslavia has an effort been made to organise units on a linguistic basis. Though the units constituting the U.S.S.R. are organised generally on this basis, there are in operation adequate constitutional, extra-constitutional and ideological correctives, which could be applied in case any regional loyalties challenge the loyalty to the party or to the State.

Constitutional relationship between the Centre and the States of the Indian Union

147. The problem of linguistic States has also to be examined in the light of the bonds of our unity and the constitutional position of the Centre.

148. It has to be realised that the political unity of India is a recent achievement. It was not, as is generally supposed, brought about by the administrative unification of India by the British. The former British areas of the present territory of the Indian Union constitute less than three-fifths of the total. The rest was under the rule of Indian princes, and it is well to remember that from 1917 at least a determined effort was made to separate "Indian India" from the rest and to bring the princely States in direct relationship with the Crown.

149. Even what was British India did not achieve a real measure of unity. It was the determination of the Indian people to rid themselves of foreign domination and to build up a life for themselves

[1]. A. J. Toynbee—The World after the Peace Conference, London, 1926, p. 18

as a free people, that created the present unity of India, sweeping away not merely the alien rule, but also the hereditary Rulers who had divided up India and thus stood in the way of that unity. But this sense of Indian unity is a plant of recent origin. It has not only to be watered and nourished, but protected against hailstorms and gales and against unfriendly climates. This was in a measure recognised by those responsible for the making of our Constitution, and consequently a number of provisions were included in it for safeguarding the unity of India. Of these the more important are:

(i) the Concurrent List of subjects in respect of which the Union Parliament has over-riding legislative authority;

(ii) provisions enabling Parliament to legislate in respect of matters in the State List in cases of grave emergency, or in the national interest when the Rajya Sabha by a two-thirds majority decides to so legislate;

(iii) provisions enabling Parliament and President to assume legislative and executive functions in States when the normal constitutional machinery fails, and provisions authorising the issue of special directives by the Centre in the event of a financial emergency; and

(iv) provisions empowering the Union Government to give directions to States to ensure compliance with the laws made by Parliament and to ensure that the executive power of every State is not so exercised as to impede or prejudice the power of the Union executive.

150. These special provisions, however, are primarily remedial in character and are meant to prevent a breakdown in the States and to safeguard the powers of the Union within its own sphere. They do not detract from the fact that under the Constitution the States constitute corner-stones of the political and administrative structure of the country with a real measure of autonomy. In fact, Dean Appleby has recently expressed the view that "the new national government of India is given less basic resource in power than any other large and important nation, while at the same time having rather more sense of need and determination to establish programs dealing with matters important to the national interests".[1] He has further observed: "no other large and important national government, I believe, is so dependent as India on theoretically subordinate but actually rather distinct units responsible to a different political control......"[2]

151. There has been a tendency during the last few years during which the new Constitution has been in force to lay more and more

[1]. Paul H. Appleby—Public Administration in India—Report of a Survey, p. 16.
[2] *Ibid*, p.21.

emphasis on the autonomy of the States. This has to be considered in relation to the encouragement to regionalism which the emphasis on language as the basis for the creation of a State is bound to give.

Group loyalties and nationalism

152. It has o be remembered that linguistic and other group loyal ties have deep roots in the soil and history of India. The culture based regionalism, centring round the idea of linguistic homogeneity represents to the average Indian values easily intelligible to him Indian nationalism, on the other hand, has still to develop into a positive concept. It must acquire a deeper content before it becomes ideologically adequate to withstand the gravitational pull of the traditional narrower loyalties. In these circumstances, further emphasis on narrow loyalties by equating linguistic regions with political and administrative frontiers, must diminish the broader sense of the unity of the country.

Other Considerations

153. Undue emphasis on the linguistic principle is likely to impede the rapid development of new areas brought under cultivation and the rehabilitation of displaced persons. If the main or the exclusive criterion for the re-demarcation of State boundaries is to be community of language, the State governments will naturally view with concern, and take measures to stop, the settlement in newly colonised areas of people belonging to different language groups, praticularly when such areas happen to be on the borders of the State.

154. A concrete case may be cited by way of illustration. The sponsors of the movement for a Punjabi-speaking State have advanced a claim to the Ganganagar district of Rajasthan which came into existence as a result of the colonisation of part of the former Bikaner State under the Gang Canal system. Apart from the fact that the Punjabi-speaking people constitute only about 26 per cent. of the population of the Ganganagar district and that the claim is, therefore, untenable even on linguistic grounds, it has to be remembered that this area is essentially a part of Rajasthan and that the Punjab has no legitimate claim to it. If, in a case such as this, the area is allowed to be separated from the parent State this would create a very unhealthy precedent; and the people not belonging to the dominant language group might be looked upon as alien settlers, who would sooner or later agitate for its separation from the State.

155. Finally, there are certain aspects of the claim for linguistic units, the implications of which should be carefully analysed and understood. The most important of these is the doctrine of an area claiming to be the "home land" of all the people speaking a particular language. Its implication is that a Bengali, an Andhra or a Malayali, wherever he is settled, has his home land in Bengal, Andhra or Kerala; that he has a loyalty to that home land, over-riding the loyalty to the area of his domicile; and that in the same way, the homeland State has claims on him, wherever he may be. We cannot too strongly emphasise the dangerous character of this doctrine, especially from the point of view of our national unity. If any section of people living in one State is encouraged to look upon another State as its true home land and protector on the sole ground of language, then this would cut at the very root of the national idea.

156. It follows from the acceptance of the doctrine of the home land that the home land itself should be demarcated with care, and it has accordingly been proposed that in determining the boundaries between linguistic groups the village should be taken as the unit. In border villages generally the population is largely mixed. If on the basis of the majority belonging to one language group, a village is separated from the administrative unit to which it is now attached, then, it follows that special provisions will have to be made to see that the language composition of such a village does not change at any future time. This is obviously impossible in what is likely to be a dynamic economy.

157. The idea that all people who speak the same language and constitute a majority, whether in a village or a taluk, should be attached to their home land will do immense harm to our national growth and must, therefore, be rejected unequivocally. The allegations that Census returns in the border areas have been tampered with illustrate the dangerous possibilities inherent in this idea.

158. The home land concept must also deepen majority and minority consciousness and thereby aggravate the minority problem. The Constitution of India guarantees common citizenship to all Indian people. There can, therefore, be only one nationality in India and the idea of majority and minority would seem to run counter to it. Unfortunately, in a number of States discriminatory practices against people from other units seem to exist even at the present time. The "home land" doctrine, if encouraged, is bound to accentuate these trends. This is a problem of considerable importance and we have dealt with it at some length in a subsequent Chapter.

Composite States

159. The question whether multilingual states will strengthen the unity of India is not easy to determine. In States having more than one developed language, there has been no marked tendency in the past to develop a sense of loyalty to the state. There was never any noticeable Madrasi sentiment when the State was a composite one. On the other hand, such loyalties as did develop- within the area were based on languages. The same holds true about Bombay and Madhya Pradesh. Marathi and Gujarati feeling grew up side by side, practically to the exclusion of any particular loyalty to the province or State of Bombay. In Madhya Pradesh, the Maha Vidarbha sentiment based on the Marathi language has been vocal for many decades.

160. The idea that the creation of multilingual States will weaken the loyalty to language groups does not, therefore, seem to be justified. There is, however, one difference between composite and linguistic States. Undoubtedly, the maintenance of multilingual units will prevent the utilisation of the machinery of the state for furthering programmes of linguistic exclusiveness, and in favourable conditions. may lead to tolerance and adjustment, especially if the importance which is now attached to economic development diverts attention from the less important questions and the barren controversies regarding culture and language.

161. A composite state in which languages are integrated territorially may have another value. National loyalties do not demand that other loyalties should be eliminated. It is, however, essential that no political values or social attitudes should be accepted at the State level which would exclude concepts around which we desire our national unity to grow. A composite state which makes adequate provision for the protection of culture and the encouragement of local languages would help to prevent the growth of anti-national trends.

Conclusion

162. We now summarise our final views on the role of language as a factor bearing on the reorganisation of States. After a full consideration of the problem in all its aspects, we have come to the conclusion that it is neither possible nor desirable to reorganise States on the basis of the single test of either language or culture, but that a balanced approach to the whole problem is necessary in the interests of our national unity.

163. Such a balanced approach would appear to be:

(a) to recognise linguistic homogeneity as an important factor conducive to administrative convenience and efficiency but not to consider it as an exclusive and binding principle, over-riding all other considerations, administrative, financial or political;

(b) to ensure that communicational, educational and cultural needs of different language groups, whether resident in predominantly unilingual or composite administrative units, are adequately met;

(c) where satisfactory conditions exist, and the balance of economic, political and administrative considerations favour composite States, to continue them with the necessary safeguards to ensure that all sections enjoy equal rights and opportunities;

(d) to repudiate the "home land" concept, which negates one of the fundamental principles of the Indian Constitution, namely, equal opportunities and equal rights for all citizens throughout the length and breadth of the Union;

(e) to reject the theory of "one language one state", which is neither justified on grounds of linguistic homogeneity, because there can be more than one State speaking the same language without offending the linguistic principle, nor practicable, since different language groups, including the vast Hindi-speaking population of the Indian Union, cannot always be consolidated to form distinct linguistic units; and

(f) finally, to the extent that the realisation of unilinguism at state level would tend to breed a particularist feeling, to counter-balance that feeling by positive measures calculated to give a deeper content to Indian nationalism; to promote greater inter-play of different regional cultures, and inter-state co-operation and accord; and to reinforce the links between the Centre and the State in order to secure a greater co-ordinated working of national policies and programmes.

Culture

164. It will be fruitless for us to go into the academic question whether the entire Indian sub-continent has only one culture or whether different regions have distinct cultures. There can, of course, be no difference of opinion on the desirability of ensuring

free and harmonious development of regional cultures, or sub-cultures as they might be called, the ideal being an Indian culture enriched both in volume and in content by a confluence of diverse cultural streams, which, while merging themselves in the main central current, preserve their individual characteristics. We have noticed, however, that in most cases the cultural argument has been pressed into service with very little justification. In fact, there was hardly a political note struck before us which did not carry a cultural under-tone.

165. Culture in its general sense is a social heritage of moral, spiritual and economic values expressing itself in the distinct way of life of a group of people living as an organised community. It covers language, habits, ideas, beliefs and even the vocational pattern of society.

166. It is obvious that the impact of the administrative activity at the state level on the citizen's life cannot possibly be so comprehensive as to have any direct bearing on cultural life in the wider sense. From the point of view of the reorganisation of States, the cultural needs of the people have, therefore, to be considered primarily in terms of the growth of the regional languages, the maintenance of customs and the popularisation of the fine arts.

167. Even in this restricted sense, claims based on cultural homogeneity should normally stand the following two-fold test:

(a) the people claiming a distinctive culture must constitute a recognisable group; that is to say, it should include a number of persons sufficient by themselves to claim, conserve and develop stable traditions or the characteristics of their culture; and

(b) such cultural individuality should be capable of being expressed in terms of a defined and sizeable geographical entity.

168. Even when these conditions are fulfilled, claims based on the cultural needs of different groups of people should be considered in proper perspective. The first point to remember is that it is neither practicable nor desirable to impede social or cultural evolution which results from increasing opportunities for social and political intercourse or from impacts such as that of modern means of communication or educational activity on pre-existing modes of living. Secondly, cultural isolation or cultural conflict are inconsistent with the traditions of this country. Indian culture, as is well-known, itself represents the synthesis of different religions and diverse modes of

thought; a healthy interplay of regional cultures is, therefore, vital to the full growth of the composite Indian national culture no less than that of regional cultures themselves. Thirdly, the Constitution provides suitable safeguards for the protection of the cultural rights of the minorities of India.

169. In these circumstances, we are disinclined to attach too much importance to cultural distinctiveness as a factor independent of the linguistic needs of the people.

CHAPTER IV

Financial Viability

170. Financial and economic considerations have always been regarded as relevant to any scheme of redistribution of territories. The important questions to consider are whether financial viability can be defined, and if so, how far it should be a factor having a bearing on the changes which we might propose.

171. In some of the memoranda which have been received by us, attempts have been made to link financial viability with concepts like *per capita* national income and *per capita* State income. These concepts involve statistical and other assumptions which may themselves be questioned. In particular, potential *per capita* income will be difficult to estimate and we may not always be justified in our forecasts of how soon and in what stages this potential growth in regional national income can be realised. It is safer, therefore, to confine ourselves to a consideration of the revenue and expenditure of the various units.

172. The term "viable" is generally understood to mean "capable of living, or existing, or developing". The two cardinal concepts of viability would, therefore, appear to be:

(a) maintenance, and

(b) growth.

Translated into financial terms, these concepts would imply that a State should have adequate financial resources to maintain itself and to develop its economy. In other words, financial viability has two aspects: the short-term aspect is the ability of the State to balance its budget over a period of time, not necessarily within each single financial year; the long-term aspect is the capacity of the State to increase its economic resources in such a way that it is possible for it to balance its budget at a higher level of development, unless it chooses, on grounds of economic policy, to have a deficit budget.

173. It has been said that in a federation it is not necessary for every unit to be self-sufficient, and that a State may be able to incur the expenditure which is necessary in order to maintain a desirable minimum standard of welfare, even without financial self-

sufficiency, the resources for this purpose being made available to it by transfers, if needed, from the wealthier units. Another view is that to lay down minimum national standards is impracticable, and that such a transfer of resources to units which are responsible for spending, rather than for the provision of the resources required, is bound to lead only to waste of public money.

174. We do not feel called upon to examine this question in any detail. Our view, subject to the findings of the Finance Commission which will presumably examine this question in greater detail, is, however, that as far as possible, units should be self-supporting. They should be so constituted that they have an incentive to raise and are able to raise, on their own initiative, at least a part of the resources needed for their development. A transfer of financial resources from the Centre to the States may be unavoidable, but such transfers should normally be utilised for development purposes and not for meeting the ordinary obligations of a State on revenue account.

175. The question of financial viability, that is to say, the ability to balance the budget over a period of time, is, as has already been stated, linked up also with the question of norms of expenditure. The Expert Committee of the Constituent Assembly on the financial provisions of the Constitution, it may be recalled, was of the opinion that it was impracticable to lay down for India a national minimum standard of expenditure. Nothing has happened since then which makes it any the easier to prescribe a pattern of expenditure in the States which can be regarded as the "norm". But several small units spend disproportionately large amounts from their revenues on general administration and administrative overheads. Obviously, it will be preferable to have units where the percentage of expenditure on general administration and overheads is not excessive.

176. We have tried to translate these general ideas into a few working principles. It seems to us that a unit to be regarded as financially self-supporting should be able to meet the following broad tests:

(i) on the average, and over a reasonably short period, a State's revenue and expenditure should be in balance—unless a deficit is deliberately being planned as a part of wider economic policy for the country as a whole; this balanced budget standard is to be attained after providing in full for servicing the State's public debt, including all the loans obtained from the Centre;

(ii) consistently with (i), the State should be able to afford such increases as are necessary in the expenditure on productive and nation-building services which are legitimately within the State sphere, *e.g.*, the extension of community projects. No all-India standards can, of course, be prescribed, but it should be possible for each State to set apart progressively more and more funds for development purposes; and

(iii) no State should be dependent on the Centre to such an extent as to cause any embarrassment either to itself or to the Centre.

177. The tests set out in the preceding paragraph may appear to state the obvious. But this is really not so, for the financial position of a number of States at the present time cannot be considered altogether satisfactory; and any change that is being made should, if possible, be an improvement on the existing state of affairs.

178. The most important test of financial viability, it will be seen, is ability, on the average, over a fairly short-term period to have a balanced budget standard. This is not, perhaps, as widely accepted as might be expected. In the memoranda which have been submitted to the Commission, there has been an attempt to argue, especially on behalf of the Part C States, that if a State is able to cover its normal non-development or rather non-plan expenditure, its financial position must be regarded as satisfactory—development being the responsibility of the Centre; an alternative approach to this question has been that the Centre must, as part of the arrangements necessary in order to improve the financial position of the States, write off a proportion of the debt due from the States to the Centre.

179. Subject to the findings of the Finance Commission, or other expert bodies which will presumably examine the claims of the different States in due course, our views are that the States of the Indian Union, which are now committed to a policy of development, should normally be in a position to meet their expenditure by raising the necessary resources to the extent agreed upon between them and the Centre from time to time. To the extent that a State fails in raising sufficient revenue to meet the expenditure which is legitimately to be borne by it, a further burden is necessarily thrown on the Centre, and this is bound to prevent the utilisation of central resources for other purposes, including grants or loans to other States.

180. It is not necessary, and it is not in any case the function of this Commission to prescribe in detail rules regulating allocations to capital or revenue account, servicing and amortisation of the public debt, arrangements for the collection or utilisation of the proceeds of the betterment levy etc. But whatever these arrangements as to detail may be, and even though some of them may vary from State to State, depending on the amount of discretion exercised by State Governments, the essential principle, namely, that over a fairly short period, the revenue budget should be balanced, every commitment being honoured as it falls due, must not be obscured.

181. It is no doubt true that all the States of the Indian Union are now dependent in varying degrees on central aid for development expenditure. However, we must not lose sight of the fact that excessive dependence on the Centre detracts from the federal principle, since a real division of political power is not possible without an adequate separation of financial powers and resources. The balance of a federal union is bound to be disturbed, if there are amongst its constituent units poor relations or mendicants, particularly if they are inclined to be extra-vagant. "If a federal system, with any real independence in the States is to continue", says Sir John Latham, formerly Chief Justice of the Australian High Court, "the States must have financial resources under their own control reasonably adequate to their responsibilities".

182. We are conscious of the fact that, with the growing need for administrative co-operation between the Central and the State Governments, the partial dependence of the State Governments upon payments from the Centre, and the fact that the Central Government, by the use of the system of conditional grants, frequently promotes development in matters which are constitutionally assigned to the States, the concept of federalism is now everywhere undergoing a change. How much importance is to be attached to inter-state co-operation rather than to the strictly constitutional aspects of federalism will depend on the needs and circumstances of the time and the context in which this problem is being discussed.

183. At the present time, however, we have thought it best to take the view that, as far as possible, the units which are created should not be saddled with an excessive burden on account of the overheads of administration and should be fully informed by a sense of financial responsibility, and, being so informed, should co-operate with the Central Government in financial matters, by raising resources within the provincial field and avoiding as far as possible non-development expenditure.

184. Financial viability as we have attempted to define it, should, in our opinion, be regarded as an important criterion bearing on the reorganisation of States. Financial considerations, however, have to be weighed with other important factors, and decisions have to be taken on a balance of arguments and advantages and in accordance with the larger national interests.

CHAPTER V

REQUIREMENTS OF NATIONAL DEVELOPMENT PLANS

185. The Resolution of the Government of India appointing this Commission states that changes which interfere with the successful prosecution of the national plan will be harmful to the national interest. In the paragraphs which follow, we take note of some of the basic requirements from the point of view of the economic development of the country on a planned basis.

186. India's development plan may increasingly take the shape of a centrally-directed effort to locate and implement projects which are intended to give the highest return within the shortest periods, the benefits accruing to the country as a whole and not merely to any particular areas or regions in it. If the maximum advantage is to be derived from any such development plan or plans, the central planning authority must operate under minimum restrictions in its choice of methods and investments, and parochial tendencies within the Union should be discouraged.

187. There are certain provisions in the Constitution which are intended to take care of these needs. The possibility that some States may develop a particularist outlook and try to take advantage of such loopholes as there are in the Constitution, or that they may in practice, though not in theory, discriminate against or interfere with the mobility of capital, enterprise and labour cannot of course be ruled out. But the effect of this is not likely to be serious; and so far as can be foreseen, it may be safe to proceed on the assumption that no State has the power to destroy the integral unity of India considered as one big development area.

188. The second point which we desire to emphasise is that no area should be in a position to impose on those who are responsible for the formulation of plans, priorities which are not otherwise appropriate, merely as a result of reorganisation or as the price of agreeing to such reorganisation. This has a bearing on claims which have been made on behalf of particular areas to the effect that a certain minimum amount of development expenditure, proportionate say to population, should be incurred in these areas.

189. It is also necessary that the direct extra cost of reorganisation should be as little as possible; and some economy in existing expenditure may even be aimed at. The claims which have been made in the memoranda submitted to the Commission are so numerous and are of such variety that, if they were to be substantially met, the burden of extra non-development expenditure on

Governors, Legislatures etc., is bound to be very heavy. It is obvious, however, that at a time when all the available resources are to be used for the purposes of the plan, and when attempts are being made to increase such resources through economy in non-development expenditure, a scheme of reorganisation which significantly increases the load of non-development expenditure, would be prejudicial to the national interests.

190. The first five-year plan period might have come to an end and the second five-year plan might be under way, by the time decisions taken on the Commission's recommendations are implemented. A natural consequence of reorganisation will, therefore, be some degree of dislocation in the second five-year plan. This is because:

(i) the new governments may alter the programmes of their predecessor governments;

(ii) existing inter-state agreements on which the programmes are based may become obsolete and new agreements may have to be arrived at;

(iii) the resources forecast at state level may be upset; and

(iv) newly-created units, being enveloped in general uncertainty for some time, are unlikely, in the normal course, to address themselves with vigour and drive to the implementation of the second five-year plan from its very commencement.

191. On the other hand, the possible advantages of reorganisation from the point of view of the plan are likely to be:

(i) the elimination of the sense of uncertainty which prevails in the disputed areas and hampers their development;

(ii) the psychological satisfaction which certain groups of people or areas might derive from reorganisation;

(iii) the possible elimination of multiplicity of jurisdictions in certain areas; and

(iv) the creation of compact States with complementary economies, which is likely to facilitate the mobilisation and a better distribution of financial resources.

192. The Commission cannot hope to be able to recommend any arrangements which will avoid any interference with the Plan altogether. Attempts may be made to minimise disorganisation, by ways and means help from the Centre in the first few years or by adjustments in the State plans which may be intended to assure the States of residual central help. But even if this is done, it will be extremely difficult for State Governments both to implement a development

plan at the same or, if possible, accelerated speed and to reorganise and stabilise the machinery of government.

193. The considerations which we might bear in mind in the light of what has been stated in the preceding paragraphs are:

(a) no change should be made otherwise than for clear and compelling reasons;

(b) the permanent advantages and possible recurring economies which can result from the scheme of reorganisation should be such as to compensate for the dislocation; and

(c) the administrative consequences of reorganisation should be clearly thought-out and suitable machinery should be devised in order to minimise the time required to deal with them.

194. We have indicated in the later portions of this report the steps which might be taken to adapt the existing agreements relating to important inter-state projects and to ensure that the execution and working of such projects are not prejudiced by any measures for the reorganisation of the States concerned. It seems desirable that, where in the interests of the orderly implementation of a project, certain financial or administrative measures have to be taken, such as those relating to soil conservation, settlement of newly-reclaimed land or the levy of betterment charges etc., the Central Government should have the power to ensure that the States co-operate in achieving the desired objectives.

195. The Government of India will no doubt consider how far these matters can be covered by legislation which will have to be promoted under Articles 3 and 4 of the Constitution, or by invoking the provisions of the contemplated Central Acts concerning inter-state water disputes and the development of inter-state rivers.

196. Apparently legislation under Article 4 will have to be confined to supplemental, incidental and consequential matters. The provisions of the Water Disputes Bill and the River Boards Bill also do not appear to confer on the Central Government adequate powers in respect of projects which are of an inter-State character. This is a matter on which we do not feel called upon to express an opinion in any great detail, but we regard it as of very great importance that the earliest steps should be taken to remove any impediments which hamper the formulation and execution of development programmes as such impediments not only retard the economic progress of the country but also tend to give rise to serious political difficulties.

CHAPTER VI

Regional Planning and a Balanced Economy

197. One of the suggestions made to us has been that it would be an advantage if administrative units could be made to conform to natural economic regions.

198. This appears to be an attractive proposition, but there are practical difficulties in the way of its implementation. As attempts to study regional patterns even in the more advanced countries have shown, the difficulty is that it is either impossible to suggest an acceptable definition of a region, or, if a definition can be suggested, to apply it in a dynamic situation, when the entire economy as in India, is undergoing a rapid change.

199. Some considerations which may be regarded as important from the point of view of national planning are, however, discussed in the paragraphs which follow.

200. The unified control of river valleys for purposes of development is, for example, desirable; and some evidence has been submitted to the Commission in support of the view that if control by two or more States can be avoided, it will promote the more orderly implementation of our multi-purpose projects.

201. A detailed examination has revealed the difficulties of this problem. The number of instances in which headworks are situated on or near the borders of existing States is so large, and there is so little chance of reducing this number substantially by adopting any scheme of reorganisation other than one based on the unity of river valleys, that multiple control of irrigation and power projects cannot be rejected in principle.

202. The gravity of the complaints made to the Commission regarding difficulties which hamper the working of joint projects need not, however, be exaggerated. The theory that every State should have access to the headworks of river-valley projects which benefit it, or be able to control the catchment area of the river or rivers in question, is also one which cannot be wholly accepted.

203. This is because firstly, with so many river valley projects being planned or In operation the question of redrawing state boundaries will become very complicated and secondly, in the case of each new proposal regarding a river valley project if the boundaries

lie outside the State, which benefits from the project, the question of altering the boundaries will arise. While this has to be the broad approach it is clear to us that where territorial adjustments intended to secure access to head-works or unified control over river valley projects do not come into conflict with other important considerations, it will be a clear advantage to make provision for them for the obvious reason that multiplicity of jurisdictions hampers smooth execution of projects and leads very often to unnecessary friction and controversies.

204. A suggestion which may be investigated is that areas which are grouped round important cities and towns or other centres of activity, nodal regions in other words, should be distinguished; and that new States should, if possible, be created so as to conform to a division of the country on these lines. The claims which have been made in favour of the theory of nodal regions are that economic activity centres round a few important places, the flow of trade and commodities being a function of distances from such central points. If these propositions were true, it might be desirable if a state which controlled the central town or area were also in command of the natural hinterland. It could be argued then that the flow of goods and services within each such natural region would be free; that the centre and its outlying area could develop in a complementary and co-ordinated manner; and that regional economic planning as a rule would be facilitated.

205. The concept of a nodal region is, however, still very vague; and it rests on insecure data. In this country at any rate, it is impossible at this stage to distinguish such regions. Even if they can be distinguished, there will be every reason to expect that as economic development proceeds apace, the regional patterns, if any, which may exist at present, will become outmoded. After some time, there may, for example, be other foci or centres of development to consider.

206. An alternative concept of an economic region is to regard it, not as a nodal region, but as an area in which the *per capita* national income is not greatly above or greatly below the national average. This is a comprehensive concept and is intended to be one. It includes other criteria which have been suggested, like a well-balanced pattern of occupational distribution; the maintenance of a proper balance between agriculture and industry; the avoidance of wide disparities in population densities, land utilisation and food production; and the availability of unoccupied land to the reorganised units.

207. It is implicit in this concept of regionalism that wide differences which now exist in such matters as population density, area, natural resources and physical endowments, will more or less disappear; and from an economic and planning point of view, this is an attractive ideal, because this will ensure that no single administrative division in the country will be too rich or too poor, having regard to the national standard.

208. The revenue and expenditure of the States in such a scheme of reorganisation may in due course become more nearly comparable than is now the case; and something like a national standard in public expenditure may ultimately emerge. The need for the transfer of resources from one administrative division to another will also be very largely eliminated at the same time; and the advantages of this in a federation, in which the units will otherwise be engaged in making claims and counter-claims regarding the distribution of revenue resources, can hardly be exaggerated.

209. There are great difficulties, however, in translating the concept of a *per capita* national income which does not deviate greatly from the national average into a scheme of redistribution of territories such as this Commission has been called upon to propose. Moreover, to the extent that the country as a whole is regarded as one economic unit, and as the Government of India moves more and more into the centre of things, the beneficial effects of central expenditure will be felt all over the country; and particular attention will be or can be paid to the needs of distressed or backward areas.

210. Consistently with what has been stated in the preceding paragraphs, the Commission cannot accept in principle the idea of economic self-sufficiency at the regional level. However, while there are obvious difficulties in the way of equating economic regions with administrative units, it would be desirable, where this does not come into conflict with other important principles, to bear in mind the need for avoiding wide disparities in natural endowments and resources between the various States.

CHAPTER VII

SMALLER *vs.* LARGER STATES

211. It would be relevant also to discuss at this stage the question whether the reorganised units should be big or small.

212. Both points of view have been placed before the Commission. Briefly summarised, the arguments in favour of small States are that in such States the administration will be more accessible to the people; and that there will be a livelier sense of local needs and appreciation of local problems on the part of the Government. Further, in such matters as public co-operation in community project areas, availability of voluntary labour for public purposes and the attitude of the people to economic development generally, the small State has an advantage. A closer link between the electorate and its representatives may help to bring about a real unity of outlook and community of interest between the people and those charged with their governance. A small State, it is claimed, may be able to administer its area intensively and to promote social welfare measures much more effectively than a large State.

213. It is undoubtedly an advantage to have compact and manageable administrative units. The merits and demerits of small States, however, have to be examined from the point of view of the progress of the plan as well as our basic conception of the status of the constituent units of the Indian Union.

214. It may be doubted in the first place whether except in the Swiss Cantons, it has been possible to realise the ideal of direct democracy anywhere. As regards the appreciation of local needs, the machinery of planning is intended to serve this purpose; and it is extremely unlikely that a small State will be able to finance on its own projects which, as matters stand at present, have no chance of being considered at the national level.

215. The question of public co-operation, assuming that it can be organised on a big scale for the purposes of the plan, would no doubt be important. But even here, there is no evidence that only a small State can succeed in enlisting such co-operation or that a large State will necessarily fail to do so. Recent experience in such areas as the Manimuthar and Tapti valleys seems to indicate that the amount of public co-operation that may be forthcoming is not governed by factors such as the size of the State but by the merits

of the projects themselves and the vigour and enterprise of the administration at the local level.

216. When it is remembered that too many small States necessarily add to the burden of unproductive expenditure, and that the view can be held that expenditure on social services cannot be regarded as more important than basic productive investment like river valley and power development schemes, which a large State will be in a much better position to undertake, the case for small states cannot be regarded as impressive.

217. The case for sizeable administrative units is based partly on a rebuttal of the claim in favour of small States and partly on other independent grounds. A sizeable State should normally be financially more stable and more able to conform to the broad requirements of financial and economic policies, as they may be formulated from time to time for the country as a whole. A further point in favour of larger units is that only the creation of relatively larger States will lead to appreciable economy in the unproductive expenditure on administration, which the country so clearly needs at the present stage.

218. Experience of the working of different administrations in this country does not lend support to the view that, in large States, standards of administration deteriorate. In actual practice, some of the larger States in India have proved to be the best-administered. In fact, efficiency of administration is seldom determined by the size of the unit. There are other factors such as economic and social conditions within the different areas; political consciousness, tempers and traditions of the people; and the political acumen and the sense of public service of the leaders in different areas, which set the pace of progress and administrative efficiency.

219. The world has travelled a great distance from the days of the Greek city states and the idea of direct democracy which they embodied. With the expansion of the requirements of organised social communities, modern States inevitably tend to grow bigger and it is difficult to reverse the process. In the existing conditions in this country as determined by territory and population, the ideal of self-government for very small units can, therefore, possibly be realised only at the level of local institutions.

220. In a matter like this, it would be unwise to be dogmatic or to rule out exceptions. When it is suggested that the weight of argument is in favour of large rather than small States, the objective

is that every State should have adequate resources to assume the responsibility devolving on a full-fledged constituent unit of the Union. This, however, does not mean that units should be so unwieldy as to be without any intrinsic life of their own or to defeat the very purpose for which larger units are suggested, *i.e.*, administrative efficiency and co-ordination of economic development and welfare activity.

CHAPTER VIII

SOME OTHER FACTORS

221. The wishes of the people, to the extent they are objectively ascertainable and do not come into conflict with larger national interests, should be an important consideration in readjusting the territories of the States.

222. The Nehru Committee regarded "the wishes of the majority of the people" as one of the two important considerations which should guide the redistribution of provinces, the other being the linguistic principle.[1] But the right of self-determination, which the Committee conceded, was subject to the important condition that its exercise should not "conflict with any other important principle or vital question".[2]

223. The Dar Commission was disinclined to impose the wishes of the majority of the people upon "a substantial minority of people speaking the same language".[3] It felt that the question of the formation of linguistic provinces was of such national importance that it could not be decided with reference to the wishes of the people who wanted these provinces, without taking into account the repercussions which they would have on the country as a whole.[4]

224. The J.V.P. Committee admitted that if public sentiment insisted on linguistic redistribution, it would have to be respected, "but subject to certain limitations in regard to the good of India as a whole"[5] and certain other conditions which included general agreement on the changes proposed.

225. It will be apparent that, while the bodies which previously went into the question of reorganisation of States, attached importance to the wishes of the people in varying degrees, none of them conceded the principle of self-determination without subjecting it to certain limitations.

226. Some of the memoranda received by the Commission, particularly those received from small units, seek the perpetuation of these units on the ground that this would meet the wishes of the people. It is not possible to ascertain with any measure of definiteness, what the real wishes of the people in these areas are. Assuming, however, that, in such cases, the majority of the people want the maintenance of the existing units, it has to be considered how

---

1. Report of the Nehru Committee, All Parties Conference, 1928, p. 63.
2. *Ibid*, p. 63.
3. Report of the Linguistic Provinces Commission, para. 10.
4. *Idid*, para. 148
5. Report of the Linguistic Provinces Committee, Congress, p. 15

far a unit which, on financial, administrative or other grounds is incapable of survival as a constituent unit of the Union, can be sustained purely on the ground that the majority of the people are disinclined to a disturbance of the *status quo*.

227. So far as the component parts of the Indian Union are concerned, there can be no question of the right of self-determination being exercised regardless of all other factors and circumstances. It may be recalled that when the former princely states were merged, the right of self-determination was demanded for these states by certain sections of public opinion. This was not agreed to on the ground that these units were incapable of survival as viable administrative units.

228. It cannot be denied that in a democratic country the wishes of the people of even small areas are entitled to the fullest consideration. But it is equally undeniable that such wishes must be subject to some essential limitations. Thus, for instance, if the principle of self-determination were to govern the internal reorganisation of States, there will be no limit to the possible demands for separate States. Every linguistic or other minority group might demand a State for itself, and the wishes of the people could be swayed by purely temporary considerations. The acceptance of such demands would lead to the division of the country into a large number of small units. The wishes of the people of different areas as a factor bearing on reorganisation have, therefore, to be considered together with other important factors such as the human and material resources of the areas claiming state hood, the wishes of substantial minorities, the essential requirements of the Indian Constitution and the larger national interests.

Historical factor

229. It has been urged in some memoranda that a common historical tradition fosters a sense of kinship and oneness and that common history, therefore, should be regarded as a factor relevant to the reorganisation of States.

230. The important part that historical association plays in creating a common consciousness cannot be denied. But in redrawing the political map of India, the question before us is, should the guidance come from the local or regional history or from the cardinal lessons of the history of the whole of India? While the history of an area, considered in isolation from the other currents of Indian

history, may indicate only the past boundaries of the States in the area or the past associations of its people, our national history tells us that the unity and strength of the country should be the first consideration. Besides, historical arguments are bound to be of doubtful validity because no conclusion could be drawn merely from the fact that the area proposed for retransfer to a State fell at one time within the administrative jurisdiction of that State. More often than not, every disputed area admits of more than one irreconcilable claim based on history, and obviously, the facts of the existing situation are much more important than the fact that in previous times the area concerned had a different administrative attachment.

231. Overemphasis on the historical factor is likely to lead to the growth of a sense of rivalry, exclusiveness and narrowness in different regions. This revivalism, which is the basis of many claims to statehood, is not in itself an evil thing so long as it is kept within bounds and is related to the main currents of Indian history. It has to be recognised, in respect of some of the States, that this is one of the basic factors governing regional spirit and not to take it into account may be somewhat unrealistic. The potentialities of the historical argument, for evil, cannot, however, be forgotten. While, therefore, we have been alive to the value of historical connections and links, we have not been disposed to attach undue importance to arguments based on them.

Geographical factors

232. Geographical contiguity of units is undoubtedly essential for administrative convenience. Contiguity, however, it must be emphasised, does not necessarily imply or involve the need for a geographical frontier, although in some of the memoranda special emphasis has been laid on physiography and it has been argued that States should ordinarily be marked off by natural boundaries like mountains, rivers and water sheds.

233. It is claimed that there are certain areas which are regarded by different groups as "areal expressions" of the collective personality of these language groups, but the actual demarcation of territories on that basis is very difficult. In these conditions, apart from geographical compactness, physical geography can at best be a factor entitled only to secondary consideration.

Administrative considerations

234. Administrative considerations have already been discussed along with certain other principles bearing on the reorganisation of

State territories. Linguistic homogeneity, geographical compactness, alignment of communications ensuring easy accessibility from one area to another and the elimination of multiplicity of jurisdictions in areas, which administratively and economically constitute integrated units, are some of the objectives which have to be borne in mind from the point of view of administrative convenience. To the extent to which it is a relevant consideration, the question of the size of the State has also been examined earlier.

Totality of circumstances to govern each case

235. Before we conclude our examination of the principles which should govern the solution of the problem of reorganisation, it remains for us to indicate how the different principles proposed by us can be applied to each case. The problems of reorganisation vary from region to region. It has to be kept in mind that the inter-play for centuries of historical, linguistic, geographical, economic and other factors has produced peculiar patterns in different regions. Each case, therefore, has its own background. Besides, the problems of reorganisation are so complex that it would be unrealistic to determine any case by a single test alone. All the committees and commissions which have previously gone into the matter such as the Dar Commission and the J.V.P. Committee have rightly expressed themselves against a monistic approach to the problem. We have, accordingly, examined each case on its own merits and in its own context and arrived at conclusions after taking into consideration the totality of circumstances and on an overall assessment of the solutions proposed.

PART III

PROPOSALS FOR REORGANISATION

CHAPTER I

Basic pattern of the component units

236. The States constituting the Union of India are very unequal in size, population and resources. As we have observed earlier, they are also unequal before the law. The present classification of States into three categories known as Part A, Part B and Part C States was adopted essentially as a transitional expedient and was not intended to be a permanent feature of the constitutional structure of this country. A preliminary but essential point to consider, therefore, is how far there is any justification for maintaining the existing constitutional disparity between the different constituent units of the Indian Union.

237. Public opinion, both within and without the Part B and Part C States, has been severely critical of the present anomalous arrangement which, it has been argued, offends against the principle of equal rights and opportunities for the people of India. We are impressed by the weight of the public sentiment on this matter. The only rational approach to the problem, in our opinion, will be that the Indian Union should have primary constitutent units having equal status and a uniform relationship with the Centre, except where, for any strategic, security or other compelling reasons, it is not practicable to integrate any small area with the territories of a full-fledged unit. If the States of the Union are to be treated on a footing of equality and if the status of the present Part A States is accepted as the standard, then the Part B and Part C States must disappear. Such a step would be justified on its own merits. Now that a reorganisation of the States has to be proposed on a rational basis, the regrouping of territories cannot be undertaken by categories. The existing distinctions cannot, therefore, be maintained.

238. If the States of the Union are to enjoy a uniform status, it is necessary that each State should be inherently capable of survival as a viable administrative unit. It should have the resources, financial, administrative and technical, to maintain itself as a modern State. It should normally be able to establish and maintain institutions to educate, train and equip its people for its administrative, technical and professional requirements. And finally,

it should be able not only to meet the day-to-day needs of the administration but also to expand its social services and other development activities.

239. It may be recalled that most of the former princely States lost their separate existence because they were not considered capable of maintaining the institutions of a modern democratic government. In the circumstances in which the integration of these States took place, this principle, however, could not be uniformly applied. It would be unfair to concede any prescriptive right in favour of any of the existing units on the mere ground that it escaped the sweep of political developments in the country owing to some favourable turn in the events or some such factor as a political concession, its geographical isolation, location on the border or economic backwardness.

Part B States.

240. The problem of abolishing the distinction between Part B States and Part A States would not present any serious difficulty. There are three factors, apart from certain minor transitory provisions of the Constitution, which distinguish the Part B States from Part A States:

(a) certain agreements in consequence of their financial integration;

(b) the general control vested in the Government of India by Article 371; and

(c) the institution of the Rajpramukh.

Of these, the agreements mentioned in (a), to the extent they are still operative, can be suitably adjusted. The Constitution provides for a review of these agreements at the end of five years and a revision is now due.

241. So far as Article 371 is concerned, with the establishment of properly constituted legislatures in Part B States, the exercise of central control over these States has been gradually falling into desuetude. Even in the past, Article 371 operated in actual practice only as a constitutional sanction behind the informal advice given by the Government of India to governments of the Part B States from time to time. A formal directive under Article 371 was issued only on one occasion and that too was withdrawn. The institution of advisers to State Governments who were appointed either by the Government of India or at their instance has also

been abolished. Bearing this in mind and the fact that the present territorial complexion of the Part B States will be radically affected by the recommendations which we make in subsequent chapters, the provisions contained in Article 371 will no longer be required.

242. The position and the role of the Rajpramukhs in Part B States are more or less the same as those of the Governors of Part A States, both being constitutional heads. While the Governor of a State is appointed by the President, the Rajpramukh has been defined in relation to Hyderabad and Mysore as the person who for the time being is recognised as the Nizam or the Maharaja, and in relation to any other state as the person recognised by the President as such. Likewise, while a Governor can be removed from office by the President, recognition can be withdrawn from a Rajpramukh.

243. The institution, however, has a political aspect and large sections of public opinion view its continuance with disfavour on the ground that it ill accords with the essentially democratic framework of the country. There are, in our opinion, some weighty considerations against the continuance of this institution. In the first place, we feel that the constitutional head of a State should not, generally speaking, be a resident of that State. The Rajpramukh being *ex-hypothesi* a person having deep-rooted local interests and influence, his position as the constitutional head of a State is altogether anomalous.

244. In view of the past associations of the Rajpramukhs with the territories of which they were hereditary rulers, it is doubtful if they can effectively discharge the essential functions of the constitutional head of a State either from the point of view of the Government of India or from that of the State Government concerned. Besides, apart from its undemocratic character, the institution of Rajpramukh tends to maintain, even where it does not create, loyalties which, in our opinion, are undesirable. We would, therefore, recommend that this institution be abolished.

245. We do not propose to go into the question of the commitments which the Government of India might have made to the holders of this office. It appears, however, that privy purses as well as most of their privileges and rights have been guaranteed to them as former rulers of their respective States, although some emoluments and amenities are also enjoyed by them by virtue of their office as Rajpramukhs. In the event of the abolition of the institution of Rajpramukh, therefore, the rights and privileges enjoyed by the rulers who hold office as Rajpramukhs at present will not for the most part be affected.

Part C States

246. We next proceed to consider the position of the Part C States, which have to undergo more radical changes in order to be brought on a par with the Part A States.

247. The governments of the Part C States have pressed, from time to time, their claim to the same status as that enjoyed by Part A and Part B States. It has been repeatedly argued on behalf of these States that there is no reason why democratic government should not function in them in the same manner as in the other States.

248. There is little that Part C States, as a category of States, have in common with each other. Separated from each other by long distances, they have greater economic, linguistic and cultural affinities with the neighbouring States than with each other. Politically, economically and educationally, they are in varying phases of development. Even in the constitutional field, they do not follow a uniform pattern in that some of them have legislatures and ministries and others only advisory councils. Two are administered through Lt. Governors and the remaining through Chief Commissioners.

249. Since these States differ so much from each other, it is hardly possible to make out a common case for their continued existence. However, some measure of community of interests has developed in political circles in these States since the commencement of the Constitution, and particularly since the appointment of this Commission. Representatives of these States have assembled together in more than one conference and have tried to impress on this Commission as well as on the country at large that, financially, the Part C States are viable; that, from a broader point of view, the experiment of democratic administration in their areas, since it was introduced in 1951, has proved to be a great success; and that any material change in their boundaries will run counter to the wishes of the people, and dislocate the implementation of their development plans.

250. That the existing position is unsatisfactory is now generally admitted. The views put forward and the resolutions passed at the recent conferences of the representatives of the Part C States make it clear, if they do nothing else, that radical changes in the existing pattern are needed. There is difference of opinion only regarding the nature of the change which is proposed and not as regards the need for the change itself.

251. Public opinion all over the country seems to favour the merger of these States in the adjoining units as the best means of eliminating the present anomaly. It may also be recalled that, in an additional note appended to the report of the Committee appointed by the Constituent Assembly to recommend suitable constitutional changes in the administrative systems of the Chief Commissioners' provinces, the representatives of Ajmer and Coorg expressed the view that "the special problems arising out of smallness of area, geographical position, scantiness of resources, attended with what may be called administrative difficulties of many a complex nature may, at no distant future, necessitate the joining of each of these areas with a contiguous unit".[1] We do not consider that the reforms introduced by the Act of 1951 could have so radically changed the whole context that the very cogent arguments advanced in favour of the merger of these States have lost their validity.

252. There is a great deal to be said in favour of the amalgamation of these States with the adjoining States. Of the nine Part C States, six have legislatures and ministries; and of these only one, namely, Coorg, has been in a position to carry on so far a reasonable system of administration without central assistance. The other five States have been increasingly subsidised by the Centre through the payment of revenue gap grants-in-aid; and these revenue gap payments (in the case of Delhi, Bhopal, Vindhya Pradesh, Ajmer and Himachal Pradesh) as estimated in the latest budget of the Central Government amount to about ten rupees *per capita*. In the case of the three remaining States, namely, Kutch, Manipur and Tripura, the budgets are still merged in that of the Government of India, but the *per capita* deficits on revenue account as now estimated are already so heavy that, if the 1951 Act were extended to these States and if revenue gap grants-in-aid from the Centre became payable to them, such grants would amount to about twenty rupees *per capita*.

253. These heavy subsidies from the Government of India compare with fixed revenue gap grants-in-aid in the case of three Part B States (Mysore, Travancore-Cochin and Saurashtra) of nine crores of rupees which works out to about four rupees *per capita*. What is more significant, the payments in the case of the Part B States are fixed or are intended to be reduced according to a sliding scale, while in the case of the Part C States the subsidies are steadily increasing.

254. The Part C States have claimed that if Article 264(b) of the Constitution did not debar the payment to them of appropriate shares

---

1. Reports of the Committees of the Constituent Assembly of India, Third Series, p. 120.

from out of the divisible pools of income-tax and central excise, and if *ad hoc* grants as in the case of the other States were also payable to them for development and other purposes they would become self-sufficient in respect of their normal expenditure.

255. The validity of this claim can be questioned. If the Part C States are to be treated like other units they will have to surrender to a greater or lesser extent the very heavy revenue subsidies which they now receive, in return for reimbursements of revenue and other payments from the Centre, which, together, cannot make up for this loss.

256. *Prima facie,* therefore, the claim that these States are financially in no worse position than the other States, that they will be able to cover their ordinary non-development expenditure if they are treated like the other States, and that they can continue to exist as independent entities, without being an undue burden on the Centre, cannot be accepted.

257. An amendment to the Government of Part C States Act, 1951, has recently been passed to enable the Legislatures of these States, where they exist, to discuss and vote the demands on account of capital expenditure within the Consolidated Fund. This amendment was intended to meet the demand for an extension of the authority of the State legislatures. The result in actual practice has been that, since October, 1954, the States have had to borrow heavily from the Government of India; and when the liability for the repayment of these loans and of the amounts which they may have to borrow in future is also taken into account, their prospective financial position can hardly be described as satisfactory.

258. On the other hand, it can be said with much more justification that the present administrative and financial arrangements have not been deliberately planned, but have been devised to meet the needs of the situation as it was found to exist after the Government of India's decision to introduce a measure of responsible government in these areas. As an *ad hoc* arrangement, the existing position is all the more unsatisfactory and cannot be continued indefinitely. The existing arrangement commits the Government of India, in effect, to a growing but uncertain liability, both on revenue and on capital accounts, and has also led to an increase in the burden of unproductive expenditure.

259. When the Government of Part C States Bill, 1951, was debated in Parliament in 1951, the extra cost of democratic administration was estimated at about half a crore of rupees. It was believed then that this would be a reasonable price to pay for a more efficient and satisfactory form of government. In the light of such experience as we have had of the working of the 1951 Act, it is doubtful whether either of the two hopes that were then entertained, namely, that the extra cost would be inconsiderable and that the administration would become appreciably more efficient, can now be regarded as having beer fulfilled. The increase in the cost of general administration, which has taken place, is already very considerably in excess of half a crore of rupees; and if the progress of the five year plan is an index of the level of administrative efficiency, the Part C States have, generally speaking, fared rather poorly.

260. The Part C States have urged that the paralysing control which is exercised by the Government of India must be held to account for this poor performance. Considering the ultimate responsibility of the Government of India to Parliament in respect of the administration of these States, Central control over them cannot be completely eliminated. But the main reason for the relatively slow progress of the plan in the Part C States is not the nature or the extent of the control exercised by the Central Government.

261. The administrative services in the Part C States have not been and are not likely to be properly manned, the main reason being that service in these States offers inadequate opportunities. Reasonably efficient state services cannot be created individually in each of these States or jointly for all of them, so long as these States, situated as they are, cannot attract or retain talent. The inadequacies of the administrative system are also shown by the existence of administrative anomalies such as the combination of offices and concentration of authority. There are instances, for example, of the head of the State functioning as the head of many other departments and of the Chief Secretary exercising the powers of the highest revenue authority. One advantage of the merger of these States in larger units will, therefore, be a general improvement of their administrative system.

262. One other reason why a merger may be desirable is that the Part C States, being in most cases unplanned enclaves, continue to have close economic links with the surrounding areas. It is not necessary to elaborate the point at this stage. We deal later with the economic affiliations of the individual States in the Chapters

dealing with the proposed new units. For the purpose of this general discussion, however, it is necessary to point out that the case for merger is reinforced, if the formulation and orderly implementation of major development plans in or near the Part C States are taken into consideration.

263. An argument often cited in support of the claim of the Part C States to separate existence is that popular government can be a reality only if the States are as small as possible consistently with the principle of self-sufficiency. We have discussed earlier the merits and demerits of the smaller states. It is true that smaller states make possible a closer personal touch between the administration and the people, but there is a point beyond which personal touch degenerates into personal rule with all that it implies. The governments of smaller areas, not having enough work in the field of policy-making, tend to undertake detailed and direct administration. When the lowest appointments are made at the highest level and those charged with the responsibility of shaping major policies assume the role of district authorities or subordinate administrative agencies, the services must lose initiative, drive and a sense of responsibility. Democratic institutions function properly, only if the respective role of each organ and agency of the state is clearly understood. Disregard of this basic principle must impede the growth of impersonal administration which is as vital for working democratic institutions as close contact between the people and the administration.

264. The analogy of some other federations where small units function along with bigger ones is inapplicable to the States of the Indian Union. The constituent units in Switzerland and the U.S.A. were pre-existing sovereign States. The States of the Indian Union, on the other hand, cannot claim to have possessed that status at least in recent history. They cannot, therefore, claim any territorial inviolability. Besides, financial resources of any of the Part C States bear no comparison with the much greater resources of the relatively small units in the U.S.A., Australia, Canada or Switzerland.

265. To sum up, the position is that there is a general consensus of opinion that the existing set-up of the Part C States is unsatisfactory. The solution suggested by the official representatives of the Part C States, namely, a constitutional status which is identical with that of the Part A States, will remove only the constitutional anomalies. These small units will still continue to be economically unbalanced, financially weak and administratively and politically unstable.

266. The democratic experiment in these States, wherever it has been tried, has proved to be more costly than was expected or intended and this extra cost has not been justified by increased administrative efficiency or rapid economic and social progress. Quite obviously, these States cannot subsist as separate administrative units without excessive dependence on the Centre, which will lead to all the undesirable consequences of divorcing the responsibility for expenditure from that for finding the resources.

267. Political institutions as well as political consciousness have been of a relatively recent origin in most of the Part C States. The choice of leadership, therefore, is necessarily limited. Besides, the smaller the forum for political activity the greater the inter-play of personal ambitions and jealousies. On the administrative side, they give rise to all kinds of anomalies and difficult situations and the size of these units is such that it does not even admit the enforcement of the salutary convention that district officers should not normally serve in their home towns.

268. Taking all these factors into consideration, we have come to the conclusion that there is no adequate recompense for all the financial, administrative and constitutional difficulties which the present structure of these States presents and that, with the exception of two, to be centrally administered, the merger of the existing Part C States with the adjoining States is the only solution of their problems.

Safeguards for the transitional phase

269. Fears are entertained in some of the economically backward Part C States that, if they join the more advanced adjoining States, their development will be impeded. The mere fact that a particular area has been economically undeveloped does not provide adequate reason for constituting or continuing it as a separate administrative unit. In fact, the consolidation of undeveloped areas into separate units will retard the constitution of States with balanced economies. However, it would be only fair to the people of those States which were placed under the Centre for the specific purpose of their economic development, if the Centre does not divest itself of responsibility for their development, until a stage has been reached when they could be left entirely to the care of the State Governments concerned.

270. This would necessitate the retention by the Central Government of some kind of supervisory power over State Governments

in respect of the development of the economically backward areas constituting some of the existing Part C States. The areas over which the Central Government's supervision may be desirable, in our opinion, are:

(a) Himachal Pradesh;

(b) Kutch; and

(c) Tripura.

271. Central authority need not be exercisable over the whole range of the administration of these areas but may be confined to matters connected with their economic development. As compared, therefore, with the provisions of Article 371 of the Constitution, which place Part B States under the general control of the Government of India, the provision made in the event of our recommendation being accepted, will be of a restricted nature. The arrangements we have proposed may be terminated either after a specified period or after the President is satisfied that the areas concerned have made sufficient progress to be on equal footing with the more developed areas.

272. The Government of India might make special allotments for the development of these areas and also exercise under the proposed arrangements, control over the disbursement of these allotments for specified purposes. The Government of India might also constitute in consultation with the Governments of the States concerned development boards consisting of officials and non-officials to look after the economic and social development of these areas.

273. Such an arrangement, while enabling the merger of a number of Part C States with the adjoining larger units, would ensure that the Centre's care and aid would be available to safeguard their legitimate interests.

274. As for the other areas, *e.g.*, Bhopal and Ajmer, we trust that the State Governments will take appropriate steps to ensure that the present pace of economic development in these areas is maintained.

275. One of the arguments advanced in favour of the maintenance of the *status quo* in the existing Part C States has been that the laws of the adjoining larger States are unsuitable in the conditions which now prevail in some of the smaller States. While there is a tendency to overstate this case, it is desirable that the laws of the larger States should be extended to the merged units with due regard to the

special needs of the people of these units. We suggest, therefore, that one of the urgent tasks of the Governments of those States into which the smaller units are to be merged should be a comprehensive examination of the existing laws in the merged units. The objective should be that the wholesale application of new laws in all the territories of the merged States does not follow as a matter of course, and old laws may be continued, to the extent that a disparity in the application of laws is desirable in the interests of the merged units, or is based on good grounds which justify such differentiation in law.

Future of remaining centrally-administered areas

276. If the existing Part C States are to be joined with larger contiguous units to the extent practicable, the question arises what the constitutional position should be of areas which, for security and other imperative considerations, might still have to be placed under the direct administration of the Centre.

277. The problem is not peculiar to India. Countries with a federal constitution do contain some centrally-administered areas besides constituent units of the federation. These are firstly, the seats of federal governments such as Washington, D.C., in the U.S.A. and Canberra in Australia, and secondly, other administered territories consisting mostly of sparsely-populated and geographically-isolated areas.

278. In the U.S.A., only the forty-eight States are treated as units of the federation and are given seats in the Federal Upper House. Alaska and Hawaii are incorporated territories not yet admitted into the federation of States. They send "delegates" only to the Lower House of Congress and the "delegates" have no votes. In Canada and Australia also, territories are treated differently from the provinces and the states in the matter of representation in the federal legislature.

279. The Part C States of the Indian Union also are centrally-administered but have certain special features of their own. Firstly, notwithstanding the fact that these states are not autonomous in the sense in which the other states are, they have been given the status of constituent units of the Indian Union and as such have full representation in both the Houses of Parliament. Secondly, they are called States. While there may be scope for difference of opinion as to other units of the Union being called States or Provinces, it is anomalous to call the areas administered by the Centre on a unitary

basis as States. The fact that these units have been called States has stood in the way of their constitutional relationship with the Centre being viewed in correct perspective.

280. The present position is that the Central Government is, for legal purposes, the repository of all power and is responsible for the entire administrative field so far as the Part C States are concerned. At the same time, in several of these States, there are local ministries responsible to their respective legislatures in the State field of administration. Conflict and blurring of responsibility are inherent in this constitutional relationship.

281. The main arguments advanced in favour of giving the Part C States a form of responsible government were:

(a) the political rights enjoyed by the people of other parts of the country had to be granted to the people of these areas also; and

(b) it was necessary to initiate the people in the principle of responsible government at the state level.

282. If the majority of Part C States are merged, the problem would be greatly simplified. However, speaking on the merits of the case, it seems to us that undue emphasis has been laid on these two points.

283. There is little justification for the assumption that if, for certain valid reasons, the Centre under a federal system of government itself administers an area, this will involve an infraction of the democratic rights of the people of the area. In fact, the people of Part C States have a clear advantage over the centrally-administered territories in other countries in that these States get representation in both the Chambers of the Union Parliament and their representatives are full members with the right to vote. The Union Parliament, representing the people of India as a whole, legislates in the wide field of Union and Concurrent items. Legislation by this body in the state field also in regard to small areas placed under the Centre's direct care should not be treated as a denial of political rights to the people of these areas. If this kind of meticulous evaluation of democratic rights is carried to its logical extreme, it would appear that the people in Part C States having legislatures and ministries are enjoying superior political rights as compared to the more populous States, in that while a State like

Coorg, with a population of 2,29,405 has a legislature and a ministry providing one representative in the legislature of the State for every 9,559 people and one minister for every 1,14,703 people, in the Uttar Pradesh there is one member in the State legislature for every 1,47,013 people and one minister for every 3,327,114 people. Judged by the criterion of absolute equality of democratic rights of the people, is it fair to the people of a district like Malabar, with a population of 4·8 millions to be treated merely as a district unit, when Coorg, with a population approximating to about one-twentieth of the population of this district enjoys the status of a State with a legislature and a ministry?

284. As for the requirements of training in public life, it is doubtful if the establishment of legislatures or of ministries responsible to them would be justified in very small areas for the mere purpose of initiating the people of these areas in the principles of responsible government.

285. Taking all the facts into consideration, we recommend that the component units of the Indian Union be classified into two categories:

(a) "States" forming primary constituent units of the Indian Union having a constitutional relationship with the Centre on a federal basis. These units should cover virtually the entire country.

(b) "Territories" which, for vital strategic or other considerations, cannot be joined to any of the States and are, therefore, centrally-administered.

286. These "territories" should be represented in the Union legislature, but there should be no division of responsibility in respect of them. Democracy in these areas should take the form of the people being associated with the administration in an advisory rather than a directive capacity. The "territories" may, therefore, have advisory bodies suitable to their requirements. If people of these areas seek a fully democratic form of government, they should be prepared to merge themselves in larger areas which can provide the full normal legislative and administrative machinery of a State.

287. The "territories" may include the existing Part C States which are not to be merged and Part D territories. Provision may be made on the lines of Sections 94 to 96 of the Government of India Act, 1935, for the President to exercise regulation-making power

in respect of some of the "territories". As stated earlier, this is the main distinction existing between the Part C States and other territories and a provision to that effect will enable the central executive to deal with these areas in an appropriate manner.

CHAPTER II

MADRAS

288. Having explained our views on the basic pattern of the component units of the Indian Union, we now proceed with the task of making our recommendations regarding the reorganisation of particular States on the basis of the principles which, we have already indicated, should govern the solution of the problem. We take up first the States in the South where the demand for the redistribution of state territories is of long standing.

289. The separation of Andhra from the composite Madras State has met the most insistent of the demands and has virtually solved the problem for a major area of this region. The residuary Madras State has been left as a fairly compact unit; this State is linguistically homogeneous except mainly for two districts, namely, Malabar and South Kanara, in a distant and outlying corner, which are not Tamil-speaking. So the problem of Madras does not present any serious difficulty.

290. The main claim advanced on behalf of Madras is for the addition of the Tamil-speaking areas of Travancore-Cochin. This claim rests mainly on linguistic considerations and grounds of geographical contiguity and relates to nine taluks, namely, Thovala, Agastheeswaram, Kalkulam, Vilavancode and Neyyattinkara in Trivandrum district, Devikulam and Peermede in Kottayam district, Shenkotta in Quilon district and Chittur in Trichur district.

291. In our scheme of reorganisation, we have adopted the district as the basic unit for making territorial readjustments. This is because we feel that districts have developed an organic and administrative unity and an economic life of their own, and any adjustments below the district level, therefore, should normally be avoided. If any such adjustments are considered necessary, they should be made only by mutual agreement. We have departed from this rule only when, for ensuring geographical contiguity or for some other important administrative or economic considerations, detachment of part of a district has become imperative.

292. The demand for Tamil-speaking taluks has a history behind it and has assumed a form that prejudices the political and

administrative stability of this area. We have, therefore, considered it necessary, in the special circumstances of this case, to examine the Tamil claims to these taluks and to make recommendations about their future.

293. As a result of the re-sorting of census slips of the Tamil-speaking taluks of the Travancore-Cochin State, the percentages of people with different mother-tongues in the nine taluks claimed by the Madras Government are now available. These figures show that in the four southern taluks, namely, Agastheeswaram, Thovala, Kalkulam and Vilavancode, situated in what is known as Nanjil Nad, the percentage of Tamil-speaking people is above 79. The wishes of the people of this area have been clearly expressed and there is no particular reason why these wishes should not be respected.

294. The Shenkotta taluk is partly an enclave in Tirunelveli district of Madras State and the percentage of Tamil-speaking people in this taluk is about 93. Physically and geographically it belongs to Tirunelveli district in which it should now merge.

295. The Devikulam and Peermede taluks stand on a somewhat different footing. These are hilly areas which, for various economic and other reasons, are of great importance to the State of Travancore-Cochin. The percentage of Tamil-speaking people in the Devikulam and Peermede taluks is 72 and 44 respectively. It has, however, been stated before us that this fairly large Tamil population of these two taluks is accounted for, in part, by a floating corps of labourers employed by plantations in this area. Recent figures for the Peermede and Devikulam taluks show that the Tamil migrant population constitutes 30 per cent. and 46 per cent., leaving behind 14 per cent. and about 26 per cent. as the non-floating Tamil-speaking population in the two taluks respectively.

296. Considering their area, which is about twelve per cent. of the whole area of Travancore-Cochin State, Devikulam and Peermede taluks have a comparatively meagre population and with the progress of development should be able to relieve some of the burden on the heavily congested littoral areas of the State. The economic importance of this locality will be discussed later, but it may be appropriate to mention here some of the natural advantages of this area, containing the high range of the Anamalais and some of the highest peaks south of the Himalayas. It is the source of the most important river of the State, the Periyar, as also of other rivers. Apart from the question of impounding the

headwaters of the rivers, it is necessary to adopt measures to afford protection to the rice fields in the valley bottoms, and to promote the special economy of the high range relating to forests, plantations and hydro-electricity; these cannot be effectively undertaken if the State is deprived of this area.

297. The Tamil side of the case is that, although much of the population of Devikulam and Peermede may have been originally migrant, it now constitutes a majority and that in the 1954 elections, the Travancore Tamil Nad Congress won both the seats to the Assembly from this area. It is important, however, to note that the Travancore Tamil Nad Congress itself recognise the special interests of the Travancore-Cochin Government in this area and is prepared to exclude from the areas sought to be transferred to Tamil Nad, the Pallivasal pakuthy of the Devikulam taluk, where the hydro-electric works are located and the Peruvanthanadu pakuthy of Peermede taluk, which includes the township of Mundakayam and the rubber estate.

298. This concedes, in effect, a part of the claim of the Government of Travancore-Cochin to these two taluks. As we have observed earlier, we do not regard the linguistic principle as the sole criterion for territorial readjustments, particularly in the areas where the majority commanded by a language group is only marginal. It may also be recalled that, on the basis of the evidence tendered before it, the Dar Commission had come to the conclusion that it would not be proper to describe any area as unilingual unless the majority of one language spoken in that area was at least 70 per cent. and that any area below that should be considered as bilingual or multilingual as the case may be[1]. We are generally in agreement with this view, but in our opinion, the mere fact that a certain language group has a substantial majority in a certain area should not be the sole deciding factor.

299. Neyyattinkara is a predominantly Malayalam-speaking taluk (86 per cent.). As regards Chittur, it was claimed that the Tamil-speaking population was 95 per cent.; the re-sorting, on the other hand, has shown that the Malayalam percentage of the taluk is 59·8. There seems to be no particular reason for separating these taluks. A portion of Chittur is now an enclave in Madras State, but if a Kerala State is constituted on the lines indicated in the next Chapter, this can be conveniently attached to Malabar which will form part of Kerala.

1. Report of the Linguistic Provinces Commission, para. 63.

300. The non-Tamil areas of Madras are the two districts of Malabar and South Kanara and the Kannada-speaking areas on the borders of Mysore, specially the Kollegal taluk of Coimbatore district. The Madras Government has not raised any objection to the separation of the two districts; as far as the Kollegal taluk is concerned, Madras had agreed earlier to its transfer to the prospective Karnataka State, but subsequently, on reconsideration, has proposed that only a northern portion, which is contiguous to the existing Mysore State, should be transferred. We have considered very carefully the arguments in favour of breaking up this taluk, but find on the whole that they are unconvincing. The entire taluk, according to our proposals, will cease to be a part of Madras.

301. Madras State thus constituted will have a population of about 30 millions, covering an area of about 50,170 sq. miles, a compact and integrated territory and will form one of the important units of the Indian Union with a history of stable administration. Neither its administration nor its plans of economic development will be affected.

CHAPTER III

KERALA

302. The formation of Kerala follows as a corollary to the proposals made in the preceding Chapter. Here also territorial adjustments have to be made around an existing homogeneous unit. The present Travancore-Cochin State is a predominantly unilingual State. Even with the Tamil-speaking taluks of the South, the Malayalam percentage is 86·3 which is higher than that of the main languages of most other States. In three of its four districts, Quilon, Trichur and Kottayam, the Malayalam-speaking population is as high as 94 per cent.

303. The main addition to the State will be the contiguous district of Malabar. Physically and culturally, Malabar district is somewhat isolated from the rest of the Madras State. Its problems are different from those of the eastern part of the peninsula. Malabar's land tenure has special features of its own characterised by a hierarchical system, from the jenmi downwards to the verumpattomdar. Rubber, coffee, cardamom and plantation and cash crops like pepper, ginger and cashew are important in the agricultural economy of the district. Calicut on the West Coast is the collecting centre for the produce exported from the Walluvanad, Ernad and Wynaad taluks of Malabar. The district has very little by way of irrigation works. Communication lines connect it closely with the West Coast; with its long coastline it is accessible to the same maritime influences as the rest of Travancore-Cochin. Inheritance is generally matrilineal and the population is predominantly (96 per cent.) Malayalam-speaking.

304. Fort Cochin, which is administratively part of Malabar, will automatically go to Kerala. It has been argued that security considerations are important in deciding its future, because of the location of a major port in this area. But that provides no justification for creating a centrally-administered area in this region. The Government of India have adequate powers in regard to ports under the Constitution, and the transfer of Fort Cochin to the proposed Kerala State is unlikely to affect materially the interests of the port.

305. The other areas to which claims have been advanced on behalf of Kerala are the districts of South Kanara and Nilgiris, Coorg and the Amindive and Laccadive Islands.

306. There is little justification for the Kerala claim to the whole of the South Kanara district. The Dar Commission had included only

the Kasaragod taluk of South Kanara in the geographically contiguous area in which the Malayalam language is largely spoken. As a result of the resorting of census slips, the language figures for this taluk are now available. According to these figures, the Malayalam-speaking percentage is about 72. Though Kannadiga opinion in South Kanara concedes the claim of Kerala up to the Chandragiri river, administratively it will be more expedient to join the whole taluk to Kerala than to break it up purely on linguistic grounds.

307. The Kerala claim to Coorg is untenable on grounds which we shall discuss later. The Laccadive Islands already form part of the Malabar district. In our opinion, the Amindive group should also form part of the prospective Kerala State. It was an accident that the Amindives ever came to be attached to South Kanara. It would be desirable and convenient, if the future Kerala State were administratively in charge of all the islands, including the Amindive group.

308. The prospective Kerala State will thus consist of the existing State of Travancore-Cochin less the five Tamil taluks of Thovala, Agastheeswaram, Kalkulam, Vilavancode and Shenkotta plus Malabar district which includes the Fort Cochin area, the Kasaragod taluk of South Kanara district and the Amindive Islands. The State thus constituted will have an area of about 14,980 square miles and a population of about 13·6 millions. It will be linguistically homogeneous; about 94 per cent. of its population will be Malayalam-speaking and the State will be geographically compact. It will be well-served from the point of view of communications.

309. There have been some suggestions that, considering its size, the density of its population, which is the highest in India, and the menacing problem of unemployment, it would be best for the whole of the Kerala area to be united with Madras to form a South Indian State. A further argument in favour of this proposal is that Travancore-Cochin, deprived of its Tamil taluks and yoked with economically-backward Malabar, would not constitute a viable unit.

310. The proposal is attractive from many points of view, but neither the Malayalam-speaking people nor the Tamilians have welcomed it. As it is frankly said to be in the interests of Kerala, one can understand the reluctance of the Tamilians to be associated with a little more than 13 million Malayalees who not only speak a different language but (except for the population of the district of Malabar) have never been united with them before. Opinion in

Travancore-Cochin itself irrespective of party affiliations is, also generally, against this proposal.

311. Yet another proposal made before us was for the formation of a West Coast Pradesh consisting of the whole coastal area from Gokarnam in the North Kanara district to Cape Comorin. The proposal is only an ambitious variant of the plan for the formation of Kerala. It rests, however, on weak foundations in that there can be little justification for adding the whole of South Kanara and a portion of North Kanara to Kerala on the ground of so-called common economic interests.

312. We have considered very carefully the arguments which have been or can be advanced against the formation of the proposed Kerala State from the financial and economic point of view. We shall first deal with Malabar. Malabar, it has been argued, is an under-developed district. The gap between revenue and expenditure in this area is already very large, but is bound to become larger, as the level of economic development is brought up to that of the rest of Kerala. The land revenue system which prevails in Malabar is, moreover, different from that of the existing Travancore-Cochin State, where the tax is or will soon be levied at a flat rate. It has been further contended that if this concession of a flat rate of tax were extended to Malabar, the financial deficit will be increased. When Malabar's deficit in food supplies is taken into account, and when allowance is made for the facts that tenancy laws in this district are different from the rest of Kerala, and that a further round of integration of services on account of the merger of Malabar will involve a great deal of time and labour, and perhaps also much additional expenditure, the transfer of Malabar to the proposed Kerala State, it is argued, will be inadvisable on financial as well as administrative grounds.

313. *Prima facie,* these arguments are not without substance. But a detailed examination indicates that there is less in these objections than may at first be thought. The financial deficit of the Malabar district, for example, seems to have been exaggerated. The Madras Government has tried to estimate this deficit during the three years ended March, 1953, and has arrived at the conclusion that the gap between revenue and expenditure cannot be in excess of Rs. 55 lakhs on an average. If some allowance is made for the facts that interest charges on account of irrigation and power projects located in this district are not considerable, the deficit, on the basis of information supplied by the Madras Government, will not be very heavy.

314. There is also reason to believe that Malabar's revenue will improve to some extent in the near future, for the existing state of Madras has since introduced an agricultural income-tax the yield of which in this district will have to be taken into consideration. Malabar's prospective financial position cannot, therefore, be described as unsatisfactory. The other objections are also not of such importance as to influence our decision regarding the future of this district.

315. It has been claimed that South Travancore or Nanjil Nad is the main rice-producing area in the State, and that the food deficit of the prospective Kerala State will be greatly increased, if this area is separated. When the substantial contribution from the Tamil taluks, and particularly from Thovala, Devikulam and Peermede, to the revenues of the existing State of Travancore-Cochin (largely because of the agricultural income-tax) is also taken into account, the argument that the transfer of these Tamil taluks might impair the economy of the State would appear to be reinforced.

316. Here again, there are reasons to believe that the financial position or economy of the Kerala State will not be adversely affected. Under the arrangements which have been proposed, the fairly heavy revenue from Devikulam and Peermede will be retained by the prospective Kerala State; and the rice production in Neyyattinkara taluk will belong to the State. Incidentally, arguments based on the assumption that Nanjil Nad is the granary of Travancore-Cochin State seem to lack substance. Estimates of food production in Nanjil Nad vary considerably. But even if the most liberal estimates, namely, those of the Travancore-Cochin Government were accepted, Nanjil Nad will not be self-sufficient in food. The result is that neither the existing State of Travancore-Cochin nor the prospective Kerala State will actually be losing a food surplus area if Nanjil Nad is transferred to Madras.

317. The power potential which is available in Devikulam and Peermede taluks will continue to be utilised by Travancore-Cochin or Kerala according to our proposals. Besides, no material changes in the Devikulam colonisation scheme of the present Travancore-Cochin Government will be necessary.

318. We should like to refer in conclusion to certain recent trends and decisions which, in our opinion, materially affect or alter the

financial picture of the prospective Kerala State as it has been presented to us. An important development is that food administration has now ceased to be the responsibility of the State Government. The effect of this is to relieve the revenue budget of the existing Travancore-Cochin State of a considerable burden (from 1943 to 1954 the total cost of subsidies has been estimated at a little less than Rs. 17 crores, of which a little more than Rs. 8 crores was met by the State). Another fact which is relevant to the present discussion is that pay-scales in Travancore-Cochin have recently been raised. This meets to some extent the objection that pay-scales in Travancore-Cochin and Madras vary so greatly that readjustment of boundaries in this area is bound to create problems. Reference has also been made already to the importance of agricultural income-tax, which has now become leviable in Malabar district. The net result of these recent developments is that the financial picture is no longer as gloomy as it was generally believed to be. Any argument, therefore, which assumed that the financial position of the future Kerala State will necessarily be worse than that of the existing State of Travancore-Cochin does not appear to be valid, and cannot, in any case, out-weigh the obvious advantages of the formation of the proposed Kerala State.

CHAPTER IV

Karnataka

319. The next area to be considered is what may be called Karnataka.

320. It has been generally recognised that, in the provincial distribution under the British, the Kannadigas suffered most, with their area split up into four units in three of which they were at the tail end and reduced to the position of ineffective minorities. The All-India Congress Committee in 1927, the All-Parties Conference in 1928 and the Indian Statutory Commission in 1930 all recognised the legitimacy of the claim of the Kannadigas to unification. The Dar Commission also expressed the view that the Kannadigas would prosper and be able to manage their affairs much better under their own government, if such a government were possible.[1]

321. There was no disagreement until recently about the territorial limits of the proposed Karnataka State. It was assumed that as soon as the question of redistribution of State territories was taken in hand seriously, and hurdles such as the special position of the former princely states were removed, the creation of a united Karnataka State would follow as a matter of course.

322. With the reorganisation of States becoming a live political issue, however, some differences of opinion have recently arisen about the territorial set-up of the proposed Karnataka State. These differences relate principally to two matters, namely, the financial prospects of the Karnataka State and the desirability of integrating, in the proposed Karnataka State, the State of Mysore which claims to have a distinct administrative and cultural tradition. It is no longer assumed, as it was, for instance, assumed in the Nehru Committee's Report, that the Karnataka areas outside Mysore will be financially self-sufficient, or that they will have a surplus of revenue over expenditure. In fact, a committee appointed by the Mysore Government known as the Fact-Finding Committee has arrived at the conclusion that the position is quite the contrary.[2] Since the Karnataka areas outside Mysore are regarded as undeveloped, and are likely to have a financial deficit, there has grown up in the last two or three years opposition to the unification of Mysore with other Karnataka areas.

---

1. Report of the Linguistic Provinces Commission, para. 150.
   Report of the Fact-Finding-Committee, Mysore, p. 133.

323. This latter view is of such recent origin, and the opinion of its sponsors is still so tentative, that this cannot, perhaps, be taken as a considered solution put forward by the Kannadigas generally. So far as we have been able to assess public opinion in Karnataka, there is a growing opposition to the proposal that two States should be created. While the general consensus of opinion outside Mysore prefers one united State to two, even within Mysore, the majority seems to value the advantages of unification above any temporary dislocation or inconvenience which may result from it.

324. It has been suggested to us that the basic reason why two States have sometimes been demanded instead of one is either political or religious apprehension, or perhaps, a combination of both. It has been estimated that Lingayats or Veerasaivas constitute about 35 to 40 per cent. of the population in the Kannada areas outside Mysore at present. The other important section of the Kannadigas, namely, the Vakkaligas, similarly constitute a little less than 29 per cent. of the population of Mysore. In the united Karnataka, it has been estimated that a little more than 20 per cent. of the population may be Lingayats, between 13 and 14 per cent. Vakkaligas, and about 17 to 18 per cent. Harijans. It is clear that no one community will, therefore, be dominant, and any one section can be reduced to the status of a minority, if other groups combine against it. These estimates of the communal composition of the new State are naturally not firm, because the figures which have been quoted vary considerably.[1] They serve, however, to illustrate the problem.

325. It is not unnatural in these circumstances for those who expect to be reduced in their relative position to view the proposed change with disfavour. It is also, perhaps, not entirely ununderstandable, if some of these minorities fear that one result of the political position which the Lingayats will occupy in the future Karnataka State may be the dominance or extension of Veerasaivism at the cost of other religious faiths. However, in the perspective of the political and economic development of the Karnataka State which we have in view, the importance of narrow communal jealousies should not be exaggerated. There is as much reason to expect that a more balanced communal distribution will be conducive to good government as there is for fears or apprehensions.

326. There will be some obvious difficulties during the period of transition to some of which the Fact-Finding Committee has drawn

[1] According to the 1931 Census the percentage of Lingayats, Vakkaligas and Harijans in the areas proposed to be included in the Karnataka State was 17, 11 and 13 respectively.

attention. But these difficulties will be no greater and the problems of the transition will be no more complex than in other areas. The deficits of Bombay and Hyderabad Karnataka will be sizeable. Indeed, our calculations suggest that they may be somewhat in excess of Rs. 1 crore, this deficit being largely explained, as in the case of Bellary, by the cost of servicing the capital outlay on the Tungabhadra project. There should be appreciable savings in overhead costs, however, which can be set off against this deficit and against the cost of revising Mysore scales of pay.

327. Rail communication in northern Karnataka, it has been stated, is now unsatisfactory. It is, however, unsatisfactory also in the Malnad area of the existing Mysore State; and in view of the scale on which railway expansion is now planned, it is hoped that northern Karnataka will soon become more easily accessible from Bangalore than it is at the present time.

328. The problems of the transition, in short, can and should be dealt with over a reasonable period; and the assumption which has sometimes been made that the Karnataka areas outside Mysore are particularly backward seems to us to be quite unwarranted. Bombay Karnataka in particular has enjoyed for a sufficiently long time the benefits of a progressive administration which has provided in this area educational facilities up to the University stage, cheap and adequate transport services run by one of the more important road transport corporations in the country and other amenities for the population. The extra cost, if any, of uniform standards of expenditure on the social services cannot, therefore, in our opinion, be very great; and on the whole, the mere fact that some administrative problems will be created and will need to be tackled in the first few years cannot be used as an argument against unification.

329. For these reasons, we recommend that one Karnataka State should be formed. This state should, in our opinion, comprise the following areas:

(a) the present Mysore State, excluding the following portions of the Bellary district as now constituted, namely, the Siruguppa taluk, the Bellary taluk, the Hospet taluk and a small area of the Mallapuram sub-taluk in which the dam and headworks of the Tungabhadra project are situated (details of the area to be transferred from the Mallapuram sub-taluk will have to be determined by the Government of India, in consultation with the State governments concerned);

(b) the four Kannada-speaking districts of the southern division of Bombay, namely, Belgaum except for Chandgad taluk, Bijapur, Dharwar and North Kanara;
(c) the districts of Raichur and Gulbarga;
(d) the South Kanara district except the Kasaragod taluk;
(e) the Kollegal taluk of the Coimbatore district of Madras; and
(f) Coorg.

The territorial limits of Karnataka, as thus proposed, broadly cover the Kannada-speaking areas, but in the case of one or two small units, linguistic considerations have been subordinated to other compelling reasons. Some explanation of the reasons why particular areas have been included in or excluded from the Karnataka State is, therefore, necessary.

330. One such area is Kolar district, which has a Telugu majority of fifty-four per cent. and a Kannada-speaking population of barely twenty-one per cent. It has intimate ties with Mysore which are of such long standing that they cannot easily be ignored. The major industry in this district is gold-mining. This has been fostered and built up by the Mysore Government, which has a direct interest in the continued existence and prosperity of this industry. The industry for its part gets the benefit of cheap hydro-electric power from Mysore. Other facilities have also been provided by the Mysore Government. The mining town itself has attracted a considerable number of immigrants from the adjoining areas, mostly Tamilians, with the result that Tamil is the largest language group in K.G.F. city today. The district is also much nearer to Bangalore than it is to Kurnool or Hyderabad. In case it is included in Andhra, it will be in the south-western corner of that State and will necessarily be somewhat remote from the main centres of Andhra. Taking into account all these factors as also the fact that the Telugu majority in this district is not large, we feel that it should remain where it is.

331. After very serious consideration we have decided to recommend the exclusion of a portion of the present Bellary district along the course of the Tungabhadra from Karnataka and its transfer to the Andhra State. We are aware that this is not in accord with the findings of an eminent judge like Shri Justice Misra and also with the decision taken by the Government of India in 1953 in respect of certain areas forming part of the present Bellary district. It is only after giving due weight to these important pronouncements and

careful examination of the merits and demerits of the different proposals that we have come to the conclusion that the change proposed is desirable.

332. It should be stated that our approach to the question is somewhat different from that of Shri Justice Misra. It seems to us that Shri Justice Misra was mainly guided by what he described as "linguistic gravity" although he took other considerations also into account. On the other hand, we have to be guided by certain principles which can be generally applied. The retention of Kolar district in the Karnataka State and the addition of the major part of Belgaum district to it will, in our opinion, be more advantageous to the new State than the continuance in it of the eastern portion of the Bellary district.

333. The arguments which have been advanced in favour of maintaining the *status quo* with regard to Bellary are almost similar to those advanced for separating the Kolar district from and not including parts of the Belgaum district in the future Karnataka state. As we have explained elsewhere, the linguistic consideration only should not, in our view, be the decisive factor, especially in settling the future of a border tract which cannot be regarded as predominantly unilingual. What has weighed with us in arriving at the conclusion to which we have referred is the cumulative effect of three main considerations, namely, administrative convenience, economic links and the importance of the Tungabhadra project to the Rayalaseema districts of Andhra.

334. There seems to be a great deal of force in the contention put forward on behalf of the Andhra Government that in view of the communication and other links of Bellary with the rest of Rayalaseema and the dependence of Bellary town on the existing Andhra state rather than Mysore in the matter of trade and commerce, these taluks have a much closer relation with the Andhra state than with Mysore. Bellary was administered as a part of the composite state of Madras for more than one hundred and fifty years, during which it developed into a sort of unofficial capital for the entire Rayalaseema area. The sudden snapping of old associations has resulted in a great deal of hardship to the people of this town. Firstly, there is the fact that many important offices serving the Andhra area were located in this town and the transfer of these offices has naturally affected many of the residents of the town who depended for their livelihood on them. There is also the consideration that the district, and the town of Bellary in particular, had and still continue to have a considerable volume of trade with the

Andhra area. Again, Bellary town continues to be connected with all the district headquarters of the Rayalaseema area by rail and road, and it is nearer to Kurnool than to Bangalore. To reach Bangalore by rail from Bellary, the shortest route lies only through Andhra territory. The importance of the area under dispute to Andhra is also evident from the fact that in the Andhra State Act, 1953, provision had to be made during a transition period for certain facilities being made available to the Andhra Government.

335. Various persons and public bodies in Bellary have claimed, in the course of their representations made to us, that the existing arrangements have caused considerable inconvenience to them. We are not in a position to say how far these grievances are real or permanent; but on a careful review of all the circumstances, we find no reason why arrangements or expedients which are plainly unsatisfactory in certain aspects should be continued, even after an opportunity for the general redistribution of boundaries has presented itself.

336. It has been represented to us that after the creation of the Andhra State, the Tungabhadra Project Board, which was set up in terms of Section 66 of the Andhra State Act, could not function satisfactorily. The complaints were so serious at one stage that it was considered desirable to reconstitute this Board. Although there are reasons to believe that the control and higher direction of the project have been facilitated as a result, it seems to us that, if the area, as proposed by us, is transferred to Andhra, the chances of friction with regard to the Tungabhadra project will be minimised to a very considerable extent.

337. It will be somewhat unsatisfactory if the Andhra Government has, even after the redistribution of States, no access to the headworks of a project in which it is vitally interested. It may be recalled that the project was originally intended, in so far as it relates to the southern side, for the benefit of Rayalaseema as an insurance against recurrent famines in that area.

338. The ayacut of the low level canal on the southern side of this project, already sanctioned, will have to be brought under cultivation as soon as possible; and it has been represented that immigration from the existing Andhra State into the eastern portion of Bellary district, as it is now constituted, is both necessary and desirable for this purpose. If we take into account the ayacut which is likely to be benefited by the proposed high level canal, the case for Andhra is considerably reinforced. The high level canal, we understand, has now been sanctioned in broad outline.

It is likely, when the localisation of the area intended to be benefited by this project has been completed, that Andhra will have a major interest in it. In view of the importance which is attached to this project and the difficulties which have been experienced, there is, in our opinion, a great deal of justification for treating this claim as a very special case.

339. We have indicated elsewhere in this report that claims to areas in which the headworks of irrigation or hydro-electric projects are situated are not necessarily to be accepted in all cases. Any such claim, however, cannot well be ignored, where other considerations are relatively unimportant.

340. It may be noted that the three taluks in question cannot be regarded as unilingual. Besides the Hospet and Bellary urban areas are fast assuming a mixed character. We have not attached any particular importance to the language factor in taking a decision on the future of the Kolar district where the Telugu-speaking people constitute about 54 per cent. of the population. Our assessment of the language factor in the area of Bellary proposed to be transferred to Andhra must be governed by similar considerations.

341. When Shri Justice Misra originally reported, Mysore had to be given a new district town of sufficient importance from which Bellary, which was transferred to it, could be administered. This latter argument is not valid to the same extent today, because it is no longer a restricted redistribution which is being considered, but a large scale redistribution; and Karnataka, which will be able to control areas which are to the north and west of those taluks of Bellary district which would still remain with it, will be able to make satisfactory arrangements for carrying on the district administration, even if Bellary town is taken away.

342. We recommend the retransfer of the areas already mentioned in the present Bellary district and the retention of Kolar in the prospective Karnataka State, on a balance of equities and advantages, in the hope that responsible public opinion, by and large, will, after dispassionately examining it, appreciate the reasonableness of this decision.

343. We trust that the Andhra Government and the leaders of the Andhra State will show vision and broad-mindedness in dealing with the Kannada population of the area in question and will provide for adequate educational facilities for them and also ensure that they are not discriminated against in the matter of recruitment to the services.

344. Coorg has retained its separate administration owing to what the Indian Statutory Commission has described as "historic causes".[1] It is a Part C State. The question of its separate existence has, therefore, to be determined by the general considerations set out in Chapter I of this part. The affiliations of this State are predominantly with Karnataka. Kannada-speaking people form the largest linguistic group in the State accounting for 35 per cent. of its population; Coorgi or Kodagu, which is spoken by about 29 per cent. of its people is akin to Kannada and is regarded by some authorities as a dialect of Kannada. Culturally, Coorg has had more links with the east, which is mainly Karnataka country, than with the west and the south, and geographically the whole of Coorg forms part of Malnad which belongs essentially to Karnataka.

345. Referring to Coorg in connection with the question of the formation of Karnataka, the Dar Commission expressed the view that if a Karnataka province was created, "it would have also solved the problem of the small province of Coorg which has been carrying on a difficult and isolated existence".[2] The future of this small State, therefore, lies with the adjoining Kannada-speaking areas in which it should merge.

346. While the case for integration of Coorg in the proposed Karnataka State appears to us to be indisputable, we wish to take note of the claim to a distinct individuality which the people of this minor administration have put forward. We suggest that a concession should be made to this sentiment by demarcating it as a separate district of the prospective Karnataka State.

347. The Chandgad taluk of Belgaum district is predominantly Marathi-speaking and it has been established as a result of the re-sorting of Census slips that the Marathi majority in the taluk is as high as 92·4 per cent. It can conveniently be administered by the State of Bombay, and Karnataka should have no objection to this proposal.

348. As regards the remaining ten taluks of Belgaum district, it has been claimed that two of them, Khanapur and Belgaum (including Belgaum town), as well as portions of Chikodi taluk, have closer affiliations with the Marathi-speaking districts of Bombay than with the adjoining areas in the proposed Karnataka State. The Marathi majorities in Khanapur and Belgaum taluks are slight, being 53·9 and 51·4 per cent. respectively. Six out of the remaining seven taluks are predominantly Kannada-speaking, and in the seventh,

1. Report of the Indian Statutory Commission, Vol. I, para. 369.

2. Report of the Linguistic Provinces Commission, para. 45.

namely, Chikodi, the Kannadigas constitute the largest single language group. All the taluks of Belgaum district have economic relations with both the Marathi as well as the Kannada speaking areas. The Belgaum town is the centre of the transit trade in this area, which is chiefly in cotton and oil seeds. Neither the Belgaum town nor the other disputed areas, however, have any particularly marked economic affiliations with the Marathi-speaking districts of Bombay. There is no case, therefore, for detaching either Khanapur or Belgaum or portions of Chikodi from the rest of the Belgaum district.

349. It has been argued that the Belgaum town has an absolute Marathi majority and that due consideration should be given to this factor. Separate mother-tongue figures for this town were not compiled during the last Census. In the past, it has, however, for a variety of reasons, attracted a steady stream of immigrants from many areas. Even if it is admitted that this town has now a Marathi majority, in view of the very slight Marathi majority in the taluk of Belgaum and the fact that economic relations are not particularly marked with any linguistic area, the future both of the taluk as well as of the town should, more properly, be decided on administrative grounds. If as many as nine out of the eleven taluks go to Karnataka (Chandgad going to Bombay and Belgaum being disputed), then, on administrative grounds, the Belgaum town, which is the district headquarters, along with the Belgaum taluk, should also go to Karnataka. We have recommended earlier that the Bellary town, along with the Bellary taluk, should go to Andhra, although the town according to Shri Justice Misra's report did not have a predominantly Andhra complexion; our recommendation in respect of the Belgaum town follows the same principles.

350. In the Kollegal taluk of the Coimbatore district about 77 per cent. of the people are Kannada-speaking. For the reasons already explained in Chapter II of this part, the whole of the taluk should, in our opinion, form part of the Karnataka State.

351. Karnataka with the territorial limits which have been indicated so far will have linguistic and cultural homogeneity and geographical integrity. Barring a few dissentients, all those who have been concerned with the Karnataka problem in some form or other will sooner or later recognise that this is so. It is impossible, however, to anticipate a similar measure of common agreement regarding the transfer to the Karnataka State of some other areas along the borders of the prospective State which have been suggested, namely, the portions claimed in the Coimbatore, Nilgiris, Salem, Chittoor, Anantapur, Kurnool, Kolhapur, South Satara and Sholapur districts. The administrative dislocation which will be inevitable

and the controversies to which any proposal to break up these districts will give rise are so great that painstaking border adjustments will not be worthwhile.

352. We have examined in some detail the economic and financial implications of the proposals which we have made, and find that, on the whole, there is much to recommend them. The proposed Karnataka State will have its own major port, for Malpe in South Kanara has already been selected as a possible site on the recommendations of the West Coast Major Ports Development Committee (1950) and preliminary examination of this project has been taken in hand. This incidentally will meet a long-standing complaint of the Bombay and Mysore Karnatàka about the absence of adequate shipping facilities.

353. The prospective financial position of Karnataka as a whole discloses a deficit of the order of one and a half crores of rupees after taking into consideration the immediate possibilities of increasing its revenue and on a realistic assessment of the rate at which public expenditure can be expected to increase. Karnataka, no doubt, will have to bear the fairly heavy burden of servicing the public debt on account of the Tungabhadra and other projects; and as the Upper Krishna, Bhima and Ghataprabha (second stage) projects are taken in hand in the next few years, the burden of the liability on account of interest charges is bound to increase. This, however, is not Karnataka's peculiar problem; and if it proves that the growth of expenditure permanently outstrips the increase in revenue resources, the problem will have to be viewed not as a by-product of reorganisation but as the result of general economic development.

354. From a broader point of view, the formation of Karnataka may go some way towards solving the problem of the development of Malnad. Ever since 1901, when the Census first disclosed a decline in population in these areas, this question has come up for consideration from time to time. But the fact that the area is under the jurisdiction of four governments has, to some extent, impeded the formulation and implementation of economic development plans in a co-ordinated manner. The character of the problem has, no doubt, changed to some extent since the last Malnad Development Committee reported in 1950. More schemes and projects are now being considered and it may be no longer true to say that the area is being depopulated. Nevertheless, the fact that practically the whole of Malnad will belong in future to one State is not an insignificant gain, and it may be expected that co-ordinated planning for these hilly areas will be easier.

355. Two important multi-purpose projects, namely, the Tungabhadra and the Upper Krishna irrigation-*cum*-hydro-electric projects are, or are likely to be, border projects as the boundaries of the States stand at present. In both these cases, the unification of Karnataka should facilitate the rapid development of the areas concerned.

356. Northern Karnataka is now on the eve of large-scale and rapid economic development. The Tungabhadra, Upper Krishna, Bhima, Ghataprabha and Malaprabha projects, when they have been completed, will convert a parched and dry area into one of the best irrigated agricultural regions in the country. The increased production of food and other commodities, after irrigation has been extended will meet the needs of Mysore, which in years of scarcity suffers from a serious deficiency of food supplies. It is not, therefore, only northern Karnataka which may hope to benefit from the unification of the two Kannada-speaking areas north and south of the Tungabhadra.

357. The agricultural, mineral, water and forest resources of Karnataka are considerable. We have no doubt that whichever way one may look at the problem, a united Karnataka will be found to have the essential unity of a culturally homogeneous and balanced economic region; and to a considerable extent, this unity is even independent of the ties of a common language.

358. The Karnataka State so constituted will have a population of about 19 millions and an area of about 72,730 square miles, possessing large forest wealth and a good soil. Also there will be no serious dislocation because the existing Mysore State provides an administrative machinery, a capital and a High Court and all the other appurtenances of a modern government.

CHAPTER V

Hyderabad

359. Further reorganisation of States in the South is dependent in a large measure on the future of Hyderabad. Hyderabad is a State with a population of 18·7 millions, of which 47·8 per cent. speak Telugu, 24·3 per cent. Marathi, 11·6 per cent. Urdu, 10·5 per cent. Kannada and 5·8 per cent. other languages. In the preceding Chapter we have already recommended the transfer of the two districts of Hyderabad, namely, Raichur and Gulbarga, to the proposed Karnataka State. The future of the rest of this State is directly relevant to the examination of certain important proposals regarding the adjoining areas. This is, therefore, one of the major problems with which this Commission has to deal.

360. There has been a general demand, with popular support behind it, that the State should be disintegrated on the basis of linguistic and cultural affinity. This demand does not rest merely on linguistic grounds. It has been argued that States like Bombay, Madras and Madhya Pradesh, though heterogeneous in character, have achieved a fair measure of progress and have acquired considerable experience in the working of the democratic form of government. In the case of Hyderabad, however, it is contended that the State has long been an artificial political unit and that the progress of the people who have remained backward cannot be accelerated unless its three component regions are attached to more advanced units. This step is also said to be necessary for the liquidation of the undemocratic tradition which, it is stated, is still deep-rooted in this State.

361. On the other hand, it has been argued before us that for more than six hundred years, from the time of the Bahmani kings, the area has been an integrated unit with common geo-political features, and that the State represents in miniature a real cultural synthesis and an intermingling of Indian people and should, therefore, be preserved as a model for other areas to imitate. A further argument for the maintenance of the *status quo* is that Hyderabad, if permitted to exist as a unit, could become a centre of north Indian culture and become the carrier of Hindi to the South.

362. It is important to bear in mind that the three areas of Hyderabad known as Telangana, Karnataka and Marathwada were substantially united only under the authority of the

Asaf Jahi dynasty. This unity was not based on a free association of the people, but rested on the weak foundation of personal rule. With the democratisation of the State, this superimposed and superficial unity has already broken down in effect.

363. Public sentiment, both within and without the State, is overwhelming and insistent on the need for the disintegration of the State. The Congress Party, though divided on the question whether Telangana should be a separate State or be united with Andhra, is unanimous regarding the issue of disintegration. The continuance of the existing unit for any considerable length of time would, in the opinion of this body, retard the growth of the people of Hyderabad. Every other organised political party that has appeared before us, however disunited on other points, has shown striking unanimity on this question. In the Marathwada area particularly, there is evidence of deep feeling in this matter born doubtless of historical reasons. From the views expressed by different parties and members of the State Legislature it is clear that only a negligible minority favours the maintenance of the *status quo.*

364. Not only is the opposition to the disintegration of the State confined to minor sections, but the arguments on which this opposition is based also do not bear scrutiny. We are not impressed by the claim that during the last two hundred years a specific Deccani culture has developed in the whole area and that this culture is a major contribution to the unity of India. The common culture of Hyderabad, like the unity of the State, is something that has been imposed from above. It is apparent, if at all, only in important towns and in no way represents a common pattern of living among the people of Hyderabad. Outside the city of Hyderabad, and to a lesser degree Aurangabad, Bidar and Gulbarga there is little that could be called a common culture.

365. Geographically, Hyderabad is divided into two distinct regions, the Deccan lavas region and the remaining region—the Deccan region corresponding more or less with Marathwada. The demographic features are also so different that a casual observer proceeding from Aurangabad to Warangal may see the differences between the people not merely in their language but also in their clothing, special customs, manners etc. The geopolitical argument and the consequent claim to unity will, therefore, be seen to have no substance.

366. As for the utility of the State for the propagation of Hindi in the South, it is true that with the background of Urdu education

Hindi can easily be made popular in Hyderabad. The obvious suggestion, however, is not only that Hindi should replace Urdu as the medium of instruction in the Osmania University, but that the former government's policy of instruction through Urdu in the primary and middle schools should be continued (now, of course, through Hindi) throughout the State. It is most unlikely that a majority of the Telugu-speaking members of the existing legislature will agree to use in the middle and secondary schools any language except Telugu. Likewise, in Marathwada education in anything but Marathi will not be tolerated. The argument that the propagation of Hindi will be easy if Hyderabad is retained in its present form takes no note of the far-reaching effects of the democratisation of the State.

367. Thus, it will be seen that the plea for the continuation of Hyderabad rests on weak foundations. As we assess political trends in the State, we are left in no doubt that if it is maintained as one administrative entity it will not acquire that minimum measure of internal cohesion which is necessary for smooth and efficient administration. Continuance of the existing structure will also keep a number of important reorganisation problems unsolved and thereby impede the stabilisation of the proposed units in the South.

368. There is one point which will have to be considered in consequence of a change in the present character of the State, namely, the position of the Urdu-speaking people of the twin cities of Hyderabad and Secunderabad who constitute 45·4 per cent. of the population. They seem to entertain the fear that if Hyderabad became the capital of either Telangana or Vishalandhra, they would stand to suffer culturally and economically. There is some justification for this fear. The remedy that some people have suggested that of making the cities a centrally-administered area does not appear to be feasible. Other measures will, therefore, have to be adopted to give adequate protection to the linguistic, cultural and other interests of the large Urdu-speaking people in the twin cities. These measures should, in our opinion, include the recognition of the special position of Urdu in the educational institutions and in the administration. Steps will also have to be taken to ensure that the Urdu-speaking people are not discriminated against in the matter of recruitment to services.

The case for Vishalandhra

369. The next question which we have to consider is the future of the Telugu-speaking areas of the existing State of Hyderabad,

with particular reference to the demand for the creation of Vishalandhra.

370. It is unnecessary for us to trace the history of the Andhra agitation in any great detail, because the Andhra State is now in existence, having been established on 1st October, 1953. In point of fact, however, the arrangements which were made in 1953 have not been regarded by the Andhras in the new State, especially in the Circars, as final; and the case for the creation of Vishalandhra has remained substantially unexamined.

371. The advantages of a larger Andhra State including Telangana are that it will bring into existence a State of about 32 millions with a considerable hinterland, with large water and power resources, adequate mineral wealth and valuable raw materials. This will also solve the difficult and vexing problem of finding a permanent capital for Andhra, for the twin cities of Hyderabad and Secunderabad are very well suited to be the capital of Vishalandhra.

372. Another advantage of the formation of Vishalandhra will be that the development of the Krishna and Godavari rivers will thereby be brought under unified control. The Krishna and the Godavari projects rank amongst the most ambitious in India. They have been formulated after a prolonged period of inactivity, during which, for various technical and administrative reasons, only anicuts in the delta area have been built. Complete unification of either the Krishna or the Godavari valley is not, of course, possible. But if one independent political jurisdiction, namely, that of Telangana, can be eliminated, the formulation and implementation of plans in the eastern areas in these two great river basins will be greatly expedited. Since Telangana, as part of Vishalandhra, will benefit both directly and indirectly from this development, there is a great deal to be said for its amalgamation with the Andhra State.

373. The economic affiliations of Telangana with the existing Andhra State are also not unimportant. Telangana has in years of scarcity a sizeable deficit in food supplies. The existing Andhra State, however, has normally a surplus which Telangana may be able to use. The existing State of Andhra has likewise no coal, but will be able to get its supplies from Singareni. Telangana will also be able to save a great deal of expenditure on general administration, in case it is not established as a separate unit.

374. The creation of Vishalandhra is an ideal to which numerous individuals and public bodies, both in Andhra and Telangana, have been passionately attached over a long period of time, and unless

there are strong reasons to the contrary, this sentiment is entitled to consideration.

The case for Telangana

375. The case for Vishalandhra thus rests on arguments which are impressive. The considerations which have been urged in favour of a separate Telangana State are, however, not such as may be lightly brushed aside.

376. The existing Andhra State has faced a financial problem of some magnitude ever since it was created; and in comparison with Telangana, the existing Andhra State has a low *per capita* revenue. Telangana, on the other hand, is much less likely to be faced with financial embarrassment. The much higher incidence of land revenue in Telangana and an excise revenue of the order of Rs. 5 crores per annum principally explain this difference. Whatever the explanation may be, some Telangana leaders seem to fear that the result of unification will be to exchange some settled sources of revenue, out of which development schemes may be financed, for financial uncertainty similar to that with which Andhra is now faced. Telangana claims to be progressive and from an administrative point of view, unification, it is contended, is not likely to confer any benefits on this area.

377. When plans for future development are taken into account, Telangana fears that the claims of this area may not receive adequate consideration in Vishalandhra. The Nandikonda and Kushtapuram (Godavari) projects are, for example, among the most important which Telangana or the country as a whole has undertaken. Irrigation in the coastal deltas of these two great rivers is, however, also being planned. Telangana, therefore, does not wish to lose its present independent rights in relation to the utilisation of the waters of the Krishna and the Godavari.

378. One of the principal causes of opposition to Vishalandhra also seems to be the apprehension felt by the educationally-backward people of Telangana that they may be swamped and exploited by the more advanced people of the coastal area. In the Telangana districts outside the city of Hyderabad education is woefully backward. The result is that a lower qualification than in Andhra is accepted for public services. The real fear of the people of Telangana is that if they join Andhra they will be unequally placed in relation to the people of Andhra and in this partnership the major partner will derive all the advantages immediately, while Telangana itself may be converted into a colony by the enterprising coastal Andhra.

379. Telangana, it has further been urged, can be a stable and viable unit considered by itself. The revenue receipts of this area on current account have been estimated at about Rs. 17 crores, and although the financing of the Krishna and Godavari projects will impose a recurring burden on the new State by way of interest charges, the probable deficit, if any, is unlikely to be large. In favourable conditions, the revenue budget may even be balanced or indicate a marginal surplus. This fairly optimistic forecast can be explained or justified by a variety of reasons.

380. One important reason is, of course, that the existing Hyderabad State and Telangana as part of Hyderabad have benefited considerably from the implementation from April, 1952, of the Finance Commission's recommendations. The increase in central payments from out of the divisible pools of income-tax and central excise which has been possible under the present arrangements and the reduction in police expenditure for which credit can be taken, as the situation in Telangana improves, more or less offset the loss on account of the abolition of internal customs duties; and if the scope which exists for raising the yield of certain State heads of revenue is fully explored, the financial position of Telangana need not cause anxiety.

The State of Hyderabad

381. The advantages of the formation of Vishalandhra are obvious. The desirability of bringing the Krishna and Godavari river basins under unified control, the trade affiliations between Telangana and Andhra and the suitability of Hyderabad as the capital for the entire region are in brief the arguments in favour of the bigger unit.

382. It seems to us, therefore, that there is much to be said for the formation of the larger State and that nothing should be done to impede the realisation of this goal. At the same time, we have to take note of the important fact that, while opinion in Andhra is overwhelmingly in favour of the larger unit, public opinion in Telangana has still to crystallise itself. Important leaders of public opinion in Andhra themselves seem to appreciate that the unification of Telangana with Andhra, though desirable, should be based on a voluntary and willing association of the people and that it is primarily for the people of Telangana to take a decision about their future.

383. We understand that the leaders of the existing Andhra State may be prepared to provide adequate safeguards to protect the interests of Telangana in the event of its integration in Vishalandhra. These safeguards may take the form of a guarantee (presumably on the lines of Sri Baug Pact between Rayalaseema and coastal

Andhra) of opportunities for employment for Telangana in the public services of the new State at least to the extent of one-third, that is to say, roughly in the proportion of population, and an assurance that particular attention will be paid to the development plans of this area.

384. We have carefully gone into the details of the arrangements which may be made on these lines. It seems to us, however, that neither guarantees on the lines of the Sri Baug Pact nor constitutional devices, such as "Scottish devolution" in the United Kingdom, will prove workable or meet the requirements of Telangana during the period of transition. Anything short of supervision by the Central Government over the measures intended to meet the special needs of Telangana will be found ineffective, and we are not disposed to suggest any such arrangement in regard to Telangana.

385. A further point to be borne in mind is that the State of Andhra was brought into existence only recently and has still not got over the stress of transition. It has, for example, still to formulate a policy on land reforms and the problems arising from the partition from the composite State of Madras have, by no means, been tackled fully yet. Integration of Telangana with Andhra at this stage is, therefore, likely to create administrative difficulties both for Andhra and Telangana.

386. After taking all these factors into consideration, we have come to the conclusion that it will be in the interests of Andhra as well as Telangana if, for the present, the Telangana area is constituted into a separate State, which may be known as the Hyderabad State, with provision for its unification with Andhra after the general elections likely to be held in or about 1961, if by a two-thirds majority the legislature of the residuary Hyderabad State expresses itself in favour of such unification.

387. The advantage of this arrangement will be that, while the objective of the unification of the Andhras will neither be blurred nor impeded during a period of five or six years, the two governments may have stabilised their administrative machinery, and, if possible, also reviewed their land revenue systems, etc., the object in view being the attainment of uniformity. The intervening period may incidentally provide an opportunity for allaying apprehensions and achieving the consensus of opinion necessary for a real union between the two States.

388. Andhra and Telangana have common interests and we hope these interests will tend to bring the people closer to each other. If, however, our hopes for the development of the environment and conditions congenial to the unification of the two areas do not materialise and if public sentiment in Telangana crystallises itself against the unification of the two States, Telangana will have to continue as a separate unit.

389. The State of Hyderabad (as we would prefer to call this unit), to be constituted for the time being, should consist of the following districts, namely, Mahbubnagar, Nalgonda, Warangal including Khammam, Karimnagar, Adilabad, Nizamabad, Hyderabad, Medak and Bidar and the Munagala enclave in Nalgonda district belonging to the Krishna district of the existing Andhra State.

390. As has been stated elsewhere in this report, this Commission have examined the boundaries of the prospective States on the principle that the administrative structure of the existing districts should be disturbed as little as possible, and that where any changes are proposed, they should either follow a substantial measure of agreement between the States concerned or be justified independently by reason of special circumstances which cannot be ignored. We believe that both the changes which we have suggested and the changes which we have not proposed can be explained on these grounds.

391. The Sironcha tehsil of Chanda district, which has been claimed for Vishalandhra and which is geographically contiguous to Telangana, has not been included in the Hyderabad State. The Telugu-speaking percentage in this tehsil is only about 51·2. The Andhra caes, therefore, rests in part on the fact that about eighty years ago this tehsil was administratively part of the Upper Godavari district. We have found no strong grounds in this case for disturbing the *status quo*.

392. The entire district of Bidar has been included in Hyderabad State on the same principles. This is a multilingual district, in which Marathi, Kannada, Urdu and Telugu are spoken respectively by 39, 28, 16 and 15 per cent of the population. Administratively, Bidar has very close links with Hyderabad and even Telangana at the present time. The major river which runs through the district, namely, the Manjira, is utilised, for example, in the Medak district. The railway system links the Marathi-speaking taluks of the district very easily with Hyderabad, and the national highway provides a direct connection between the Kannada-speaking taluks and this

city. The undoubted Kannada areas are also somewhat remote from Bangalore and Mysore; and the north-western strip, which is Marathi-speaking, is likewise far removed from Bombay. Consistently with our general view that districts should not be broken up, except when compelling reasons for doing so exist, we have recommended that Bidar should not be disintegrated merely in order that linguistic claims in the north-west or in the south may be respected. We consider that it should remain with the residuary Hyderabad State.

393. The Hyderabad State with the boundaries which we have indicated will be a compact and well-knit unit with an area of about 45,300 sq. miles and a population of about 11·3 millions.

CHAPTER VI

ANDHRA

394. The boundaries of the existing Andhra State will be determined in the light of what has been said in the preceding Chapters. It is only necessary to deal with two or three minor matters, namely, the rectification of the Andhra-Orissa and Andhra-Madras borders and the adjustment of the Andhra-Karnataka border, with particular reference to the claims of the Andhra State in all these areas.

395. We deal later on, in Chapter XVIII, with the Andhra-Orissa border. Here, it is only necessary to indicate that no changes are being proposed. The boundary of the Andhra State in the south has already been the subject-matter of discussion, and the Prime Minister's statement in Parliament, dated March 25, 1953, made it clear that a boundary commission would in due course demarcate the southern and south-western boundaries of the Andhra State. The Andhra Government has also conceded in the memorandum presented to us that the claims of the Tamilians to areas in the Puttur, Chittoor and Tiruttani taluks of the Chittoor district may be considered after the census slips have been sorted and village-wise language figures are available.

396. Some progress has now been made in this direction and the Madras-Andhra border disputes may be settled satisfactorily by negotiation between the two governments. We do not feel called upon in these circumstances to make any particular recommendation.

397. The Andhra-Karnataka border may also be settled perhaps in the same manner. In the absence of agreement between the parties concerned, however, we see no reason to depart from our general principle that as far as possible district boundaries should be respected. We have considered at some length only two important points, namely, the future of the present Bellary district of Mysore and that of the Madakasira taluk of Anantapur district.

398. The Andhra claim to portions of the existing Bellary district of Mysore has been examined in detail in Chapter IV of this part on Karnataka. We have also dealt with the question of the future of the Bidar district, portions of which have also been claimed by Andhra. The position regarding the Madakasira taluk is somewhat complicated. Portions of this taluk, being enclaves within the existing Mysore State, were merged in Mysore in 1950 in terms of the Provinces and States (Absorption of Enclaves) Order,

but a substantial area of this taluk which has a Kannada majority of about 64 per cent. still juts out in Mysore and is surrounded on three sides by areas which will belong to the prospective Karnataka State.

399. There is, however, a great deal to be said in favour of not breaking up the Anantapur district. This would be in accord with our general principle, and since it is also accepted that the integrity of Rayalaseema must as far as possible be respected, this argument applies with additional force. It will be illogical to break up the Anantapur district for the purpose of adding the Madakasira taluk to Karnataka but to decline to break up Kolar for the purpose of adding the predominantly Telugu portion to Andhra.

400. We now come to the question of the future of Madras city. In the memorandum which has been submitted to this Commission, the Andhra Government has reopened this question and has presented elaborate arguments in favour of special arrangements being made for Madras city, relying in particular on the early history of the city in order to prove its Telugu origin and affiliations. The arrangements proposed, which envisage a kind of joint control for Madrss city are, however, patently unworkable. The Tamil-speaking population of the city exceeds two-thirds of its total population at the present time and the case for its separation from the predominantly Tamil-speaking State of Madras rests on weak foundations. The future of Madras city, therefore, must now be regarded as finally settled; and, in our opinion, it will be neither necessary nor desirable to go back on a decision which has already been taken after due consideration of the various points of view. We should like to add, without expressing any opinion on the merits of the historical account of the growth of Madras city as it was presented to us, that according to the general principles which have already been discussed in Chapter VIII of Part II, historical origins cannot be regarded as directly relevant at the present time.

401. The area and population of the Andhra State after minor adjustments will be a little more than 64,950 square miles and about 20·9 millions respectively without taking into account any adjustments which may be made by agreement between Andhra and Madras regarding the rectification of the southern border.

CHAPTER VII

BOMBAY

402. The formation of the proposed Karnataka State involves the separation of the Karnataka districts of the existing Bombay State. We now consider the important question whether there is a case for recommending a further disintegration of this State in order that separate Maharashtra and Gujarat States may be formed.

403. We should like to make a few preliminary observations regarding the existing Bombay State before the case for breaking it up is discussed in detail. Although it has been contended that in multilingual areas the stress of internal friction within the administration retards efficiency, Bombay is undoubtedly one of the best-administered States of the Indian Union. It has the highest percentage of literacy amongst the Part A States and has made a promising start in introducing compulsory primary education, and judged by the measure of success it has achieved in enforcing land reforms and ameliorative legislation, it must rank amongst the most progressive States in the country.

404. It is also noteworthy that its financial position continues to be sound and satisfactory, in spite of the heavy development expenditure which the State has incurred in recent years. The question, therefore, of further disintegration of this State which, on the whole, has done so well must receive very serious thought.

405. The urge for further disintegration of the State comes firstly from the sponsors of the movement for Samyukta Maharashtra and secondly from a section of the Gujarati-speaking population.

406. Though not as old as the demand for Andhra and Karnataka, nor even as old as the movement for Maha Vidarbha, the demand for a United Maharashtra comprising the Marathi-speaking areas of the existing States of Bombay, Madhya Pradesh and Hyderabad, with the city of Bombay as its integral part, has, of late, gathered considerable momentum and has been pressed with great vigour by influential sections of the Marathi-speaking people.

407. Alongside the Samyukta Maharashtra movement there has also grown up a demand for the formation of Maha Gujarat by uniting the States of Saurashtra and Kutch with the Gujarati-speaking areas of Bombay. This demand, however, cannot be regarded as

pressing, because, by and large, the Gujarati-speaking people would now seem to be content to remain in the composite State of Bombay, if it continues more or less as at present constituted.

408. Linked with these two important demands is the future of the following areas:

(i) the Marathwada areas of Hyderabad;

(ii) the eight Marathi-speaking districts of Madhya Pradesh;

(iii) the city of Bombay, where, owing to its multilingual character and its importance as the nerve-centre of trade and business, the question requires serious thought and consideration; and

(iv) the Saurashtra and Kutch States.

409. The demand for the separation of the Marathi-speaking areas and their consolidation into one administrative unit rests on the arguments which are generally advanced against the continuance of composite States and in favour of the formation of linguistic States. These are internal tension, discriminatory and unequal distribution of development expenditure and favouritism in services. Finally, it is emphasised that the Marathi-speaking people, who are claimed to be a distinct cultural group with a common historical tradition and political and economic interests, can legitimately claim a State of their own.

410. As we have observed earlier, we are not inclined to concede any demand on the sole ground of language. We have, therefore, to weigh the linguistic factor with other relevant considerations bearing on the well-being of the people of this region.

411. We are conscious of the fact that opinion in the northern and southern Maharashtra districts in general seems to be in favour of the creation of the United Maharashtra State. At the same time, we cannot ignore the fact that important sections of public opinion in the Marathi-speaking districts of Madhya Pradesh do not subscribe to the ideal of Samyukta Maharashtra. We deal separately in the next Chapter with the merits of the demand for the formation of a separate State of Maha Vidarbha and with the reasons for which we recommend the formation of such a State. Here we refer to it only to indicate that Maharashtra opinion is by no means unanimous on the formation of Samyukta Maharashtra.

412. The most difficult problem, however, which the separation of the Maharashtrian and Gujarati regions of Bombay would pose is the future of the city of Bombay.

413. The case for and against the integration of the city in Samyukta Maharashtra was presented to us by the contending parties very ably and in great detail. The case for the integration of Greater Bombay in Maharashtra briefly is that it does not deserve to be treated differently from other important multilingual cities like Madras; that it is geographically an integral part of Maharashtra; that if it is deprived of its hinterland its further growth would be arrested; and that as a separate State it will become an arena of ideological and political conflicts. On the other hand, it is argued that the case of Bombay city stands by itself; that it is not a predominantly Marathi-speaking unit; that it has acquired its present commanding position by the joint endeavour of the different language groups and that it cannot legitimately be claimed by one language group; and that its integration in Maharashtra will lead to a rapid decline in its importance.

414. The Dar Commission and the J.V.P. Committee, it may be recalled, paid particular attention to the future of the Bombay city and came to the conclusion that in the event of the disintegration of the Bombay State, Bombay city should be constituted into a separate unit. The conclusions arrived at by them are summed up in the following extracts:

> "The city of Bombay stands in special relation to Maharashtra, Gujarat, and to India as a whole . . . Industrially and commercially, it is the hub of India's financial and industrial activity. And altogether it excites some of the deepest emotions in Marhatha and Gujarati hearts, and its failure is the thorniest problem which the linguistic provinces are required to solve.
>
> In all the non-Maharashtrian evidence that came before us there was practical unanimity that the city of Bombay should be formed into a separate province, either Centrally administered or with a Government of its own and in no case should it be placed under a unilingual Government. Some expert evidence was also led before us to show how the commercial and financial interests of the Bombay City and of India as a whole would be affected by a sudden change in the form of the government in Bombay.
>
> The best fortune that we can see for the city of Bombay is that it should continue as it is today, the meeting-place of all communities, their source of pride and affection and

a convenient centre for their joint labour and enterprise. It will be incongruous to make this multi-lingual, cosmopolitan city the capital of a unilingual province." (Report of the Linguistic Provinces Commission, paras. 57, 65 and 67.)

"The question of the City of Bombay has not only risen but has been fiercely debated. And yet in our opinion, there can be little room for argument about this great city. It is not only one of the greatest cities of India but is essentially a cosmopolitan multi-lingual city, the nerve-centre of our trade and commerce, and our biggest window to the outside world. It is quite impossible for us to entertain any idea or any proposal which might injure the many-sided life and activity of this great city, which has been built up by the labour of all kinds of people and communities. We cannot consider it as belonging to any one linguistic group and attach it to a purely linguistic province. That would undoubtedly mean its rapid deterioration from its present commanding position. The population of Bombay has grown rapidly during the past years. It is very much a mixed population and there can be little doubt the Maharashtrians in Bombay are a minority of the population. But even if they were in a slight majority, that would not take away in the least from the cosmopolitan character of the city. We are, therefore, of opinion that, in case the present province of Bombay is split up, and separate Maharashtra province is formed, the City of Bombay should be constituted into a separate political unit. It should be remembered that the Congress even when it formed the Maharashtra, Gujerat and Karnataka Provincial Congress Committees, made Bombay City a separate Provincial Congress Committee.

. . We feel, therefore, that it should be stated clearly and emphatically that Greater Bombay will not become just a part of a purely linguistic province, and that if such linguistic provinces are formed out of the present Bombay Province, the area of Greater Bombay will have to be constituted as a separate unit." (Report of the Linguistic Provinces Committee, Congress, pp. 12, 13.)

415. It would be generally agreed that these weighty expressions of opinion could not be easily disregarded.

416. During the course of our enquiry, a vast majority of persons who appeared before us and did not belong to either of the two contending language groups expressed themselves strongly in favour of placing the Bombay city under a separate administration in the event of the disintegration of the State. We also noticed serious misgivings in the minds of large sections of the inhabitants of Bombay as well as persons outside about the future of the city, if it formed part of a unilingual State.

417. It has been argued before us that all this may be irrelevant to the main issue, namely, whether Greater Bombay should merge in Maharashtra. Constitutional provisions, it has been stated, will ensure that there will be freedom of trade, commerce and intercourse between Greater Bombay and the other areas of the Indian Union. Discriminatory treatment of minorities is also forbidden by the Constitution, and there may be no particular reason to expect that any future government of Maharashtra will be so short-sighted as to create an atmosphere of tension, suspicion and unrest thereby injuring its own long-term interests.

418. We are impressed by the cogency of these arguments, but we cannot lightly brush aside the fears of the other communities. The Maharashtrians in the city, according to the 1951 Census, still remain a minority, being only 43.6 per cent of the population. The position of the city, therefore, is different from that of Madras and Calcutta, where the dominant language groups account for about two-thirds of the population. After taking into account the mixed population of the city, the fact that its future development depends on the co-operation of the different language groups, and the views and apprehensions of the minor language groups even though these may appear to be exaggerated, we have come to the conclusion that its special position should be recognised.

419. The alternative suggested by the Dar Commission and the J. V. P. Committee, namely, the constitution of Greater Bombay into a separate administrative unit will also not be free from serious difficulties. Having regard to the population and the size of the area as well as the fact that it is primarily a city unit, it will not, in our opinion, be entitled to be treated as a full State of the Union. On the other hand, Greater Bombay has been the hub of the political life of a democratically advanced State and its administration as a central enclave may be regarded as a retrograde step.

420. Another point to bear in mind is that Greater Bombay now depends for power and water supplies, no less than for its further

expansion, on the Maharashtra areas. The natural links of the city with its hinterland in Maharashtra are, therefore, another argument for not constituting Greater Bombay into a separate administration.

421. If the separation of the city from Maharashtra is administratively not desirable, the effects on the growth and development of the city in future may prove to be equally adverse, if Greater Bombay were to form part of Maharashtra, but were administratively independent of Gujarat. The likely psychological dissatisfaction of the Gujarati and other communities, in the event of Greater Bombay forming part of Maharashtra, may be very great, and it will be unwise to hope that the industrial and commercial life of the area will remain unaffected. We feel that the importance of Greater Bombay is such and the possible loss either to Gujarat or to Maharashtra considered individually and to the country as a whole might be so great that it would be prudent not to take any risks.

422. A very important factor bearing on the question of the separation of Greater Bombay from Maharashtra and Gujarat is the dependence of both the Marathi and Gujarati-speaking regions on the financial surplus of Greater Bombay.

423. The figures published by the Bombay Government indicate that Greater Bombay's average surplus during the three years ending March, 1953, was of the order of Rs. 12 crores. It is probable that this surplus will increase rather than diminish in future.

424. It has been stated that this somewhat embarrassing surplus of Greater Bombay and the equally embarrassing deficits of the other areas may be corrected in the normal course in the event of the separation of Greater Bombay. It has been pointed out in this connection that some portion of the tax on sales for export from Greater Bombay may cease to be available to the city. It has also been suggested that in the event of the separation of Greater Bombay, it may, in view of its unique financial position, allot a portion of its surplus or relieve the deficit areas of a major share of their debt and interest-bearing liabilities, by means of an *ad hoc* settlement which may form part of the scheme of separation.

425. On an examination of these suggestions we feel that it will be difficult to devise in practice satisfactory arrangements for the routing of Greater Bombay's surplus to the deficit areas of Gujarat and Maharashtra.

426. We are so greatly impressed on the one hand by the difficulties of making Greater Bombay's surplus available to the deficit areas of Gujarat and Western Maharashtra or Samyukta Maharashtra and on the other hand by the argument that Western Maharashtra and Gujarat, if they are constituted, will themselves be deficit respectively to the extent of about Rs. 6·0 crores and Rs. 2·5 crores or more, that, on financial grounds alone, we would view with concern the separation of Greater Bombay from the other two regions of the State.

427. A number of suggestions were made to us for finding a solution of the financial problem which we have just discussed and for reconciling conflicting interests in this area. These include the constitution of three sub-States, representing Bombay-Maharashtra, Bombay-Gujarat and Greater Bombay within a composite State; joint administration of Greater Bomby by Maharashtra and Gujarat; and enhancement of the powers of the Bombay Municipal Corporation. We have examined all these proposals with the care they deserve, but have come to the conclusion that any improvised devices which depart from the normal constitutional pattern may create more difficulties than they may solve and in the conditions in which such expedients are sought to be tried may not achieve the object in view. The conclusion is, therefore, forced on us that no alternative can really be so conducive to the welfare of all the people of the State as the maintenance of its composite character.

428. We recommend, therefore, that the reconstituted State of Bombay may comprise the areas of the existing Bombay State *minus* the Abu Road taluk of the Banaskantha district, the Karnataka districts of Dharwar, Bijapur, North Kanara and the district of Belgaum (except the Chandgad taluk), *plus* the following areas:

(i) Osmanabad, Bhir, Aurangabad, Parbhani and Nanded districts of the existing Hyderabad State;

(ii) Saurashtra; and

(iii) Kutch.

429. The integration of Marathwada with Bombay follows necessarily from our proposals in regard to Hyderabad. We considered the possibility of the northern part of these areas being joined with Vidarbha but popular sentiment is strongly in favour of integration with Bombay, and as there is no over-riding administrative and economic objection to such integration we see no reason why the wishes of the people should not be respected in this case.

430. Saurashtra, a Part B State, is, to our mind, too small a unit to be treated as a State of the Union. The covenant establishing Saurashtra itself provided that the formation of this State was not intended to prevent it from negotiating a union with other Gujarati-speaking areas. Important sections of public opinion in Saurashtra State have expressed themselves in favour of joining the Bombay State.

431. Kutch is a small Part C State, which was placed under Central control because of its economic backwardness and geographical position. For the reasons we have discussed in Chapter I of this part of our report, we do not consider it necessary that this unit should continue to be a separate centrally-administered area. We, however, regard the State as one of the units to which the safeguards which we have proposed for some of the centrally-administered areas like a special development board may be extended.

432. The State thus reconstituted will have an area of about 151,360 sq. miles with a population of 40·2 millions.

433. In arriving at this conclusion we have carefully considered how far the proposals which we are making will give satisfaction to the Marathi and the Gujarati-speaking peoples. The Maharashtrians are a virile and patriotic people with a past in which they take legitimate pride. Their achievements form an important chapter in the history of India. We have been anxious to ensure that their legitimate aspirations are met. The present position is that while they are the largest single language group in the existing State of Bombay, with a percentage of 44, in the other two States in which they are to be found in substantial numbers, namely, Hyderabad and Madhya Pradesh, they constitute the second largest language group with a percentage of 24 and 29, respectively. The proposals which we are making will have the effect of bringing into existence a new unit, namely, Vidarbha, in which the Maharashtrians will be the predominant linguistic group with a percentage of 75; and of consolidating the rest of them in the new Bombay State (of which Greater Bombay will form an integral part) where their percentage would increase to about 48. Further, it may be noted that the population of the predominantly Marathi-speaking districts of the proposed Bombay State will be 21·3 millions out of the total population of 40·2 millions. The Maharashtrians will, therefore, enjoy a position of some advantage in the proposed State.

434. The case of the Maharashtrians is very different from that of the Kannadigas who, as we have already stated, are at present

dispersed over a number of States, constituting ineffective minorities in all except one of them. We hope that when all the facts mentioned by us are fully considered, public opinion in Maharashtra will find in the arrangements we have proposed a substantial fulfilment of their aspirations.

435. What we have stated in the preceding paragraphs might seem to be unsatisfactory, from the point of view of the Gujarati-speaking people. These proposals, it may appear, constitute a total and summary rejection of the case for Maha Gujarat. It is not that we have not weighed carefully the merits and demerits of our proposals regarding Bombay from the point of view of the Gujarati people. Our assessment of Gujarati sentiment, as has been mentioned earlier, however, is that influential sections amongst the Gujaratis would prefer to stay in a composite State even after the separation of the Karnataka districts. We are strengthened in this belief by the categorical assurance of the Gujarat Pradesh Congress Committee to the effect that important elements amongst the Gujarati-speaking people would be prepared to live and to work together in one State with their Maharashtrian brethren in the larger national interests, as also in the interests of the city of Bombay, to which they seem to be greatly attached.

436. Our own view of the prospective development of the Bombay State does not lend support to the fear that the two linguistic areas which will be left in the State after the separation of the Karnataka districts will not receive fair and equal treatment. On an unbiassed view of the relevant facts the existing State of Bombay cannot, in our opinion, be accused of having been partial to the interests of any particular area or group to such an extent as to justify its being broken up. We feel, therefore, that both the Gujarati-speaking and the Marathi-speaking people would, after a careful consideration of our proposal, realise that it is to their mutual advantage to be partners in a great co-operative venture.

437. In the Chapter dealing with language we have expressed the view that where satisfactory conditions exist and economic and administrative considerations favour composite States, these States should be continued, with such safeguards as may be necessary to ensure that all sections enjoy equal rights and opportunities. Bombay, in our opinion, is a State which undoubtedly fulfils these conditions.

438. We have recommended elsewhere an agency to be set up to go into the question of fair and equitable distribution of develop-

ment expenditure in the different areas of the proposed States. To remove all suspicion of possible neglect, the agency we contemplate, should take special note of the requirements of the two important regions of the new State and see that development plans are equitably distributed. We also hope that the Government of the State will devise suitable means of adequately safeguarding the special interests of its two regions.

439. Having regard to these recommendations and to the traditions of tolerance which have so far been characteristic of the existing Bombay State, the arrangements proposed by us, which bring together all the Gujarati-speaking people and also a great majority of the Marathi-speaking people will, we hope, be worked in an atmosphere of mutual understanding and goodwill.

CHAPTER VIII

VIDARBHA

440. We now deal with the demand for the separation of the Marathi-speaking districts of the present State of Madhya Pradesh.

441. The origin of the movement for Maha Vidarbha can be traced back to 1905. In the circumstances which prevailed about fifty years ago, the demand for the creation of Maha Vidarbha inevitably took the form of a claim for separation from the Hindi-speaking areas. In recent years, however, the question whether this separation should lead to the formation of Maha Vidarbha or the integration of this area with a larger Marathi-speaking unit has assumed importance.

442. The first issue to be settled is whether there is a case for the reorganisation of the present composite State of Madhya Pradesh. It is not necessary for us to go in any detail into the charges made by those demanding the separation of the Marathi-speaking areas from the rest of the State, regarding the alleged discriminatory and unequal distribution of development and welfare activity over the two regions or the relative share of the two language groups in the State services. Judged by the evidence submitted to us on behalf of the Madhya Pradesh Government, the distribution of expenditure as between Hindi and Marathi speaking areas, at any rate in recent years, has, by no means, been unfair. However, whatever the merits of such charges and counter-charges may be, it seems to us that the demand for the separation of the Marathi-speaking areas from the Hindi-speaking areas of the State can no longer be ignored. This demand has gathered such momentum that maintenance of the *status quo* will involve an increasingly severe strain on the political life and the administrative machinery of the State. The Hindi-speaking people of the State seem to be more or less reconciled to this proposition. In the circumstances, the separation of the Marathi-speaking areas from the rest of Madhya Pradesh would appear to be unavoidable.

443. The second question which is more controversial is what should be the future alignment of the eight Marathi-speaking districts of Madhya Pradesh. The case for the integration of these areas with western Maharashtra rests primarily on the ground of linguistic homogeneity, although it has also been claimed that the

economies of the two regions are complementary. On the other hand, the arguments advanced in favour of a separate State are historical, cultural, administrative and financial.

444. We shall first deal with the four Berar districts, namely, Akola, Amravati, Buldana and Yeotmal. The history of Berar falls into certain distinct periods; and it may be useful to indicate briefly the political fortunes of Berar in each one of these periods, since it will facilitate an understanding of the demand for autonomy.

445. Before the beginning of the fourteenth century, Berar was under the domination of Deccan kingdoms like the Satavahana empire and the Vakataka, Chalukya, Rashtrakuta and Yadava kingdoms. The area was conquered for Delhi early in the fourteenth century. But about four hundred years later, it passed into the possession of the Nizam of Hyderabad, and was administered by him or on his behalf under various treaties till it was attached in 1903 to the then Central Provinces. From 1903 onwards the link with Hyderabad was, however, merely nominal. With the enactment of the present Constitution even this nominal connection with Hyderabad has come to an end.

446. The Marathi-speaking districts of the existing State of Madhya Pradesh other than the Berar districts cannot be dealt with independently of Berar. The historical links of these districts with Berar have been intimate. Geographically, economically and culturally, the Marathi-speaking districts of Madhya Pradesh outside Berar cannot be distinguished from Berar itself.

447. Historical accidents are to a large extent responsible for the feeling in favour of separation which exists today in the major part of Vidarbha. Vidarbha's financial history under the bankers, to whom the revenues were farmed out, was also so unusual that there has been understandably a certain degree of suspicion ever since of persons from outside the area.

448. Vidarbha's traditional financial surplus, so far as we are aware, continues. The size of this surplus in future will depend on a variety of factors but so far as it can be estimated, it may be a crore and a half of rupees or possibly more. In view of the satisfactory financial position of Vidarbha and since Maharashtra without Greater Bombay is likely to be a deficit area on revenue account to a very much greater extent, there is, some reluctance in this area to join Maharashtra. There seems to be some *prima facie* justification for the suspicion that if Vidarbha joins Maharashtra,

it cannot be certain that its resources will be spent within its own area on suitable development schemes and projects.

449. The position will, of course, be different if Greater Bombay forms part of Maharashtra. In view, however, of our recommendation in regard to the future of Bombay State, this expectation would no longer be valid.

450. We should also like to mention certain other reasons in favour of the creation of a separate Vidarbha State which are either explicitly stated or are implied in the memoranda submitted to us. One of these is the fear that Nagpur will be completely overshadowed by the Bombay city, which would be the natural capital of a single Maharashtrian State, if it were created. Communalism, it has been stated, may also be introduced into the political life of Vidarbha if it joins Maharashtra. Land and tenancy laws in this area will have to be modelled on those of Bombay State; and a period of transition, during which Vidarbha may be struggling to maintain and safeguard its interests, may be unavoidable. Important sections of the people in Vidarbha, in these circumstances, are not willing to run this risk.

451. We have described the conditions in which the demand for the creation of a separate Vidarbha State has come into being. That there is deep-rooted regional consciousness in Vidarbha is conceded even by the leaders of the movement for Samyukta Maharashtra who have offered to make concessions to allay the fears of the people in Vidarbha. The Akola and Nagpur agreements, which aim at reconciling the different points of view, go so far as to provide for a tract-wise allocation of a defined share not only in the cabinet and the executive and judicial services, but also in educational institutions. They also contemplate the establishment of a High Court at Nagpur, the recognition of two capitals and the distribution of development expenditure on an agreed basis. As we have observed in the Chapter on the new Hyderabad State, these arrangements are not workable, and if our assessment of public opinion is correct, are no longer regarded by a section of leaders as a satisfactory means of finding a solution.

452. Without necessarily accepting all that has been urged, and after weighing the merits and demerits of the contending views, we have come to the conclusion that it will be in the interests of all concerned if the Marathi-speaking districts of Madhya Pradesh, which form a compact unit, are constituted into a separate State.

453. We recommend, therefore, that a new State should be formed in this area consisting of the following Marathi-speaking districts, namely, Buldana, Akola, Amravati, Yeotmal, Wardha, Nagpur, Bhandara and Chanda. The area and population of this State will be 36,880 square miles and 7·6 millions respectively.

454. It will be noticed that we do not propose to break up the existing districts of Nimar, Betul, Chhindwara and Balaghat to the north and Bastar to the east in order to recognise the claims made on behalf of Vidarbha mainly on linguistic grounds. As we have indicated earlier, as far as possible, adjustments below the district level should be avoided except where important administrative, economic or other considerations would justify a departure. In our view, there are no special circumstances and we are, therefore, unable to concede these claims.

455. The new State of Vidarbha will be much smaller than the other units which we have proposed. But in view of the special circumstances to which we have referred and the fact that it appears that the economy of this area will be more or less balanced and prosperous, we are not disposed to attach too much weight to mere area or numbers as such.

456. Vidarbha will be one of the most important cotton-growing areas in the country. It will, however, be reasonably industrialised at the same time. The cotton textile industry of the existing State of Madhya Pradesh is heavily concentrated in this area. Only minor and medium irrigation works have been undertaken in this area so far. But in view of the proposals to utilise the waters of the Kanhan, Penganga and Wainganga rivers, large scale development may hereafter be possible. The further opening up of the Pench and Kanhan valley coal fields will benefit this State.

457. It is difficult to forecast the details of the development plans which may be undertaken in future and it is not necessary to do so. There is enough *prima facie* evidence to suggest that Vidarbha can be a stable and prosperous State even if it stands by itself.

CHAPTER IX

MADHYA PRADESH

458. The separation of the eight Marathi-speaking districts of Madhya Pradesh brings us to the question of the future of the remaining districts of the State. This has to be considered along with the future of the other Hindi-speaking units of Central India, namely, Vindhya Pradesh, Bhopal and Madhya Bharat.

459. The proposals made to us about these areas range from the consolidation of all of them into one administrative unit, on the one hand, to the maintenance of the *status quo,* on the other. Public opinion in the Hindi-speaking areas of Madhya Pradesh seems to assume that the formation of a larger Hindi-speaking unit follows as a necessary corollary from the disintegration of Madhya Pradesh. The Mahakosal Pradeshik Congress Committee has thus suggested the formation of a State consisting of the Hindi-speaking areas of the present Madhya Pradesh, the Malwa portion of Madhya Bharat and the whole of Vindhya Pradesh and Bhopal. The main question to be considered is whether it would be feasible to form one State by the unification of all the Hindi-speaking areas of Central India.

460. Historically, the area considered in this Chapter has never been administered together, at any rate long enough for a tradition of common loyalties and sentiment to have come into existence. The question is, however, one which should be determined primarily by economic and administrative considerations and not by the history of individual principalities. Judged by these considerations the formation of a large unit will have clear advantages.

461. We have already recommended in Chapter I of this part of the report that, to the extent practicable, territories now constituting Part C States should be integrated in the adjoining larger units. Apart from the fact that there will be a recurring saving, there are some additional reasons in favour of the proposed merger of the uneconomic and small units of Bhopal and Vindhya Pradesh in a new central Indian State.

462. The State of Bhopal owes its separate existence to a commitment made to the Ruler, at the time of the merger of the State, that it would be administered as a Chief Commissioner's Province

for a period of five years. Speaking in Parliament on 26th May, 1951, about the future of Bhopal, the then States Minister, Shri N. Gopalaswami Ayyangar, observed:

> "Even in Bhopal there is a small group which is not in favour of merger and which would like the State to be a separate unit but I believe at the present moment the great majority of the people in Bhopal do want a merger. But we cannot effect a merger because of our commitments to the Nawab and unless I am able to persuade the Nawab to agree to a merger even before the period for which he is entitled to demand that the present position should continue, we have got to wait in the case of Bhopal also."[1]

This period has expired and, therefore, the difficulty alluded to no longer stands in the way of the merger of Bhopal. One advantage of this merger will be that economic development of the region will be facilitated. The Narbada serves as the boundary between this State and Madhya Pradesh but a number of projects to be sited on or near this border, but within the existing Madhya Pradesh State have recently been investigated. There are proposals, we understand, to build a high dam on the Narbada river in the Jabalpur district of Madhya Pradesh; and it is likely that one of the two principal canals leading off from this project will serve an appreciable portion of Bhopal territory.

463. Vindhya Pradesh, likewise, is in a position to benefit from the projects for the utilisation of the Narbada waters. This State initially came into existence as a Part B State but was subsequently converted into a centrally-administered unit, because it was thought that, owing to its economic and political backwardness, it could not be administered as a Part B State. The intention of the Government of India, when this decision was taken, was to divide Vindhya Pradesh and to merge it in the adjoining States. The considerations which led the Government of India to propose the abolition of the State as a separate administrative unit still hold good.

464. We mention all this to reinforce the general conclusion already reached in Chapter I of this part. There can be no doubt that the advantages, from the point of view of Bhopal and Vindhya Pradesh, of becoming an integral part of a richly-endowed State will more than compensate for the initial disadvantages, if any, such as the loss of revenue gap grants-in-aid from the Centre or the temporary unsettlement regarding development plans.

---

1. Parliamentary Debates, 26th May, 1951, 9462-3.

465. The future of Madhya Bharat presents a more real problem. Madhya Bharat, it has been stated, is relatively undeveloped, and is, therefore, not yet in a position to join the residuary areas of the Madhya Pradesh State. The case for special assistance to Madhya Bharat was recognised in the federal financial agreement and in pursuance of an undertaking which was then given by the Central Government, the needs of this area have been investigated, and an *ad hoc* grant has recently been made to it by the Government of India. It has also been urged that the position has not radically changed since then; and that it would be unwise to introduce any degree of unsettlement regarding the future of a State which has just achieved a certain measure of political and administrative stability and is beginning to concentrate on the real problems of economic and social development.

466. There is also the fear that a new unit, which includes both the Hindi-speaking areas of the present Madhya Pradesh State and Madhya Bharat, will tend to concentrate on the development of the areas in the east where potentialities for development are much greater. If this actually turns out to be the case, Madhya Bharat's special needs and problems will, it is argued, be ignored or neglected.

467. We have carefully examined from this point of view the proposals which have been made for the retention of Madhya Bharat in its existing form, with or without minor boundary adjustments. On the whole, we find that the case against the merger of Madhya Bharat, as it has been presented to us, is not very strong. On the other hand, there are a number of important reasons why in the long run the formation of the bigger unit will be desirable.

468. In the first instance the basic assumption that Madhya Bharat is relatively undeveloped may itself be questioned. It is true that the federal financial agreement recognised the claims for special assistance from the Centre only in the case of some Part B States. The Part B States (Special Assistance) Enquiry Committee, however, found that the progress made by Madhya Bharat in the preceding four or five years compared favourably with that made by some of the Part A States. Even in the matter of *per capita* expenditure the position of Madhya Bharat was better.

469. The unsettling consequences, from an administrative point of view, of the merger of Madhya Bharat also seem to us to have been exaggerated. We understand that in some cases pay scales in Madhya Bharat are already in line with those in Madhya Pradesh;

and in any case the inconvenience regarding the integration of services will be minimised if the suggestions made later are followed.

470. From an administrative point of view, it seems to us that Madhya Bharat, like Bhopal or Vindhya Pradesh, can only gain by joining a large and resourceful unit. One clear advantage of the proposed merger will be that controversies regarding the distribution of development expenditure between the north and the south, which are linked to some extent with the traditional rivalries between Gwalior and Indore, will lose their edge, if a bigger unit which may have its capital at a more central place, is formed. Since this bigger unit is also likely to have the resources needed in order to provide for the balanced and equitable development of all the areas which may be included in it, Madhya Bharat, we feel, can have no reasonable ground for any apprehensions regarding the future.

471. There is reason to believe that these facts are more widely appreciated and accepted than may be supposed. On the whole there has been a remarkable consensus of opinion in favour of the formation of a large State comprising the Hindi-speaking areas of Central India.

472. The suggestions made to this Commission regarding the exact extent of this State have been various and conflicting. In particular, the following claims and counter-claims have been made:

(i) it has been argued on behalf of Maha Vidarbha that the boundaries of Mahakosal should be so drawn as to exclude the following areas, namely, the Marathi-speaking portions of the Nimar, Betul, Chhindwara, Balaghat and Bastar districts;

(ii) it has been suggested that the four northern districts of the existing State of Madhya Bharat, namely, Bhind, Morena, Gird (Gwalior) and Shivpuri, cannot appropriately be included in the proposed State, as they do not form part of Malwa;

(iii) the district of Mandsaur, which is surrounded by Rajasthan for the most part and has an enclave which is a very small and tiny island in Rajasthan territory, as also portions of the Rajgarh and the Guna districts of Madhya Bharat have been claimed by Rajasthan;

(iv) the Sironj sub-division of the Kotah district is an enclave in Madhya Bharat and it has been suggested that it should merge in the new State; and

(v) the Andhra State has claimed the southern half of Bastar district below the river Indravathi; a portion of this district has also been claimed by the Utkal Sammilani.

473. We have already dealt in Chapter VIII of this part with the southern boundary of the new unit, which will be the northern and north-eastern boundary of Vidarbha. We have there recommended that the five districts of which portions have been claimed for Vidarbha should not be broken up.

474. As for the four northern districts of Madhya Bharat, there seems to be no particular reasons why they should be separated from the proposed State. Rajasthan has not claimed these four districts, which are predominantly Hindi-speaking, with ninety to ninety-nine per cent of the population in each district speaking this language. We are not recommending the formation of any other Hindi-speaking State, of which these four districts may form a part. On the other hand, these districts have fairly close economic and administrative links with the Mahakosal area.

475. The law and order situation in the area immediately to the south of the Chambal river is such that the creation of one single administration will be desirable. The terrain of the country is difficult; and the existing State borders are so artificial that the establishment of a common agency has been found necessary to deal with unsocial elements. The consolidation of the entire area into one unit, therefore, will be a clear gain from the administrative point of view.

476. One illustration of the links of the four northern districts of Madhya Bharat with the rest of the proposed State is that the Matatila dam on the river Betwa, which is one of the biggest projects undertaken so far in Bundelkhand, is intended to serve the Gird (Gwalior) and Bhind districts in Madhya Bharat, the Datia and Tikamgarh districts in Vindhya Pradesh, and Jhansi in Uttar Pradesh. As matters now stand, however, some difficulty seems to have been experienced in its working because of the existence of more than one government in this area. Our proposals will incidentally eliminate, to a large extent, this multiplicity of jurisdictions.

477. It has been pointed out to us that there is no direct rail communication from Ujjain or Indore in the south of Madhya Bharat to Gwalior in the north; and that the northern part of Madhya Bharat in consequence is rather cut off from the rest of the State. We understand, however, that the Railway Board have already under consideration the question of constructing a new line from Gwalior

to Ujjain *via* Shivpuri, Guna and Agar. With the construction of this line, the four northern districts of Madhya Bharat will become more closely linked with the rest of the State than they are at present.

478. The demand which has been made on behalf of Rajasthan to the Mandsaur district and the Madhya Bharat claim to Kotah and Jhalawar rest more or less on the same grounds, namely, historical association, administrative convenience and cultural affiliations. These claims are to some extent interlinked. An argument which has been urged by both the governments is that the areas jut out inconveniently into the territories of the States claiming them and that territorial readjustments would ensure greater geographical compactness. Barring the Sunel and Sironj enclaves, however, the disputed areas are geographically contiguous to their respective States and have been administered as part of these States for a long time. Public opinion has not expressed itself in favour of the disturbance of the *status quo*. In these circumstances, we would confine our recommendations only to the transfer of the Sunel town which is an enclave now belonging to the Mandsaur district to Rajasthan and of the Sironj sub-division of the Kotah district of Rajasthan to the proposed State of Madhya Pradesh.

479. The portions of the existing Rajgarh and Guna districts, which Rajasthan has also claimed, are contiguous to the rest of Madhya Bharat. The arguments put forward in favour of the transfer of a portion of these districts are even weaker than in the case of Mandsaur. It is, therefore, unnecessary to recommend that Rajgarh or Guna should be broken up.

480. The Andhra claim to the southern half of Bastar has been pressed on the ground that Telugu is the prevailing language in this area. It has also been pointed out that administratively south Bastar used to be part of the former Upper Godavari district. The Andhra State has also claimed that the economic development of southern Bastar is linked with that of Vishalandhra. This claim to Bastar, however, **cannot be conveniently conceded**, if, as is proposed later, the claim to Koraput is rejected.

481. The linguistic affiliations of this area are not very clear. Telugu, it has been contended, is only a language which is used and understood in what is naturally a bilingual area. Halbi, Bhatri, Parjhi and Gondi are the real indigenous languages. The Andhra Government, however, does not accept this position and has not only questioned the results of the 1951 Census, but has also sought to prove that Hindi has been forced on the residents of this area from 1949 onwards.

482. We have no means of checking these statements in detail. It seems to us, however, that if the *status quo* is to be disturbed, and an existing district is to be split up, the onus of proof regarding its linguistic, economic, or other affiliations must clearly be on the party which claims the area. The linguistic, economic, administrative and other affiliations of the area must be so unmistakably established that it will be advantageous to disturb the existing arrangements. No such case has been made out by Andhra.

483. The Utkal Sammilani's claim to portions of the Bastar district is based, among other reasons, on an alleged affinity between Halbi and Parjhi on the one hand and Oriya on the other, which in our opinion has not by any means been adequately proved. Besides, our more general remarks in the immediately preceding paragraph are also applicable in respect of this demand.

484. The claim which has been advanced on behalf of Maha Vidarbha to Bastar, it is interesting to note, is also based on the argument that Halbi is a dialect of Marathi. Eminent linguists like Grierson and Sten Konow have, however, differed on this point; and Vidarbha's claim cannot, therefore, be considered to be stronger than that of Andhra or Orissa which we have found it necessary to reject.

485. The result of this brief examination is that the proposed State, according to our recommendations, should include the following areas, namely,

(i) the 14 districts of the residuary Madhya Pradesh;

(ii) the whole of Bhopal;

(iii) the whole of Vindhya Pradesh;

(iv) Madhya Bharat except the Sunel enclave of the Mandsaur district; and

(v) the Sironj sub-division of the Kotah district of Rajasthan.

486. The new State, which can appropriately be described as Madhya Pradesh, will be a compact unit. It will bring almost the whole of Bundelkhand and Baghelkhand under one administration. Jabalpur will be situated at a central place in this unit and has or will soon have some important facilities like water supply and availability of electrical power. It will, in our opinion, be a suitable capital.

487. Partly as a result of the decision to erect certain new steel plants, but partly also because of general economic expansion and the growth in traffic, the route and track mileage of the railway

system within the proposed unit will have to be increased and certain proposals have already been sanctioned or are under consideration. We would, however, like to mention more particularly in this connection the demand that Jabalpur should be connected with Lalitpur or Jhansi. With two new rail links from Jabalpur to selected points in the south-west and the south-east on the Central and South-Eastern Railways respectively, and another line running east to west through Vindhya Pradesh, the proposed State of Madhya Pradesh will be much more satisfactorily served by the railway system than it is at the present time. The suggested links in our opinion seem to be essential; and the Government of India will no doubt take this into consideration.

488. With relatively greater scope for the reclamation of virgin or jungle land and a preponderence of zamindari areas in which land alienation has now been abolished, the proposed State is expected to be agriculturally prosperous. The new State will have virtually the entire wheat and rice belts of the existing Madhya Pradesh State. There will also be a very rich concentration of minerals in this area; and with the development of the hydro-electric power potential in the Narbada and Betwa valleys which is now being planned, there are possibilities of large-scale industrialisation, particularly in the Nimar-Hoshangabad and Durg-Bilaspur areas.

489. Bhilai in the Durg district of Madhya Pradesh has already been selected as the site of one of the new steel plants and both the Central and State Governments have formulated plans for the industrialisation and development of Bilaspur and Hoshangabad. Central and provincial expenditure in the new Madhya Pradesh State in the next five-year plan period will, in all probability, be very considerable; and opportunities for employment and income in the new State will be very greatly increased. Madhya Pradesh may, therefore, become one of the richest States in the Indian Union.

490. Financially, the new State, on the basis of such judgments as we have been able to form about the future, will have a comfortable revenue surplus. Even if allowance is made for an accelerated rate of development expenditure, it seems likely that the revenue budget of the State will be balanced. At the least, the financial position will be such as to cause the minimum embarrassment to any newly-constituted government.

491. The scales of pay in this area, as has already been stated, have been upgraded to the Madhya Pradesh level in many cases; and since there will be considerable savings under overheads and a great

deal of scope for increasing the yield of the provincial heads of revenue, our general conclusion as to the financial position of the new State seems to be reinforced.

492. The creation of a State in this part of India and the breaking up of the State of Madhya Pradesh, which has been in existence since 1861, is bound to cause some administrative problems during an initial transition period. But there is no need to exaggerate the difficulties. In the long run, the advantages of having a compact, strong and prosperous unit in Central India will be so great that we have no hesitation in recommending the formation of a new State with the boundaries which have been proposed earlier.

493. The reconstituted State of Madhya Pradesh will have an area of about 171,200 sq. miles, with a population of 26·1 millions.

CHAPTER X

RAJASTHAN

494. We have in the preceding Chapter disposed of the claims for territorial readjustments between Rajasthan and Madhya Bharat. We now proceed to deal with the other major proposals bearing on the future of Rajasthan as well as its territorial limits.

495. The State of Rajasthan was brought into existence as a result of the integration of nineteen former princely states between March, 1948, and May, 1949. It has been claimed in some of the memoranda that the Union which was ultimately brought into being has no integral character and that, in the interests of more efficient administration, it would be better to split up the existing State into two or even three units, namely,

(i) Western Rajasthan (to be called "Maru Pradesh") which will be a border province;

(ii) Eastern Rajasthan which may include certain areas bordering on Delhi and Uttar Pradesh; and

(iii) Southern Rajasthan which may be bounded by the Aravalli range in the west, the Sambhar lake in the north and by the borders of the proposed Madhya Pradesh State in the east.

496. The formation of these three units, it has been stated, will be necessary if all the areas are to be effectively administered; and it will incidentally meet the criticism that the public offices of the new State have not been located in accordance with the recommendations of the Committee which went into this question soon after the formation of the present State and that development expenditure is not being equitably distributed.

497. We should like to make it clear, before we take up the question of disputed areas, that there seems to be little justification for the disintegration of Rajasthan. There was a substantial measure of agreement in 1948 and 1949 in support of the mergers which then took place. Indeed, the Government of India were so anxious to associate public opinion with the changes which were being made that, in the last stage, namely, before the Matsya Union was merged in Rajasthan in May, 1949, a Committee with Shri Shankarrao Deo as Chairman was appointed to ascertain the wishes of the people of

this area. There is no reason to believe that public opinion has changed in the last five or six years or that any significant advantages, either from the point of view of the country as a whole or from that of the areas concerned, will result from partition on the proposed lines.

498. We should like to say a few words, in particular, regarding the proposal to form a Maru Pradesh along the Indo-Pakistan border. If this State is formed, it is unlikely to have adequate resources in manpower or material to police a seven-hundred mile frontier, and financially it will be a weak unit. Moreover, if a comprehensive scheme for the control of the Rajputana desert is to be taken in hand, the proposed State of Western Rajasthan will not be able by itself to implement the scheme. We can see no advantage in forming a unit, the major portion of which will be an unreclaimed desert.

499. Having indicated our reasons against the disintegration of Rajasthan, we now pass on to the consideration of the major claims and counter-claims for territorial readjustments. The Government of Rajasthan has claimed the following areas, namely, the whole of the Ajmer State, the Abu Road taluk of the Banaskantha district of Bombay, the Mandsaur district and small portions of the Guna and Rajgarh districts of Madhya Bharat, the Loharu sub-tehsil of the Bhiwani tehsil of the Hissar district of the Punjab and the Mohindergarh district of PEPSU. In the paragraphs which follow, these claims are discussed in the order mentioned.

500. Ajmer is a one-district Part C State surrounded on all sides by territories of Rajasthan. It has retained its separate existence so far because of historical reasons. The question of its merger in a larger unit has been agitated from time to time since 1921, when a Committee went into it. The fact that Ajmer was a convenient British outpost in Rajasthan and that it could not very well be included in the then United Provinces, from which it was far removed, accounted for the State's separate existence in British days.

501. Ajmer is no longer geographically isolated. Nor does it any longer play the role of a sentinel. We, therefore, agree with the Rajasthan Government that the linguistic, cultural and geographical links of Ajmer with Rajasthan must be respected, and that, for several reasons, for example, the likelihood that the law and order situation may improve as a result of the elimination of dual control, the proposal to merge Ajmer will be justified. It may be recalled that the representative of Ajmer on the Committee on the Chief Commissioners' Provinces, which was appointed by the Constituent Assembly in 1947, had himself envisaged the joining of this area with the contiguous unit "at no distant future".

502. The controversies regarding Abu Road taluk are much more real. This portion of the former Sirohi State was merged in Bombay in January, 1950, in the belief that the partition of the State on the lines mentioned in the States Merger (Bombay) Order, 1950, would be acceptable to the people. Unfortunately, however, the decision to break up Sirohi has not been welcomed either in Gujarat or in Rajasthan.

503. The Rajasthan Government seems to attach very great importance to the retransfer of this area to Rajasthan. We have now reconsidered the position very carefully and, after a great deal of deliberation, we have come to the conclusion that Rajasthan has a legitimate claim to the Abu Road taluk and that this claim should be recognised.

504. In making this recommendation we have taken into consideration the fact that arguments based on trade affiliations or on the need for more effective control of the Western Banas river have been advanced on behalf of both the parties and do not appear to be conclusive. Rajasthan's claims to the area which is now in Bombay, however, rest, in the last resort, on two main grounds, namely, local feeling, and the fact that Rajasthani is the mother-tongue of 65 per cent. of the population of the Abu Road taluk.

505. It may be argued that no clear case has been made out either on administrative or economic grounds for the separation of the Abu Road taluk from the district of which it forms a part. There are, however, two important facts bearing on this question, which cannot be overlooked. Firstly, this area was only recently separated from an administrative unit with which it had a long association and which now forms part of Rajasthan. Secondly, apart from the fact that a majority of the people of this area have not so far reconciled themselves to this separation, the Government of India had decided in 1952 to reopen this question and they had also set in motion the process contemplated in Article 3 for readjustment of state territories. After taking all this into consideration we have reluctantly been compelled to recommend a review of the decision taken in 1950.

506. Loharu is now part of the Hissar district, having been merged in 1948. It has been represented to this Commission that, for at least three and a half centuries after the State was founded, it had intimate links with Rajasthan and that, even in the period which immediately preceded the merger, the association with Bikaner was

very close. Loharu, it has also been stated, has rather intimate trading connections with Rajasthan, the wool trade being particularly important. The area is geographically contiguous to Rajasthan, and it would, perhaps, be easier to administer it from Jhunjhunu, with which town Loharu is incidentally intimately connected, than from Hissar. On a review of all the circumstances in which the claim has been made we recommend that Loharu should be transferred to Rajasthan.

507. Rajasthan's claim to the Mohindergarh district of PEPSU seems to us to be much less reasonable than the claim to Loharu. Apart from the fact that Mohindergarh is outside Rajasthan from the linguistic point of view, the primary ground on which the claim is made, namely that Mohindergarh is an enclave cut off from its parent State, will no longer be valid if our recommendation regarding the amalgamation of PEPSU with the Punjab is accepted Mohindergarh, incidentally, may benefit in future from the Punjab Government's scheme for the utilisation of the waters of the Sutlej or the Jumna. There is, therefore, no case for disturbing the *status quo.*

508. We have already dealt with Rajasthan's claims on Madhya Bharat in the preceding Chapter.

509. We now pass on to a brief examination of the claims made on Rajasthan by other States. The demands are various and conflicting. But, for all practical purposes, we need consider only two proposals which have been made, namely, the suggested transfer of Banswara and Dungarpur to Bombay and the inclusion of Bharatpur and Alwar either in Greater Delhi or in Brij Pradesh. The claim to Banswara and Dungarpur rests on two main arguments. Historically, this so-called Vagad area used to be part of Gujarat. This historical connection with Gujarat, it has been stated, has now been reinforced by the fact of Gujarat's interest in the Mahi river which flows through the Vagad area and the utilisation of which is of very great importance from Gujarat's point of view.

510. In view of the recent history of Banswara and Dungarpur, we are not inclined to attach undue importance to the ancient affiliations of the Vagad area. As far as the utilisation of the Mahi river is concerned, both Gujarat and Rajasthan are interested, and while it is not necessary to anticipate any difficulties, such problems as may arise can be dealt with independently of territorial adjustments.

511. As regards Alwar and Bharatpur, apart from the fact that we have not recommended the formation of the proposed Greater Delhi or Brij Pradesh, we do not think there has been any appreciable change in the state of opinion since the Shankarrao Deo Committee went into the question in 1949, which may justify the disturbance of the *status quo.*

512. It does not seem to be necessary to enter into the details of various other claims and counter-claims which have been made. Public opinion has not expressed itself clearly in favour of these minor changes.

513. The State of Rajasthan will include, according to the recommendations which we have made, the present State less the Sironj sub-division of the Kotah district, plus the Sunel town of Mandsaur district, the Abu Road taluk of the Banaskantha district, the Loharu sub-tehsil of the Hissar district and the State of Ajmer. The area of this unit will be about 132,300 square miles and its population about 16 millions. The financial position and economy of the existing State will be more or less unaffected.

CHAPTER XI

THE PUNJAB

514. While reviewing the northern and eastern boundaries of Rajasthan, we have dealt with the future of certain territories which now form part of the Punjab and PEPSU. We shall now examine the major proposals bearing on the future of these two States and the adjoining Part C State of Himachal Pradesh.

515. We first examine the demand for the formation of a Punjabi-speaking State. The case for the creation of this State, as set out in the memorandum submitted by the Shiromani Akali Dal, rests mainly on the arguments generally advanced in favour of linguistic States. But it has some features of its own and poses problems which require very careful consideration.

516. The main arguments urged in favour of the proposed Punjabi-speaking State are:

(i) it will remove all causes of unrest and discontent, eliminate language controversies, enable the imparting of education in the mother-tongue and help the people to grow and advance;

(ii) it will be a geographically compact unit, financially viable, surplus in food and rich in resources;

(iii) it will be a homogeneous State inhabited by sturdy people, and as such would strengthen the defence of the north-western border; and finally

(iv) it will secure for the country a contented Sikh community.

517. The areas which are claimed to be Punjabi-speaking, and are, therefore, suggested for inclusion in the proposed State are:

(i) *Punjab.*—The districts of Gurdaspur, Amritsar, Ferozepore, Ludhiana, Jullundur, Hoshiarpur, Ambala, Karnal (except Panipat tehsil) and tehsils Sirsa and Fatehabad, and sub-tehsil Tohana of Hissar district;

(ii) *PEPSU.*—The districts of Patiala, Barnala, Bhatinda, Kapurthala, Fatehgarh Sahib and Sangrur (except Jind and Nirwana tehsils);

(iii) *Rajasthan.*—Ganganagar district.*

518. The agitation in favour of the proposed Punjabi-speaking State has been the subject-matter of a serious controversy, a regrettable consequence of which has been the inflammation of communal passions in this region. One strange result of this has been the repudiation by large sections of the Hindu community of the Punjabi language as their mother-tongue. This led during the last Census operations to a situation in which the separate tabulation of Hindi and Punjabi-speaking people had to be abandoned.

519. A peculiar feature of the demand for a Punjabi-speaking State has also been that, while other demands for separation from existing composite States have had the backing of an overwhelming majority of the people of the language group seeking such separation, the demand for a Punjabi-speaking State is strongly opposed by large sections of people speaking the Punjabi language and residing in the areas proposed to be constituted into a Punjabi-speaking State. The problem, therefore, is *sui generis*. It has to be examined against its own peculiar background.

520. We first examine the linguistic considerations urged in support of the demand. As has been stated earlier, our approach to the linguistic principle is governed by practical administrative considerations. Linguistic homogeneity, in our opinion, has to be aimed at as an instrument for facilitating social and political intercourse amongst the people and for ensuring the closer association of the people with the government. If this criterion is applied, it will be found that there is no real language problem in the State of Punjab as at present constituted. This is so because the Punjabi and Hindi languages as spoken in the Punjab are akin to each other and are both well-understood by all sections of the people of the State. Nobody has seriously argued before us that the present set-up presents any difficulty so far as the communicational needs of the people are concerned.

521. It is also of interest to note that while the substratum of Punjabi is a language of the outer circle akin to modern Lahnda, its superstructure is a dialect of western Hindi. According to Grierson, "the superstructure is so important and has so concealed the foundation, that Punjabi is rightly classed, at the present day,

* During the course of the discussion with the Commission on the 12th April 1955, the General Secretary, Shiromani Akali Dal, intimated that the organisation no longer wished to press the claim for any parts of Karnal district or for parts of the Ganganagar district other than the tehsils of Hanumangarh and Ganganagar.

as the language of the central group". The line of demarcation between the Punjabi and the Hindi spoken in the State has, therefore, been more theoretical than real. In recent years, moreover, with the large-scale influx of Punjabi-speaking people from Western Punjab into all the districts of the State this line has been further blurred.

522. Likewise, the present arrangements do not stand in the way of the growth of Punjabi language and culture. There are no distinctive cultural zones in the existing State. As for literary activity, the figures cited in the Akali Dal memorandum would themselves rebut any contention that in the existing Punjab State there is any impediment to the development of the Punjabi language.

523. The feelings of those sections which advocate the creation of a Punjabi-speaking State seem to be that Punjabi is a distinct and developed language with a script, different from the Nagari script, devised to suit the phonological and inflectional pecularities of the Punjabi language; that this language is the language of the region which is proposed to be constituted into a Punjabi-speaking State; and that those who oppose the demand are motivated by communal considerations because the Punjabi-speaking State will "improve the position of an under-dog of democracy which they at present are".

524. Those opposed to the movement argue on the other hand that basically the demand is a communal one and that cultural and linguistic arguments have been pressed into service merely to camouflage the real motives. The Hindus as a whole, it is argued, have never accepted Punjabi as their medium of expression, to the exclusion of Hindi, because while at home they speak the Punjabi language, in their religious ceremonies and festivals, in their schools and colleges they use Hindi. In any case, they have never accepted the Gurmukhi script.

525. For assessing the merits of these contending views, it is necessary to take note of certain special features of the linguistic composition of the Punjab. The first point to remember is that, although Punjabi has been the spoken language of the greater part of the eastern half of the undivided province of the Punjab, the position before the partition was that Urdu and not Punjabi was regarded as the official language for purposes other than those for which English was used. This position still holds good. It is only recently under the decision known as the Sachar-Gyani Kartar Singh formula that Punjabi and Hindi are proposed to be introduced as regional languages for official and educational purposes in the two language zones into which the Punjab has been demarcated.

526. There is also no denying the fact that the demand that Punjabi written in Gurmukhi script alone should be recognised as the Punjabi language is of relatively recent origin. Not only have some of the reputed Punjabi writers like Warris Shah written in a script other than Gurmukhi with which Punjabi is now sought to be related, but even the University of Punjab had been giving before partition an option to candidates taking various Punjabi examinations to adopt either the Gurmukhi or the Persian script.

527. The problem of language in the Punjab is, therefore, primarily one of scripts; and in this battle of scripts, sentiment is arrayed against sentiment.

528. We have to consider how far the formation of the proposed Punjabi-speaking State will help to solve this script problem. The first point to be considered is naturally whether there is any justification for the exclusive use of the Gurmukhi script in writing Punjabi. It has been contended that no practical difficulties were experienced even when the Persian script, which is quite distinct from the Gurmukhi script, was used for writing Punjabi. The Devanagari script, it is claimed, is even more suitable, because it has marked affinities with the Gurmukhi script, and is fully equipped to meet all the phonological needs of the Punjabi language.

529. The Hindus, as a community, seem to be strongly opposed to the imposition of the Gurmukhi script on them in disregard of the past practice as also their own sentiment. In these conditions, it may create more problems than it would solve, if this area is constituted into a unilingual state, in which only one script, namely, Gurmukhi, is recognised.

530. Assuming for the sake of argument that a settlement of the problem is to be sought by conceding the demand that Punjabi written in Gurmukhi script should be the language of the region proposed to be constituted into a Punjabi-speaking State, the long-term prospect, from the point of view of all those who are interested in the growth and development of the Punjabi language, can hardly be described as happy. In the proposed State, people claiming Hindi as their mother-tongue will still be entitled to receive instruction in Hindi. Under the arrangements made at present, in implementation of the resolution regarding the interests of linguistic minorities that was adopted by the Provincial Education Ministers' Conference of August, 1949, and approved by the Central

Advisory Board of Education and the Government of India, the State Governments are required to provide facilities for the instruction of children in the primary stage in their mother-tongue, if it is different from the regional or State language, provided that there are at least 40 pupils speaking that language in the whole school or 10 in one class. Facilities must also be provided in the secondary stage, if there is a sufficient number, usually one-third of the total number of pupils, whose mother-tongue is different from the regional or State language.

531. Having regard to the background of the language controversy in this area, it is not unlikely that large sections of Hindus would seek instruction in Hindi if a Punjabi-speaking State is formed. Whatever the legitimacy of such a demand may be, there is no method by which a person can be compelled to adopt a mother-tongue other than that for which he himself shows his preference. In these circumstances, even if a Punjabi-speaking State is formed, the entire area will still be bilingual, in the sense that instruction in Hindi will have to be arranged on an extensive scale, and for official purposes also Hindi will probably have to be given special recognition.

532. That the demand for the due recognition of Hindi as the spoken language of the region has not been stimulated only by the recent controversy, is clear from the fact that, of the total number of candidates who appeared during the last five years in the Hindi and Punjabi examinations of the Punjab University from the Jullundur division, 62·2 per cent appeared in the Hindi examinations and 37·8 per cent in the Punjabi examinations; these figures relate to the six Punjabi-speaking districts of the present Punjab State in which, according to the 1931 Census, the percentage of Punjabi-speaking people was 97·2 and of Hindi-speaking people only 1·3. It is also of interest to note that, out of 1,03,758 candidates appearing in the matriculation examination of the Punjab University during the last four years who had the option to answer history and geography papers either in Hindi or Punjabi, 73·5 per cent. elected to answer in Hindi and 26·5 per cent. in Punjabi. Motives cannot well be attributed to examinees at university examinations who must have exercised their option on the basis of their own literary needs and family traditions. For this reason, the conclusion which seems to be indicated cannot be ignored. Hindi will not by any means be unimportant in the Punjabi-speaking zone and Punjabi and Hindi will have to exist and develop side by side.

533. An arrangement such as that contemplated under the Sachar-Gyani formula, based on the recognition of the bilingual character of this area would provide, in these circumstances, a more effective solution of the problem of language than the separation of the Punjabi-speaking areas from the rest of the State. It may be pointed out that Punjabi has now been given, under this formula, a place of honour in that it is accorded the same treatment in the Hindi-speaking zone as has been conceded to Hindi in the Punjabi-speaking zone. If, therefore, in consequence of the formation of a Punjabi-speaking State, the Punjabi language secures an advantage in one direction, namely, in the enforcement of the Gurmukhi script in the Punjabi-speaking zone, it may lose in another direction, namely in its dissemination in areas now known as the Hindi-speaking areas.

534. There is another important aspect of the problem which should be taken into account in considering a further division of the Punjab on linguistic grounds. According to Grierson, the line between western Hindi spoken in the Hindi-speaking area of the Punjab and Punjabi could be taken as the meridian passing through Sirhind. The territorial claims for the proposed Punjabi-speaking State, however, ignore this line of division. They go so far as to include the whole of Ambala, the district of Karnal *minus* one tehsil, and portions of Hissar. A claim has also been made to the Ganganagar district of Rajasthan which never formed part of the Punjab. With the large-scale dispersal of Punjabi-speaking people from the Punjab (Pakistan) in the eastern Punjab and with the colonisation of the area under the Bhakra project, the division between the two linguistic zones in the Punjab is progressively becoming less and less real. The Akali Dal memorandum itself states that the Punjabi-speaking people carry their culture and language with them.[1] Quite clearly, with this widespread dispersion of the Punjabi language in recent years and the intermingling of Hindi-speaking and Punjabi-speaking people, it would be impossible to create a compact unilingual State.

535. The results of this brief examination may now be summarised. The creation of a Punjabi-speaking State would offer no solution to the language problem, the present arrangements for the recognition of both Punjabi and Hindi could not be done away with, and the controversies would not in all probability come to an end, and while no major problem would be solved, both the languages might suffer.

---

1. Memorandum of the Shiromani Akali Dal.

536. We now come to the important question whether the proposed State will secure an improvement from the point of view of peace and contentment of the people of the area. There are no complaints from those sponsoring the movement for a Punjabi-speaking State about economic or political exploitation of the Punjabi-speaking areas by the representatives of the so-called Hindi-speaking region. If anything, the complaint is from the hilly areas and the Hariana tract.

537. There is undoubtedly internal tension in this area. But this tension follows communal and not territorial lines. There is little likelihood that the creation of the proposed State will lead to greater communal harmony and concord.

538. The sponsors of the Punjabi-speaking State argue that a majority of the people inhabiting the area are in favour of a Punjabi-speaking State and that opposition is confined to certain communal elements. The results of the recent elections to the Shiromani Gurdwara Prabandhak Committee have been cited as evidence of the popular backing which the demand has amongst the Sikh masses. On the other hand, the results of the last general elections and the subsequent by-elections are cited in support of the view that the demand for the Punjabi-speaking State is confined to communal elements in the Sikh community.

539. We do not propose to express any opinion on the relative influence and popularity of those supporting or opposing the movement for a Punjabi-speaking State. But it is quite obvious that the minimum measure of agreement necessary for making a change in the present set-up does not exist so far as the proposal for the Punjabi-speaking State is concerned. The Dar Commission rightly expressed the view that no linguistic State should be imposed on substantial minorities opposing them.[1] In this particular case, we may actually be imposing the wishes of a substantial minority on the majority.

540. The case for a Punjabi-speaking State falls firstly, because it lacks the general support of the people inhabiting the area, and secondly, because it will not eliminate any of the causes of friction from which the demand for a separate Punjabi-speaking State emanates. The proposed State will solve neither the language problem nor the communal problem and, far from removing internal tension, which exists between communal and not linguistic and regional groups, it might further exacerbate the existing feelings.

1. Report of the Linguistic Provinces Commission, para. 10.

541. We now come to the demand for the separation of the so-called Hariana area of the Punjab. The complaint from this area is one of inadequate representation in the civil administration of the State and relative economic backwardness.

542. The Punjab Government placed before us some facts and figures in repudiation of the allegation of discriminatory treatment of this region. It has been argued that schemes have recently been formulated or implemented for extending the irrigation system of the Punjab so as to serve the dry areas of Hissar and Rohtak. The Gurgaon Canal project now under consideration is a major project intended to benefit Hariana. The Bhakra-Nangal project will materially benefit this area and the contention that the original plan has been varied to the disadvantage of the area has no basis in fact.

543. We do not wish to express any opinion on these two contending views, but we are convinced that the separation of the so-called Hariana areas of the Punjab which are deficit areas, and are, according to the memorandum submitted by the Akali Dal, "only a liability which can be better borne by their neighbours with whom they have greater affinity in language and culture" will be no remedy for any ills, real or imaginary, from which this area at present suffers.

PEPSU

544. The next question we have to consider is the future of PEPSU. The decisions regarding the proposed Punjabi-speaking State and the Hariana tract which have been indicated in the preceding paragraphs do not dispose of the contention of the PEPSU Government that having regard to the special background against which this State was created the *status quo* should not be disturbed. We now examine how far the claim to the separate existence of PEPSU is justified.

545. Physically and geographically PEPSU is very much a part of the Punjab. From the point of view of population PEPSU is the smallest of the Part B States and is comparable to an existing Part C State, namely, Vindhya Pradesh. The area of the State is less than one half of that of Vindhya Pradesh and even this small area is not geographically compact. It consists of five disconnected bits which are surrounded mostly by the territories of the Punjab. This lack of geographical contiguity has naturally stood in the way of a real political integration of the people of the State and it is not surprising that demands for merger in the adjoining areas have been voiced

from time to time in the outlying enclaves of Kapurthala and Mohindergarh and the hilly tracts of the State. It is because of this anomalous geographical position that it has often been argued that PEPSU is an artificial unit and cannot continue under any scheme of reorganisation.

546. There is considerable force in these arguments. We feel that even with its present territory the State cannot be regarded as a sizeable unit, and with the merger of its outlying pockets in the adjoining areas, which should follow as a natural corollary of territorial readjustments in this area, it will become very difficult for this State to maintain its separate existence.

547. As it is, the State is not in a position to maintain separate cadres of All-India Services and the proposal for having a common cadre with the adjoining State of Punjab has been under consideration for some time. Administratively the States of the Punjab and PEPSU have a number of common problems to face and devices such as a Joint Advisory Council and periodical conferences have to be adopted to achieve a certain minimum degree of co-ordination between the two States. It would be simpler and more economical, besides being conducive to more efficient administration, if the State were merged.

548. The main arguments advanced in favour of the continuance of the State are, firstly, that PEPSU is a home land for the Sikhs and should, therefore, be allowed to continue as such, and secondly, that the alternative to this would be to concede either the demand for a Punjabi-speaking State or the demand for a Maha Punjab, both of which, it is stated, are communal in character in that they are intended to tilt the balance in favour of one or the other of the two main communities.

549. In an earlier Chapter we have discussed at some length the implications of the home land concept. Here we would only add that while we view the doctrine of a linguistic home land with serious misgivings, we consider that the concept of a communal home land is fraught with even more dangerous potentialities.

550. As for the possible unfavourable repercussions of enlarging the present State of Punjab on the existing communal equilibrium, the position is that the proposal which we make about this region will no doubt result in the formation of a larger unit, but the Sikh percentage in the enlarged unit will not be adversely affected as compared with their percentage in the existing State of Punjab.

The Sikh percentage in the proposed State will in fact show a small improvement of a little more than 1·5 per cent. resulting in a corresponding decrease in the Hindu percentage.

551. It is no doubt true that the percentage of the Sikh community in PEPSU is 49, but for the reasons already stated, this unit cannot be considered to be administratively viable and we do not find it possible to overlook this fact.

552. During the course of our discussions with the representatives of the PEPSU Government we noticed that it was appreciated that on account of clear geographical and administrative compulsions, PEPSU could not continue as a separate administrative unit for any length of time. It was, however, suggested to us during these discussions that for some time to come the State might be maintained as a separate unit in order to ensure that the present pace of its development was not impeded. We are not impressed by this argument. We feel that the people of PEPSU are as resourceful and enterprising as those of the adjoining areas of the Punjab and there is no reason why the immediate formation of the larger unit should in any way prejudice the development of the areas now included in this State.

553. It seems to us that one important reason why the proposal to merge PEPSU in the Punjab has not been as popular as it might otherwise have been is the feeling that Patiala city, which has grown appreciably in size and importance since the partition of the country, may be overshadowed by Chandigarh and Simla. A great deal of money has recently been spent on the improvement of the city, and if it were to be reduced after merger to the status of a mere district headquarters or the headquarters of a Commissioner's division, much of this investment might turn out to have been a waste.

554. It would be reasonable to take note of this feeling. We do not foresee that the government of a united Punjab will ignore the claims of Patiala, which has so far enjoyed the status of an important State capital, or that any future administration will deny itself the use of the facilities which are now available in Patiala city. By way of caution, however, and as a concession to the sentiment in Patiala, we would recommend that the special position of the city of Patiala might be recognised and that some important offices of the Punjab Government might be located there. This would involve no departure from the general principle which is referred to elsewhere in this report, namely, that administrative convenience must be the main consideration to be taken into account in deciding the location

of government offices. The claims of Patiala can be supported on the ground that Chandigarh has still to develop and that the location of some offices in Patiala which is situated at a short distance from Chandigarh, will be both popular and convenient.

Himachal Pradesh

555. Our decision regarding the future of the Himachal Pradesh and the general considerations on which it is based have already been indicated in Chapter I of this part of the report. We shall now examine certain arguments advanced by the Himachal Pradesh Government against its merger in a larger unit.

556. Himachal Pradesh is relatively backward, and having regard to its small population, the percentage of literacy in these areas which is much lower than in the case of the Punjab, and the very great need for development, it is argued that this State as part of a bigger unit will be a neglected area with few opportunities, if any, for economic or social advancement. The alleged indifference of the Punjab Government to the needs of the eastern portion of the Kangra district is quoted in support of this argument. Himachal, as it happens, is also a border State, with an international boundary which is partially undefined. It is contended, therefore, that the existing position, under which the State has a separate administration but is actively supported by the Centre, should continue.

557. We have examined these arguments with sympathy and understanding because the area is backward, and will need special attention for quite some time to come. We are extremely doubtful, however, whether direct administration by the Centre, within the framework which we propose for centrally-administered territories, is the best solution which is possible or whether this solution will be acceptable to those who have been advocating the continuance of Himachal Pradesh as a separate unit.

558. Himachal is relatively poor largely because of the poverty of its resources. The lack of trained personnel is also at present a serious impediment. It is not, therefore, a unit which can stand by itself.

559. One of the main arguments in favour of separate existence is that the area has a cultural individuality and that the interests of the relatively backward people of this area will suffer by association with the more advanced people of the adjoining plains. We are unable to accept this argument, because it does not seem to us

to be desirable that states should be formed in this or any other region consisting exclusively of hilly areas. For one thing, it is not correct to say that all hill people are necessarily backward. It is also implicit in the demands for separate hill states that the interests of the hill people, on the one hand, and the interests of the people of the adjoining plains on the other, are mutually exclusive and that the former can develop economically and politically, only if they are segregated from the people of the adjoining plains. These assumptions are unwarranted by facts.

560. The economic and administrative advantages of Himachal Pradesh being integrated with the adjoining States are on the other hand quite clear. The catchment area of the Sutlej and the Beas, for instance, is mostly in Himachal Pradesh; and from the point of view of the Bhakra project, this fact is of such great relevance that the need for the transfer of some area to the Punjab has been accepted in principle and a Committee appointed by the Union Ministry of Irrigation and Power has already gone into the details of this proposed transfer. The links between the hills and the plains are really much more intimate than even this report suggests. Soil conservation in the hills is vitally important from the point of view of the plains. Integration of these areas will, therefore, be to the mutual benefit of the people of the plains and of the hills.

561. Another argument urged in favour of the claim of Himachal Pradesh to separate existence is that the Government of India in the Ministry of States had intended at the time of the formation of this unit that it should continue as a separate centrally-administered unit. It is doubtful if any firm assurance to that effect was actually given. Quite apart, however, from the merits of the evidence on which this argument is based, the arrangements which were made at the time of the integration or merger of the former princely states, including their classification as Part B and C States, must, as we have observed earlier, be regarded as transitional expedients. If we were to accept them as final and binding settlements, it would be impossible to reorganise the States on a rational basis. The declaration by the Government of India of their intentions about the future of the units known as Part B States rests on a more formal basis than those made in respect of Part C States. Since, however, our terms of reference do not exclude from the purview of our enquiry any category of States, we have recommended substantial alterations in the existing structure of even the Part B States. It will, therefore, be invidious to lay particular emphasis on any assurance assumed to have been given in the case of Himachal Pradesh.

562. Our own impression, formed as a result of our tour of this area, is that opposition to the integration of this unit in the Punjab is not so strong as is generally made out. While we undoubtedly noticed some sense of uneasiness in certain sections of the people about the merger of the State, it was clear to us that vested interests were actively fostering this. Taking this into account, we see no reason why all other important considerations should be subordinated to the alleged feeling of the hill people against amalgamation with the adjoining areas.

563. In view of what has been stated in the preceding paragraphs the right course would be to merge Himachal Pradesh with the Punjab and to make at the same time suitable arrangements to ensure that the economic development of this area is not impeded. We have already recommended in Chapter I of this part that the Central Government should retain supervisory authority over this area and that the flow of central aid for its development should not be disturbed for another period of, say, ten years.

564. We also suggest that the Punjab cabinet should include at least one member elected from one of the constituencies of the Himachal Pradesh.

565. The India-China border in this region admits of easy infiltration and the defence and security requirements of the region must remain a special concern of the Central Government. These considerations of security in our opinion require the establishment of a stronger and more resourceful unit than the present Himachal Pradesh.

566. We do not propose to go in any detail into the proposal for the formation of a larger hill unit by integrating with the present Himachal Pradesh the adjoining hill territories of the Punjab, the Uttar Pradesh and PEPSU. For one thing, there has been no reliable evidence of any desire on the part of the people of the areas claimed from other States to join the people of Himachal Pradesh. In fact, if one were to judge by the results of the recent elections in Bilaspur, which according to the winning group constitute a clear popular verdict against the merger of Bilaspur in Himachal Pradesh, the claim that in the adjoining hill areas there is a popular movement in favour of integration with Himachal Pradesh would stand repudiated. Quite apart from these considerations, it is clear that if even a larger hill unit is brought into existence, it will not form an administratively viable unit.

Maha Punjab

567. It now remains to dispose of the demand sponsored primarily by certain Hindu organisations in the Punjab for the formation of a larger Punjab unit comprising not only the territories of the States of Punjab, PEPSU and Himachal Pradesh but also of portions of the existing Delhi State and two or three neighbouring western districts of the Uttar Pradesh. On administrative and economic grounds, there is no case for the further addition of territories to the proposed Punjab State. From a political point of view, the acceptance of the proposal is likely to have very undesirable repercussions.

The new State of Punjab

568. We have now considered all the important proposals regarding the future of the Punjab. By a process of elimination we have arrived at the conclusion that the merger of the existing States of the Punjab (except the Loharu sub-tehsil of Hissar district), PEPSU and Himachal Pradesh in a single integrated unit is the most satisfactory solution which can be proposed. This new State will have an area of about 58,140 square miles and a population of 17·2 millions.

569. We have approached this problem with every desire to assess the merits of the alternative proposals, because of our anxiety to consider and examine these alternatives as objectively as possible. Our final conclusion has been reached as a result of discarding all other alternatives. We would like to make it clear, however, that this final solution is not in the nature of a mere *pis aller*. It is not only the least unsatisfactory of several unsatisfactory alternatives There is a great deal that can be said positively in favour of the formation of a united Punjab.

570. The whole of the Punjab from the Sutlej to the Indus was obviously intended by nature to be a single natural area. Even after the division of the State, the areas within the Union of India commanded by the Ravi, Beas and Sutlej constitute a compact unit fertilised by a single river system. The central part of this unit consists of an area on both sides of the rivers Beas and Sutlej. This central part, however, has vital economic links with the hill districts of Himachal where the catchment areas of this river system are located; and the portion which is to the south also has important economic links with this central part, because the most important irrigation work which has been undertaken since Partition is intended to serve this southern portion, either directly by means of new

irrigation canals, or indirectly by means of augmenting the available supply in the old canals. An important instance of the links of the south with the north is provided by the Mohindergarh district. Situated in a remote corner of this region, it is likely to receive electricity from Bhakra, and if plans which have been under investigation materialise or are extended, this district, which has had no irrigation so far, may get water from the Jumna. Apart from the fact that the irrigation system of the whole of the Indian Punjab is thus one and indivisible, the power potential of this region, which is also dependent on this system, is also immense; and the Uhl and Bhakra-Nangal electrical power grids together are intended to command the entire area of united Punjab.

571. It is impossible to overlook the fact of this natural and economic unity; and in recent years, as more and more attention is being devoted to economic development, this essential unity of the region has been illustrated in various ways. We have already referred to the Joint Advisory Council and to the Hejmadi Committee's report regarding the transfer of some area from Himachal to the Punjab in the interests of the Bhakra project. Other instances can also be quoted. The system of road communications in Mandi, Mahasu, Lahul, Spiti and Kulu is centred, for example, on Simla; and trade flows along these routes. The allotment of evacuee agricultural property under the resettlement scheme had to be handled at Jullundur as a regional problem. The prosperous central belt moreover is the granary of the Punjab; and the Hariana tract of the Punjab, which experiences periodical famines in food and fodder, derives considerable advantage from the fact that it can draw on the resources of this central belt.

572. During the past few years new problems calling for coordination have arisen as a result of the Punjab undertaking commitments in respect of the Bhakra project. These problems are the rehabilitation of persons displaced by the project and the orderly implementation of the agreements regarding the rivers of the Punjab which have been or are likely to be arrived at as the result of negotiations between India and Pakistan. In our opinion, the formation of a united Punjab will facilitate planning of the kind which seems to be so obviously indicated.

573. Before we conclude, we should like to emphasize the important fact that whether the proposed Punjabi-speaking State is formed or not, the Hindus and the Sikhs in the Punjab have to live together in amity. The two communities are so interspersed in this region that no form of reorganisation can be a real substitute for

communal harmony. To base a decision regarding the future of this area on the assumption that the Hindus and Sikhs are destined to drift apart will be both shortsighted and unwarranted in these circumstances.

574. The Punjab has, during the recent years, passed through the very severe ordeal of Partition. It is only by the joint and heroic effort of the Hindus and the Sikhs that it has been possible to rehabilitate the political, social and economic life of the province which was so completely disorganised as a result of Partition. It would be most unfortunate if a number of complex problems were created at this time by a further division of the State with all its undesirable consequences.

575. From the point of view of the Sikhs themselves, the solution which we have proposed offers the advantage that the precarious or uncertain political majority which they seek will be exchanged for the real and substantial rights which a sizeable and vigorous minority, with a population ratio of nearly one-third, is bound to have in the united Punjab in the whole of which they have a real stake.

576. Numerically, the Sikhs are a small community, but they are an enterprising and vigorous people. Their creative energy needs greater opportunities than those which a small unit can offer. Those amongst them who have pinned their faith to a home land which cannot be justified on important administrative grounds, and in which the political power of the Sikh community is likely to be evenly balanced by the power and influence of the other major community, seem to disregard this fact.

577. We realise that important sections of the Sikh community seem to nurse a sense of grievance and seek its redress in a Punjabi-speaking State of their conception. We are in no position to say how far the allegations made about discrimination against the Sikhs have any real basis in fact. One complaint is that the Sachar-Gyani formula itself has not been implemented effectively. This formula had the support of all the political parties in the Punjab legislature at the time it was adopted. We see no reason why the arrangements proposed under it should not be worked in the right spirit. Another grievance which has been voiced relates to the relative share of the Sikh community in the services of the State. The validity of this complaint has been questioned. It is not for us to express any

opinion on this or any other grievance of the community or to suggest measures for the solution of the communal problem in the Punjab. All that we would say is that, given a measure of goodwill, an amicable settlement should not be difficult.

578. If the political settlement which we propose is accepted as a fair and lasting solution, a great deal of time and energy, which are now spent on the reconciliation of divergent points of view, will be released for implementing the far-reaching development plans which the various governments in this region have now under consideration. We would conclude in the hope that these anticipations would prove to be correct.

579. Our Chairman is unable to subscribe to the recommendation we have made about the merger of the Himachal Pradesh in the Punjab. He would prefer the administration of this unit by the Centre as a territory. A separate note containing his views on the subject is appended to this report. On all other issues discussed in this Chapter, including the abolition of Himachal Pradesh as a Part C State, the recommendations made are unanimous.

CHAPTER XII

DELHI

580. The proposals which have been made in the two preceding Chapters involve a rejection of the demand for the creation of the Hariana prant or a Greater Delhi State. Quite independently, however, of any decision affecting the areas adjoining it, the future of Delhi has to be determined primarily by the important consideration that it is the seat of the Union Government.

581. The present set-up of Delhi State, it may be stated, is even more anomalous than that of other Part C States in that, within the narrow ambit of powers delegated to these States, the legislative authority of Delhi is subject to certain special limitations. The subjects specifically excluded from the purview of the State Legislature include law and order, local self-governing institutions, the Improvement Trust and other statutory boards regulating certain public utility services in Delhi and New Delhi.[1]

582. This peculiar diarchical structure represents an attempt to reconcile Central control over the federal capital with autonomy at State level. It is not surprising that these arrangements have not worked smoothly. On the one hand, it is contended that the development of the capital is hampered by the division of responsibility between the Centre and the State Government and that there has been a marked deterioration of administrative standards in Delhi since dual control was introduced in 1951. On the other hand, there is persistent complaint from the State Government about the inadequacy of the powers vested in it. How unrealistic the present situation is, will be clear from the strong opposition of the State Government to the establishment of a corporation in Delhi, in spite of the fact that there is every justification for setting up a corporation for a big urban area like Delhi, which is rapidly growing in importance and where health and sanitation are raising immense problems. It is interesting to note that the main ground on which opposition to a corporation is based is that, with the creation of a legislature and a popular government in this predominantly urban State, establishment of a corporation is not feasible. This, in a way, illustrates the problem of Delhi State.

583. That the present arrangements cannot endure is admitted even in the memorandum submitted on behalf of the Delhi Government which states that "Delhi is a Part C State and it is difficult to

---

1. The Government of Part C States Act, 1951, Section 21.

see any future for such States". According to the basic pattern of component units of the Indian Union which we envisage, an existing Part C State must in future become either part of a State or a centrally-administered territory. In making a choice between the two alternatives we must take into account the following special factors:

(i) Delhi is the seat of the Union Government; and

(ii) it is basically a city unit, 82 per cent. of its total population being resident in urban areas.

584. It is hardly necessary to discuss in any detail the reasons why Delhi, if it is to continue as the Union capital, cannot be made part of a full-fledged constituent unit of the Indian Union. Even under a unitary system of government, the normal practice is to place national capitals under a special dispensation. In France, for example, there is a greater degree of central control over Paris than over other municipalities. In England, the police administration of the metropolitan area is directly under the control of the Home Secretary, who does not exercise similar powers in respect of other municipal areas. Apart from reasons which are peculiar to each country or city, there are some general considerations necessitating special arrangements in respect of national capitals. Capital cities possess, or come to possess, some degree of political and social predominance. They are seats of national governments, with considerable property belonging to these governments. Foreign diplomatic missions and international agencies are located in these capitals. They also become centres of national culture and art. So far as federal capitals are concerned, there is also an additional consideration. Any constitutional division of powers, if it is applicable to units functioning in the seats of national governments, is bound to give rise to embarrassing situations. Practice in other countries, administrative necessity and the desirability of avoiding conflicting jurisdictions, all point to the need for effective control by national governments over federal capitals.

585. It may be recalled that the desirability of excluding the seat of the Central Government from the jurisdiction of a provincial government was one of the main considerations which led to the transfer of the Imperial capital from Calcutta in 1912. It was then considered essential that the Supreme Government should not be associated with any particular Provincial Government and it was also felt that the removal of the Central Government from Calcutta would materially facilitate the growth of local self-government on

sound and safe lines. "It is generally recognised", observed the Government of India in their Despatch to the Secretary of State dated 25th August, 1911, "that the capital of a great central Government should be separate and independent, and effect has been given to this principle in the United States, Canada, and Australia". The Secretary of State for India, in his reply to this Despatch, put the case for undivided Central control over the capital more succinctly:

> "The arrangement, as you frankly describe it, is a bad one for both Governments, and the Viceroy for the time being is inevitably faced by this dilemma, that either he must become Governor-in-Chief of Bengal in a unique sense, or he must consent to be saddled by public opinion both in India and at home with direct liability for acts of administration or policy over which he only exercises in fact the general control of a supreme Government. The local Government, on the other hand, necessarily suffers from losing some part of the sense of responsibility rightly attaching to it as to other similar administrations".

586. The weighty considerations urged in these Despatches should not be lightly brushed aside on the ground that they relate to a period when India was under a foreign government. If anything, these arguments are more valid in the present circumstances, because there is a greater need for avoiding the blurring of responsibility under a democratic form of government based on the federal principle than under a bureaucratic system of government, which allowed each higher unit to exercise overriding authority over the lower units.

587. That the capital of the Union Government should be directly administered by it has not been disputed either in the memorandum submitted on behalf of the Delhi Government or by the official representatives of the State during the course of their discussions with us. It has, however, been suggested that New Delhi should be regarded as the national capital over which the Union Government might have full control. The real issue, therefore, so far as the future of Delhi is concerned is whether a line of demarcation should be drawn between New Delhi and Old Delhi and the two units be placed under two separate administrations.

588. It may be recalled that, when in 1912 the Imperial capital was transferred to Delhi, the question of the extent of territory to be included in the Delhi Province was discussed between the Central Government and the Punjab Government. "The extent of territory to be included in the new province" was determined, according to the Government of India, "by the impossibility of excluding old

Delhi, whose interests are intertwined with those of the new city, and by the expediency of including a small margin over and above the actual limits of the Imperial capital".[1] The total population of the two areas, old Delhi and new Delhi taken together, at that time was only 2,32,837.[2] Since then the two parts of the city have rapidly developed and Delhi is now an integrated and vast metropolis with an urban population of nearly a million and a half.[3] From the point of view of law and order, the social life of the people, trade and commerce and common public utility services, old Delhi and New Delhi now constitute one integrated unit and it will be wholly unrealistic to draw a line between the two. Both the areas are rapidly expanding and satellite townships are developing on the outer peripheries of both old Delhi and New Delhi. The anomaly of treating the two areas separately is illustrated by the fact that even under the existing arrangements Delhi Fort had to be declared as an area outside the jurisdiction of Delhi Government for purposes of the Warrant of Precedence. It will also be of interest to note that, when in 1949, the Government of India decided to exclude New Delhi from the jurisdiction of the corporation proposed for old Delhi, the kind of corporation envisaged was regarded as 'truncated', 'moth-eaten' and not 'sufficiently inspiring'. If there is objection to the two areas being treated as two distinct units in the civic field, there will be even less justification for the assumption that administratively they can be placed under two different governments.

589. If it is conceded that the national capital has to be under the effective control of the national government and both New Delhi and old Delhi have to be treated as a single unit for administrative purposes, there will be little scope for difference of opinion on its future administrative pattern.

590. As we have observed earlier, Delhi is essentially urban in character. It has a rural belt which was acquired to meet its requirements as the seat of the Imperial Government. The rural areas, however, to the extent that they are not indispensable for the future urban expansion and development of Delhi, can be retroceded to the parent state or states.

591. In devising a system of government for Delhi, therefore, we must take into account primarily the requirements and aspirations of a cosmopolitan urban population. Urban problems such as slum

---

1. Memoranda submitted by the Government of India to the Indian Statutory Commission, Vol. IV, p. 356.
2. 1911 Census.
3. Exact figure—1,437,134 according to the 1951 Census.

clearance, reconstruction, city planning, recreation, transportation, and primary and secondary education, all fall within the domain of municipal finance and enterprise. If we are to be guided by these clear considerations as well as by the experience of other advanced countries, municipal autonomy for Delhi in the form of a corporation would appear to be the most appropriate method of meeting and reconciling the broader requirements of the national Government as well as the local needs and the wishes of the people.

592. One of the main reasons advanced by the Delhi Government against the establishment of a municipal corporation is that the financial resources of Delhi State cannot maintain a popular government as well as a municipal corporation. As under our recommendations, a separate state government for Delhi will no longer be required, this objection will cease to have any validity.

593. We have given careful consideration to the argument that a denial to the people of Delhi of the benefits of popular government at state level would be a retrograde step. It has to be realised that, if Delhi is to continue to be the seat of the Central Government, it must adopt a model which is sound in principle and administratively workable in practice. People residing in national capitals enjoy an advantageous position and they must be prepared to pay some price for it. It may be pointed out that the legal residents of the District of Columbia in the U.S.A. are at present totally disfranchised and do not in any way participate in government at either the federal or State or even the municipal level. As we have stated elsewhere, the people of centrally-administered areas in India are more advantageously placed than those of the centrally-administered territories in other important federal countries in that they have full representation in the Union Parliament. There is, therefore, no question of disfranchising the people of Delhi or any other Centrally-administered area. Having taken all these factors into account, we are definitely of the view that municipal autonomy in the form of a corporation, which will provide greater local autonomy than is the case in some of the important federal capitals, is the right and in fact the only solution of the problem of Delhi State.

594. We do not feel called upon to go into the question whether, in the event of our recommendation being accepted, the municipal set-up of Delhi should follow a two-tier model on the lines of the London County Council or whether there should be one or two corporations of the pattern already under the consideration of the Government of India. These are matters for the consideration of the Government.

CHAPTER XIII

UTTAR PRADESH

595. We shall now consider the future of the Uttar Pradesh. The proposals made in the preceding Chapters leave the western and southern boundaries of the Uttar Pradesh unaffected. No major proposals regarding the eastern boundary have been made to us, except for certain claims on behalf of a Vishal Vindhya Pradesh, which we have already disposed of in Chapter IX of this part. The recommendations which we have made so far, therefore, do not affect the territorial limits of the existing State of Uttar Pradesh. But an important question which still remains to be decided is whether Uttar Pradesh itself should be divided.

596. The case for division was presented to this Commission by an *ad hoc* body described as the Western U.P. M.L.As.' Central Committee for the Reorganisation of the Uttar Pradesh. A memorandum urging the division was originally signed by ninety-seven members of the local legislative assembly representing sixteen western districts. But about seventy members subsequently dissociated themselves from this memorandum. The State Government moreover has strongly expressed the view that a division of the State will be both unwarranted and undesirable.

597. The arguments in favour of dividing the State are mainly three or four. It is claimed that physically and geographically, the hill and plateau regions of the Uttar Pradesh have little in common with the Gangetic valley. The present size of the State is also unwieldy. The inevitable result is that the administration is, generally speaking, not too efficient. It has also been urged by those representatives of the western districts, who continue to press their claim, that their areas have been neglected, and that the financial surplus which accrues to the State from its western half is now mostly being spent on the development of the eastern areas. Finally, they have expressed sympathy with a point of view which has sometimes been presented to this Commission, namely, that the States of the Union should be roughly equal in size and importance, so that no one unit is in a position to exercise a dominant influence in all-India affairs.

598. We have carefully considered these arguments, and we have also reviewed at length the information which has been placed before

us bearing on this subject. Our conclusion is that on the whole the size of the State has not affected the standard of administration; and that the allegations of neglect of the west or, indeed, for that matter of any other portion of the State cannot be sustained.

599. The existing State of Madhya Pradesh has, and the proposed States of Bombay, Madhya Pradesh and Rajasthan will have after reorganisation, a much bigger area than that of Uttar Pradesh. Undivided Bengal before the partition of the country, and the composite State of Madras before the separation of Andhra, had each a population which was not far short of that of the Uttar Pradesh at the present time. The circumstances under which Bengal and Madras, which were nearly as large in size and population as the Uttar Pradesh, were broken up are well-known. No similar circumstances exist in the Uttar Pradesh and, knowing the repercussions of the partition of Bengal we have to adopt a cautious approach and to refrain from doing anything which may lead to unnecessary agitation or create problems which do not exist at present. We are satisfied that in the State itself there is no demand on any large scale for its being broken up. On the other hand, we think that the vast majority of the people are likely to view with very great disfavour and concern the partitioning of a State which has remained as a unit by itself for a very long period.

600. It cannot well be claimed that mere size as such is undesirable and there is in fact no clear or necessary connection between the size of a State and the quality of its administration. This conclusion is also borne out by the facts. The law and order situation in Uttar Pradesh, particularly in Bundelkhand, is generally supposed to be very unsatisfactory, but official statistics of crime in the various States, recently published for the first time, do not by any means indicate that Uttar Pradesh has a particularly bad record in this respect. Literacy in this State is, no doubt, low. But the *per capita* figures of expenditure on security and social services, which are usually produced in support of the argument that the administration of the State is not very efficient, are now somewhat out of date. The rate at which expenditure on the nation-building departments has been stepped up in recent years is impressive; since 1950-51, for example, expenditure on education has gone up by a little less than fifty per cent. With the relatively greater increase in the size of the State's revenue budget, the expenditure on the overheads of administration, considered as a proportion of the total expenditure of the State is already fairly low, and is likely to be reduced even further. Uttar Pradesh has been a pioneer in certain

respects, for example, in the abolition of zamindari. On the whole, therefore, there is little, if any, justification for the partition of the State on the ground of mere administrative necessity.

601. Statistics over a period of ten years furnished by the Uttar Pradesh Government indicate that the distribution of expenditure has been more or less in the ratio of the population of the sixteen western districts and this disposes of the allegation that the Meerut, Agra and Rohilkhand divisions have been neglected. We only wish to add that a case such as that which some of the members of the State legislature from the western districts have sought to make out, of intentional and deliberate neglect justifying the partition of the State, can hardly be made to rest on stray instances like the reduction in the number of Commissionerships at one stage or delay in the formulation of certain costly and controversial projects.

602. The political objection to the continuance of Uttar Pradesh is in a way extraneous, because it is in no way related to the internal administration of the State. Nevertheless, it is of considerable importance because it reflects a sentiment which is fairly widely shared in some non-Hindi-speaking areas. The contention is that a fair balance between its constituent units is an essential condition for the working of a federal union; it has further been argued that the present commanding position of the Uttar Pradesh, with its representation in both the Houses of Parliament broadly reflecting its numerical strength, violates this important principle.

603. We readily concede that in the interests of national unity, it is of the utmost importance that no unit should nurse a sense of grievance that its point of view is not adequately represented in Parliament or properly reflected in the Central Government's policies or programmes. The feeling, therefore, that the Uttar Pradesh today exercises a powerful influence in all-India affairs, whether justifiable or not, should not be lightly brushed aside. If, however, we examine the question in the light of the current political trends in certain important federal unions, it will be seen that the influence of any particular State in national affairs under a federal system of government, is not determined by its size. We feel, therefore, that the case for the division of the Uttar Pradesh on the ground of its position in all-India affairs is somewhat overstated.

604. In all the federal constitutions the representatives of the Lower House are elected on a population basis, but in most of them there is equality of representation in the Upper House. It must, however, be remembered that in India, the Union is not a federation of sovereign states and the Rajya Sabha does not enjoy the same powers as the Lok Sabha. This is an important distinction between the Indian Union and some other democratic federations where the federating units existed before the formation of the federal unions as sovereign independent units and could, therefore, insist on coming into these federations on their own terms. In our Union, representation on the existing basis in the Upper House is due to the considered decision of the Constituent Assembly in which all the States were represented. If there is any merit in the contention that there should be equality of representation in the Upper House, the mere breaking up of the Uttar Pradesh will not solve the problem. The disparity in the size and population of the various states will continue. If, therefore, there is any remedy at all, it lies in the amendment of the Constitution. Besides in view of the limited powers enjoyed by the Rajya Sabha, equality of representation will not do any good to the smaller states.

605. After a great deal of thought we have come to the conclusion that it is not possible to form only such states as are equal to one another in size and population. In fact, there is no country in the world where one can find mathematical uniformity in regard to size and population among the component states; and some disparity is unavoidable in this country also. Some states will be large and some comparatively smaller. The mere size of the Uttar Pradesh, therefore, should not necessarily drive us to the extreme measure of breaking it up.

606. Considering the restricted powers that this House exercises as compared to the powers enjoyed by the Lok Sabha, unequal representation of the States in the Rajya Sabha, it may be stated again, has no particular significance. In other countries also, where the Upper Houses enjoy relatively wide powers, political forces have so operated that the old concept of states as such being represented in the Upper House has undergone a radical change. Finer, on a close study of the working of the principle of equal representation of States in the United States of America, has come to the conclusion that "if America, as it is today, were to give itself a new Constitution, it is very doubtful whether it would adopt equality in the Senate"[1]. According to him, the Senate of the United States

[1] Herman Finer: The Theory and Practice of Modern Government, Vol.1, London 1932, p. 304.

has been converted into "a forum where the States may be very much talked of, but where the preservation of the identity of the States has become forgotten or a fictitious thing,........................"[1]. The factors which explain this development include the following:

(a) "in the actual evolution of the Federation the small states have never been allied against the large states or *vice versa*";

(b) "owing to the growth of party the country has been divided, not into states, but into opposed political organisations which have reconciled the states within their fold to each other and to the Union"; and

(c) "owing to the industrial and commercial evolution of the nation the rival interests have been and are, Sections rather than states,....................."[2].

607. In Australia also party divisions, in Professor Wheare's words, "have usually proved stronger among Senators than state divisions. Votes in the Senate are cast more on strict party lines than upon a regional basis"[3]. In fact, the control of the Senate by Labour for many years has had the result of converting the Upper House in Australia into an instrument for weakening the power of the States and for promoting party programmes as against States' rights.

608. The constitutional and political structure of the U.S.S.R. exhibits certain special features. The conditions in that country are, therefore, not comparable to those of this country.

608. The main objection seems to be that the Uttar Pradesh being a very large state, all its representatives are apt to combine in pressing their point of view in Parliament. There is no guarantee, however, that even if the Uttar Pradesh is split up the representives of the newly-created units, who have been associated together for a long time, will not vote on the same side. We should not also forget that, sometimes, the complaint is that most of the representatives of the Hindi-speaking areas vote on the same side.

610. It will be unrealistic to think that any State *qua* State is, or will be, able to influence the Centre to any considerable extent under a system of Cabinet government under which party loyalties must override state loyalties. We are, therefore, not disposed to attach

---

[1] Herman Finer: The Theory and Practice of Modern Government, Vol. I London, 1932, p. 300

[2] *Ibid.*, p. 299.

[3] K. C. Whoare : Federal Government, London, 1953, p. 94.

much importance to the view that either the present size of the Uttar Pradesh or its representation in the Upper House, by itself, secures for this State any dominating influence in the Union Parliament or executive.

611. Whatever the historical origin of the Uttar Pradesh and the justification for the formation of this State might have been, the State has now been administered as a single unit for a long period. There is considerable force in the State Government's contention that the economy of the whole region has, in consequence, become integrated. Thus, the two main irrigation or power projects in the State, namely, the Ganga and Sarda Canal systems cover both the eastern and the western parts of Uttar Pradesh. The Yamuna hydel project is to be located in Dehra Dun, and the Ramganga Canal is intended mainly for the west; but even in these cases, a considerable area in central and eastern Uttar Pradesh, as far eastwards as Fatehpur, will be served by the projects which are now under consideration. It will not be desirable, therefore, in the absence of any strong or compelling reason, to create a situation in which the headworks of all the three or four major projects will be left in the west, though some of these have also to serve the benefit areas in the eastern districts.

612. The existing State has been able to avoid a great deal of expenditure which might otherwise have been necessary, if two or more States had been created. We see no reason for imposing this unnecessary expenditure on this area. Besides, we must bear in mind the facts that the State has now committed all its resources to its economic development, and that the scope which may exist for increasing the revenue in the immediate future seems to be limited. The State has, for example, entered into a contractual obligation with the bhumidars not to revise land revenue settlements for a period of forty years. Partition of the State in these circumstances is bound to lead to the dislocation of the administration, besides creating financial difficulties for one or more of the new units.

613. In view of what we have said above it is not possible for us to recommend that the dislocation and disturbance which will inevitably be caused by the division of the Uttar Pradesh must be faced as incidental to a major reform which is independently justified. The existing unit should, therefore, continue.

614. Our colleague Shri K. M. Panikkar does not subscribe to the recommendation contained in this Chapter regarding the future of the Uttar Pradesh. His views on this subject are contained in a separate note which is appended.

CHAPTER XIV

BIHAR

615. The proposals regarding Uttar Pradesh leave the western boundary of Bihar unchanged, but claims and counter-claims in the north, east and the south are numerous, and the case for or against the changes proposed has been argued in considerable detail. We propose to deal only with the more important and controversial issues, namely,

(i) the formation of a Jharkhand State in south Bihar;

(ii) the Orissa claim for the restoration to it of the Seraikella sub-division of the Singhbhum district;

(iii) the border adjustments proposed by West Bengal; and

(iv) the Bihar claims to Darjeeling, Jalpaiguri, Malda and West Dinajpur in the north and to Sundargarh, Keonjhar and Mayurbhanj in the south.

616. The proposal to split up Bihar into two units, so that the Chota Nagpur division and the Santhal Parganas may be formed, independently or together with other areas, into a new Jharkhand State, has an interesting background. Before the present Constitution was brought into force, the Sub-Committee of the Constituent Assembly on the excluded and partially-excluded areas (other than Assam), which went into the question of drawing up a scheme for the administration of tribal and backward areas, considered very briefly the suggestion that a new province should be created in South Bihar. The Sub-Committee expressed itself against this proposal, although it did not deal with the question in detail, as the formation of new States was outside its scope.

617. Since then, there have been only two major developments of interest. One is that the Jharkhand Party fought the last general elections on this issue and claims to have secured a substantial verdict in favour of the proposal to form a new State. The other recent development is that thirty-three members of the local legislature from the Chota Nagpur division and the Santhal Parganas district have presented the case for the division of Bihar to this Commission, this representation being supported by other parties and organisations. The members of the Bihar Legislative Assembly from the Chota Nagpur division and the Santhal Parganas, who have supported the

case for the formation of the new State, do not, however, represent the majority view, and it is also of some interest to note that the Jharkhand Party did not obtain a clear majority within the Chota Nagpur division and the Santhal Parganas during the last general elections. This is, in our opinion, significant. We need hardly add that public opinion outside South Bihar is not in favour of dividing the State. Even in South Bihar parties other than the Jharkhand party were in general opposed to a division.

618. We cannot overlook this volume of opposition. If the Chota Nagpur division and the Santhal Parganas are taken together, the tribal population is only a little more than one-third of the total population and is divided into several language groups. Even if it is assumed that Adivasis are solidly in favour of the formation of a Jharkhand State, a major issue of this kind cannot, in our opinion, be decided on the basis of the views of a minority. There seems to be no warrant, however, for the assumption that even Adivasi opinion can be considered to be unanimous on this point.

619. The separation of South Bihar will affect the entire economy of the existing State. The plains are predominantly agricultural and the Chota Nagpur plateau provides an industrial balance. The sugar factories of the State are situated outside the Chota Nagpur division, but the coal-bearing areas and the major industrial zones are in South Bihar. Bihar's biggest thermal power station is also located at Bokaro in the Jharkhand area. The residual area can hardly afford to lose the benefits derived from this station.

620. The separation of Chota Nagpur will upset the balance between agriculture and industry in the residual State which will be a poorer area with fewer opportunities and resources for development. At the same time, the centres of higher education, like the Patna and Bihar Universities, will be outside the Jharkhand area. Obviously, it would be very inconvenient for the north as well as for the south if the State were to be broken up.

621. It has sometimes been suggested that Chota Nagpur is bound to benefit from the separation, because it has been neglected so far by the Bihar Government. We have gone into this complaint carefully. While it is true that irrigation works in Chota Nagpur are not many or important, there is little evidence, on the whole, of lopsided economic development. It was, in our opinion, natural and inevitable, having regard to the resources of the two areas, that irrigation should have been important in the north and industrialisation in the south. A comprehensive plan for irrigation in the south has recently been prepared and a broad-based development plan is now

under consideration. A Tribes Advisory Council has also been constituted.

622. The ultimate objective, in relation to the inhabitants of what are at present "scheduled areas" under the Constitution, is that normal administration should be introduced as early as possible and that distinctions between Adivasi and other citizens, in so far as they impede the economic and political advancement of the tribal areas, should be progressively removed. From the point of view of the long-term interests of the Adivasis themselves, the present arrangements, as set out in the Fifth Schedule to the Constitution, read with Scheduled Areas (Part A States) Order, seem to be fair and satisfactory.

623. The Sub-Committee of the Constituent Assembly on the excluded and partially-excluded areas (other than Assam), to which reference has already been made, was of the view that tribal people should be associated adequately with all branches of administration "including the Cabinet" and that "this tract must be dealt with not only by economic and educational improvements but also by remedies which recognise its political and psychological aspects". Their observations have the same force today as they had about seven years ago and we commend them for special attention. We also recommend that question of a special development board for the Chota Nagpur division and the Santhal Parganas district of Bihar along the lines suggested in Chapter III of Part IV be considered.

624. The controversies over Seraikella and Kharsawan are comparatively more recent. The Orissa claim to these areas rests mainly on the ground that Oriya is the largest single language group. The two states, however, have formed part of the Singhbhum district since May, 1948, and the historical affinities of the two states with the Porahat raj in Singhbhum district, on the one hand, and with the administration which was in charge of the Chota Nagpur division, on the other, are held to justify the decision to include them in Bihar.

625. The major question which we have had to consider in the course of our examination of this problem is whether the position of Oriya in the Seraikella sub-division is, by itself, an adequate ground for disturbing the existing arrangements. As has been pointed out elsewhere in this report, language, by itself, does not, in our opinion, provide sufficient justification for breaking up a district. In this case, moreover, the Oriya percentage in rural portions is only about 26; and those speaking this language do not

seem to be concentrated, anywhere within the sub-division, to such an extent that linguistic affinities can be regarded as clear and unmistakable. Above all, in view of the recommendations which we make in the next Chapter for the transfer of part of the Manbhum district to West Bengal, the transfer of the Seraikella sub-division, or any portion thereof, to the State of Orissa will convert the Dhalbhum sub-division in the east into an enclave which will not be physically contiguous to the rest of Bihar.

626. This can be avoided only if the whole of Singhbhum is transferred to Orissa. Such a transfer, however, will not be justified on administrative and other grounds. It may be recalled that in 1932 the O'Donnell Committee considered the question of the transfer of this entire district as it then was to the proposed Oriya-speaking State, but declined to recommend its inclusion in Orissa, on the ground, amongst others, that its geographical position and lines of communication favoured its retention in Chota Nagpur. We see no reason why the decision reached on the basis of this recommendation should now be reconsidered.

627. We deal with the claims of West Bengal on Bihar in the Chapter which follows.

628. The Bihar Government's claims to Darjeeling and some other districts of West Bengal and to three districts of Orissa which are contiguous to Bihar, to which reference has been made in the opening paragraphs of this Chapter, are not justified on the ground of linguistic or cultural affinity, administrative necessity, or any other special reason. It is not, therefore, necessary for us to examine them in any detail.

629. The results of our examination of the border disputes in the north, east and south of Bihar can now be summarised. Subject to the recommendations which are made in the Chapter which follows immediately, the boundaries of the existing State of Bihar will remain unchanged.

630. After taking the recommendations in the next Chapter into account, the State of Bihar will have an area of about 66,520 square miles and a population of a little less than 39 millions. The administrative structure and economy of the existing State are unlikely to be affected materially by our proposals.

CHAPTER XV

WEST BENGAL

631. The material which has been submitted to this Commission from West Bengal is voluminous, and the claims or counter-claims of the other governments concerned, namely, Bihar, Assam and Orissa, have also been supported in considerable detail. Although these states are predominantly unilingual, the reorganisation of the border areas has not become any the less difficult or controversial. Indeed, as the incidents in Goalpara and the emotional upheaval that followed the appointment of this Commission in some of the disputed areas have indicated, the readjustment of West Bengal's borders has now become a major problem. We do not foresee that, with the passage of time, this problem will disappear. It must, therefore, be dealt with as part of the general settlement of the problem of reorganisation.

632. Obviously, without a clear appreciation of the conflicting points of view no lasting or satisfactory solution can be proposed. It is necessary, therefore, to indicate briefly the background to these disputes.

633. Partition has created many problems for West Bengal. Apart from the influx of refugees from Pakistan, which may now be estimated at about three and a half millions, the entire communications system of Bengal has been disrupted since 1947. The northern districts of the Presidency division have become less easily accessible from Calcutta; and West Bengal is now the only Part A State which is geographically not a compact and integrated unit.

634. To some extent, West Bengal's difficulties are also shared by Bihar and Assam. Communication links between the north and the south in this part of the country have not been as satisfactory as may be desired. The reasons for this deficiency are various. There is in the first place the problem of bridging the Ganga. The major rail bridge across this river was at Paksi in East Pakistan; and since this has been lost to India, a crossing at Mokameh Ghat is now being provided. The Mokameh Ghat bridge when it is completed will, however, relieve the congestion in traffic only partially. The break of gauge north of the Ganga, the inadequacies of the Assam rail link, and the comparative inaccessibility of the eastern areas of the Malda

and West Dinajpur districts of West Bengal will still remain problems which will have to be solved independently of the Mokameh project.

635. Various proposals have been put forward in order to improve communications between Calcutta and the north-eastern portion of India which is now somewhat isolated. One proposal is that a road-*cum*-rail bridge and a barrage across the Ganga at Farraka in West Bengal should be built. It has also been suggested that a new railway line from Dhubri in Assam *via* Alipur Duar to Siliguri should be laid and that line capacity should be doubled from that point onwards. Rail links are also proposed to be provided *via* the contemplated Farraka crossing, connecting the southern districts with Darjeeling, Jalpaiguri and Cooch-Behar through the Barsoi-Siliguri railway line; and links with suitable points in the east in the middle portion of the West Bengal State have also been proposed.

636. In order to supplement the transport capacity which will be provided by these new railway lines, two road links which will be part of the national highway system are also being constructed within or just on the borders of the West Bengal State. The West Bengal case is that all these projects should be given priority; and that such territorial readjustments should be made as will give to the State control over the areas through which the main lines of communication are to pass.

637. Geographical contiguity, in order to ensure the more orderly development of its communication links, is thus the main argument on which the West Bengal claims in the north, that is to say, in the Purnea and Santhal Parganas districts, are based. As regards the area which is to the south, the basis of the claim is that river control and irrigation development are now being projected on a very large scale in the Burdwan division of West Bengal. This development, it is claimed, will be helped by the transfer to West Bengal of a portion of the Santhal Parganas and the whole of Manbhum. The rivers which have been particularly mentioned in connection with these territorial claims are the Ajay and the Kasai, dams on which are proposed to be built in or on the borders of Bihar. The West Bengal Government has asked for the catchment areas of these two rivers, in order to ensure that its programme of river control and development is not jeopardised.

638. We have dealt so far with what apparently are the most important points in West Bengal's case. But it will be wrong to assume that the claims are based only on administrative grounds.

West Bengal, so far as we have been able to judge, feels that it has been treated unjustly. This feeling is based partly on the fact that from 1905 onwards the State has steadily lost territory; the result of the latest change has been to create a disconnected unit, and West Bengal thinks that its difficulties have not been appreciated.

639. The "areal extent" of Bengal, it has been stated, was always larger than it is at the present time. It is not surprising, therefore, that arguments drawn from history have also been considered to be relevant. The West Bengal Government and the Pradesh Congress Committee have relied to some extent on the fact that considerable portions of the areas now claimed were previously under the Government of Bengal. Reliance has also been placed on the definition of the limits of the Madarun Sarkar of the Moghul empire; on a resolution passed by the Congress in 1911; and on a statement reported to have been issued by some prominent leaders of Bihar in 1912, conceding West Bengal's claims to the territory east of the Mahananda, the whole of Manbhum and the Dhalbhum portion of the Singhbhum district.

640. The last-mentioned statement has been challenged and counter-arguments drawn from history have been produced in order to rebut West Bengal's claim. The Government of Bihar has also pointed out that no great importance need be attached to geographical contiguity, in view of the fact that the Constitution of India contains adequate provision to facilitate inter-state co-operation, even if such co-operation cannot be assumed in the normal course. The other grounds on which the claims have been made are, it is argued, not substantial.

641. A more or less extensive bilingual belt, it is stated, is unavoidable. Attempts to establish the precise linguistic and cultural affiliations of such areas can never be quite successful and may also be unnecessary since a completely unilingual area cannot always be created. Hindi is either the predominant language or at least a very important language in this bilingual border belt; and since Hindi is not only the regional official language in the disputed areas, but also the national language, proficiency in which is necessary and desirable, the grievance that Hindi is being "imposed" cannot be regarded as legitimate. The Bihar Government has also stated that the natural predominance of Hindi in these areas has been obscured in the past by attempts to impose Bengali; and it has been pointed out that a number of typically Bihari castes are to be found in the territory claimed.

642. Many of the arguments advanced against the proposal to create a Jharkhand State are also regarded as relevant to the proposal to transfer the rich mineral-bearing and industrialised areas of Rajmahal, Manbhum and Dhalbhum to West Bengal. This transfer, it is argued, is bound to dislocate the economy of residuary Bihar, and it will upset the balance between agriculture and industry.

643. Finally, it has been contended by Bihar that there is no popular demand in this disputed fringe for a rectification of the boundary.

644. The linguistic complexion of the disputed areas is unfortunately not quite clear. The mother-tongue data of the 1951 Census have been challenged by both Bengal and Bihar; and only a broad judgment as to the relative numerical strength of various linguistic groups in the districts of Purnea, Santhal Parganas, Manbhum and Goalpara seems possible. Neither West Bengal nor Bihar has, in these circumstances, confined itself to arguing from past figures. Both the governments have relied on a number of subsidiary factors in order to prove the cultural affinity of the disputed areas.

645. The arguments advanced by the Bihar Government in favour of the maintenance of the *status quo* are not without force. It has also to be recognised that bilingualism in the area under consideration has to be accepted as an inevitable fact and that no great importance can, therefore, be attached to mere linguistic affinity.

646. We feel, however, that quite apart from the special background of the West Bengal claim and its psychological aspect, there is no denying the fact that the present distribution of territories between Bihar and West Bengal is such as to give rise to some real administrative difficulties from the point of view of West Bengal. It may be possible, as the Bihar Government has contended, to mitigate these difficulties within the existing constitutional and administrative framework. However, now that an opportunity for a general settlement has presented itself, it will be desirable in our opinion to find more lasting solutions.

647. We shall first examine the claims made on the Purnea district. The mother-tongue data of the census returns for this district, as has been mentioned already, have been challenged by West Bengal. The main controversy in this district, however, relates to the classification of the dialect or dialects spoken to the east of the river Mahananda. Grierson. and following him O Malley, classified them as North Bengali, but the Bihar Government, relying among other evidence on the views of Gait, the Census Superintendent in 1901, has challenged this classification.

648. We do not feel called upon to review or to decide this question. The affinities between Kishanganjia or Sirpuria as spoken in the extreme east of Purnea district, on the one hand, and Bengali on the other, seem to be close. But this dialect is written in the Kaithi script, which is allied to Hindi, and as one proceeds westwards its affinities with Maithili and Hindi become more marked. Arguments based on linguistic affiliations, whether advanced by Bihar or by Bengal, are thus far from being conclusive.

649. The main argument in support of the West Bengal claim on this area is the desirability of making the State a geographically contiguous unit. The Bihar Government has represented that it is not necessary to transfer to West Bengal the area through which the national highway connecting the northern districts to the rest of West Bengal passes. The highway, it is stated, is now and will remain the responsibility of the Central Government, and whichever State functions as the agent of the Centre, the general principles which have already been laid down regarding the maintenance or the use of national highways will go a long way towards ensuring the interests of all those who may be using them. The Government of Bihar has also dealt at some length with the allegations of lack of co-operation in facilitating transport and communications between the southern and northern portions of West Bengal.

650. We feel that this is a matter which should be examined on its merits rather than on the basis of complaints or counter-complaints against one state or the other. We attach great importance to the geographical compactness of administrative units, because we are of the view that the physical integration of such units is vital to their real political and administrative integration. Apart from the inconvenience in administering geographically detached areas we must take note of the fact that the continued isolation of the northern districts from the rest of West Bengal will tend to foster and accentuate separatist trends in these districts. West Bengal, therefore, has a good case for a geographical integration of the northern areas.

651. Besides, even if the Bihar Government extend full co-operation in facilitating traffic between the north and the south of West Bengal, certain difficulties are inherent in the existing arrangements. These difficulties will be eliminated if portions of the Kishanganj sub-division and the Gopalpur revenue thana are transferred to West Bengal. This will enable West Bengal to construct feeder roads connecting the national highway to its other territories and to control road traffic with Darjeeling and other places in the north, by eliminating avoidable delays and cumbersome and inconvenient administrative arrangements, and by liberalising, if necessary, the

present practice relating to road transport. West Bengal will also acquire control of the Indo-Pakistan border in this region along its entire length. From an administrative point of view this will be both convenient and desirable.

652. We have carefully examined the suggestion that the entire area to the east of the river Mahananda in the Purnea district should be transferred from Bihar to West Bengal in order to provide for geographical contiguity between the two disconnected parts of West Bengal. We do not consider it necessary, however, to recommened the transfer of any area which may not be absolutely essential in order to achieve the object in view. Taking all the relevant factors into consideration we propose that

(i) the portion of the Kishanganj sub-division which is to the east of the river Mahananda; and

(ii) a portion of the Gopalpur revenue thana contiguous to the territory mentioned in (i) and extending down to national highway in this thana,

should be transferred to West Bengal. The actual delimitation of the new boundary will have to be settled after a detailed survey. The details of this transfer will have to be left, therefore, to the Government of India, acting in consultation with the State Governments concerned. But it should be ensured that control of the national highway in the Gopalpur revenue thana is vested in the Government of West Bengal.

653. While making this recommendation we have to take note of the fact that the eastern portion of the Kishanganj sub-division is predominantly inhabited by Muslims who would view with concern the transfer of this area to West Bengal on the ground that their linguistic and cultural rights might suffer and that the possible resettlement of displaced persons from East Bengal might dislocate their life. These fears are not without justification. It would, therefore, be necessary for the West Bengal Government to take effective steps such as the recognition of the special position of Urdu in this area for educational and official purposes. The density of population in this area is such that there is little scope for any resettlement of displaced persons. The West Bengal Government would, therefore, do well to make a clear announcement to the effect that no such resettlement would be undertaken. This would go a long way in our opinion in dispelling doubts and fears.

654. In the Santhal Parganas, the Santhals are, according to the 1951 Census, numerically the second most important linguistic group.

The West Bengal claims in this district seem to be based on a number of subsidiary arguments, such as that Santhals have affinities with West Bengal, and that the revenue history of this district indicates its administrative links with Birbhum and Murshidabad. These claims, however, are not convincing.

655. Bengali influence in the entire Santhal Parganas district is very slight. The percentage of the Bengali-speaking people is meagre in all the sub-divisions, excepting Rajmahal and Pakur, where they constitute about 16 and 13 per cent. of the population respectively. Rajmahal was for brief periods the capital of ancient Bengal. Even so, the Hindi-speaking population in Rajmahal, as the Bihar Government has pointed out, far outnumbers at the present time that speaking Bengali. That this is not an accidental or manipulated result is clear from the records of earlier censuses.

656. The areas claimed by West Bengal are an integral part of Santhal Parganas as it was constituted in 1855. It will be inconvenient to Bihar if this eastern fringe of this district were now detached from it. Apart from the administrative complications which may be created, Bihar will lose the Rajmahal coalfields to West Bengal if the area claimed were transferred. Santhali opinion has not declared itself in favour of the West Bengal claim.

657. We have considered very carefully the question whether a portion of the Santhal Parganas alongside the Ganga, which is reported to be partially unsurveyed in this neighbourhood, can be transferred to West Bengal, in order to enable that State to control entirely one or more points at which this river can be crossed. We have also examined in some detail the case for the transfer of the catchment areas or a portion of territory along the course of the river Ajay. As has been stated elsewhere in this report, a claim which is based on the desirability of access to the proposed site of a river valley project will be admissible only if other factors are more or less evenly balanced. This is not the case so far as this district is concerned. We have, therefore, come to the conclusion that the transfer of any portion of the Santhal Parganas district to West Bengal will be difficult to justify.

658. In Manbhum, which is further to the south, the position is different. Manbhum is really composed of two different areas which are divided by the Damodar. These areas are now treated as two sub-districts, but with a population of 732,000 and 1,548,000 respectively, they are for practical purposes separate districts and are administered as such. Dhanbad which is the industrialised area, in

which incidentally Hindi is predominant, differs from Purulia which is comparatively less industrialised, and has a much greater concentration of the Bengali-speaking people.

659. There is no case for the transfer of Dhanbad to West Bengal. The Hindi speaking majority in this sub-district is 65 per cent. Coal-fields along the course of the Damodar river and the D.V.C. industrial belt are situated mostly in this sub-district, and there are indications that Dhanbad, like Jamshedpur further south, may soon attract a mixed population from all over India as it is further developed. The West Bengal claim to this area is, therefore, untenable.

660. In Purulia on the other hand, there is unmistakable evidence of Bengali influence even today. This sub-district has the largest concentration of Bengali-speaking people outside West Bengal.

661. The transfer of Purulia can be justified on the ground that it will facilitate the implementation of a flood control-*cum*-irrigation project which has recently been taken up in West Bengal. The Kangsabati (Kasai) river, which rises in Purulia, is of no real importance from the point of view of Bihar, but West Bengal has already utilised it to some extent in its lower reaches, and now proposes to build a dam on this river near the Bihar border.

662. If flood control and irrigation in the Burdwan division are to be efficiently carried out in future it will be desirable to transfer to West Bengal a major portion of the catchment area because this will facilitate soil conservation measures and also provide perhaps a more appropriate dam site.

663. The importance of the Kasai to West Bengal will be apparent from the fact that it is supposed to derive its name of "the butcher" from the annual devastation which its flood waters cause in and round Midnapore. This may not be a conclusive argument justifying the proposed transfer. But in this case, as in the case of Bellary, which has been dealt with in Chapter IV of this part, the other arguments are either unimportant or are more or less balanced; in these circumstances, it cannot be regarded as a minor question that the implementation of a project to which West Bengal attaches considerable importance will be helped by the transfer.

664. It has been claimed by West Bengal that the linguistic tabulation of the 1951 Census cannot be regarded as satisfactory and that if we disregard the Census of 1951 and take into account the two previous Censuses at which the linguistic distribution of the people was recorded, the Bengali-speaking percentage was of the order of two-thirds of the total population in the entire district; in Purulia, which as has already been stated has even today a considerable

population speaking the Bengali language, it was, perhaps, more impressive.

665. We do not feel called upon to enter into the controversies relating to the figures of the preceding Censuses. We must, however, take note of the fact that even according to the 1951 Census, the Bengali-speaking majority in the rural areas Purulia will be about 55 per cent. (as against 28 per cent. of the Hindi-speaking people) if the Chas revenue thana, which is contiguous to Dhanbad is excluded.

666. Considering the circumstances referred to above in which the West Bengal claim to Manbhum has been made, we propose that the Purulia sub-district excluding the Chas thana should be transferred to West Bengal. Such a transfer will not seriously upset either the economy or the administrative structure of Bihar, but will, on a balance of considerations, be justified. It may be pointed out incidentally that since the area proposed to be transferred is virtually a district, the initial inconvenience, if any, as a result of the transfer will be negligible.

667. We pass next to Dhalbhum. From a linguistic point of view, Singhbhum district is the meeting ground of Ho, Oriya, Bengali, Hindi and Santhali. These languages are important roughly in the order named. In the Dhalbhum sub-division considered separately, Bengali is the largest language group but it cannot by any means be considered to be predominant; and a *prima facie* case for a boundary adjustment in favour of West Bengal has not been made out either on the ground of linguistic affiliation or on any other grounds. The historical links of this district with West Bengal, as in the case of Goalpara, are tenuous. It is also impossible to overlook the fact that in an important portion of the area claimed, that is to say, in and round Jamshedpur, the population is so mixed that no State can legitimately claim the city on cultural or linguistic grounds. Indeed, the West Bengal Government has itself recognised this fact. There is no case in our opinion for transferring to West Bengal either the Jamshedpur city or any other area by breaking up Dhalbhum.

668. We next deal with the West Bengal claims on Assam. These claims do not seem to us to be sound. There is no evidence, according to the 1951 Census, that the Goalpara district is predominantly Bengali-speaking. Although the figures have been challenged, and reference has been made to the considerable Muslim population in Goalpara which is claimed to be Bengali-speaking, we do not have enough evidence on the basis of which the mother-tongue data of 1951 can be disregarded. It is true that the latest Census figures show, as compared to the figures of 1931, very striking variations which cannot be satisfactorily explained. But we find it difficult

to admit on that ground alone any claim by West Bengal to Goalpara or any part of it. Such historical connection as there has been between Goalpara and West Bengal has been intermittent and tenuous. The district has now been part of Assam for such a long time that there is no justification for disturbing this position.

669. Our findings regarding the border disputes between West Bengal and Bihar and West Bengal and Assam can now be summarised. We have conceded the claim of West Bengal to the whole of the Purulia sub-district of Manbhum district, with the exception of the Chas thana, and have also admitted its claim to some territory east of the Mahananda in the Purnea district. The existing Bengal-Bihar and Bengal-Assam boundaries will continue except to the extent indicated.

670. The area and population of West Bengal as a result of these recommendations will be about 34,590 sq. miles and about 26·5 millions respectively.

671. We have already referred, in the opening paragraphs of this Chapter, to the long history and complicated nature of the border disputes. The claims which have been made on Bihar by or on behalf of West Bengal have not only been numerous but have also been conflicting.

672. The New Bengal Association, which submitted a representation to the Constituent Assembly in 1948, was broadly in favour of the addition of a little more than 10,000 sq. miles from Bihar to West Bengal. But a memorandum prepared at about the same time by the late Shri N. R. Sarker for the Government of West Bengal claimed an area of almost 16,000 sq. miles.

673. In a resolution passed by the West Bengal Legislative Assembly in August, 1952, this demand was more or less reiterated. The official representation which has now been made to this Commission on behalf of the Government of West Bengal is confined to a smaller area of about 11,840 sq. miles involving a population of about 5·7 millions. The West Bengal Pradesh Congress Committee on the other hand claims at present an area of about 13,950 sq. miles involving a population of about 6·7 millions.

674. Our recommendations relate to two bits of territory which have been mentioned in every claim during the last seven years; and even in these two cases, they are confined to areas, the transfer of which can be regarded as absolutely essential. The proposals

which we have made will involve the transfer only of an area of about 3812 sq. miles and a population of about 1.7 millions. This is roughly about one-fourth and one-third of the area and population which have now been claimed in Bihar by the West Bengal Pradesh Congress Committee and the West Bengal Government respectively.

675. The redrawing of these boundaries has been one of the most difficult problems with which this Commission has been faced. We have tried to arrive at decisions which are in our opinion fair and equitable. We have been anxious to ensure, if possible, that the sterile and unfortunate controversies which have claimed a great deal of the time and energy of the leaders of Bengal and Bihar should be brought to an end as early as possible.

676. Our Chairman, Shri Fazl Ali, because of his long connection with Bihar, has not considered it desirable to concern himself with investigating and deciding the territorial disputes to which Bihar is a party.

CHAPTER XVI

ASSAM

677. We now proceed to consider the proposals for the reorganisation of States in north-eastern India with particular reference to the future of Assam. In the preceding Chapter we have examined the claims of the West Bengal Government to the Goalpara district of Assam. Before we deal with the other problems concerning this region, it may be desirable to describe briefly the background against which the various demands should, in our opinion, be considered.

678. The State of Assam is made up of the Brahmaputra (Assam) and Surma river valleys and the hilly areas to the north, south and east of these two river basins. The Brahmaputra valley, which is the most important and fertile tract in the State, contains six out of the seven plains districts. Communications between this area and the rest of the State, or for that matter with the rest of India, are still relatively undeveloped. Indeed, a former Governor of the State during the British period described the Brahmaputra valley as a broad central corridor or hall, from which small rooms corresponding to the hill districts open out on both sides, with, however, no connecting doors between them. This description remains substantially true to this day. The hill districts have to-day even more intimate administrative and economic links with the plains, in which incidentally about seven lakhs of tribal people are to be found.

679. From a historical point of view, Assam and north-east India seem to have been intended by nature to be the meeting place of many tribes and races. Right through its history, there has been immigration into and settlement in the state from various sources, with the result that till comparatively very recent times, that is to say, up to 1931, when linguistic tabulation was last undertaken, Assamese was not in fact a language spoken by a majority of the inhabitants of the State.

680. Assam also owes a great deal to capital and enterprise from outside the State; and its tea, coal and oil industries have been built up mainly as the result of such enterprise. The Tea Districts Emigrant Labour Act, which is intended to regulate the recruitment of labour in the other States of India for the tea gardens in Assam, is a notable but not an isolated illustration of this statement.

The contribution which permanent or temporary immigrants into the State can make to the development of its economy is important even at the present time.

681. The major proposals regarding the eastern and southern boundaries of Assam will need to be considered in this perspective. These proposals as presented to the Commission can broadly be summarised as follows. The Assam Pradesh Congress Committee, the local Communist party, the Tripura State Congress Committee, and the Government of Assam are broadly in favour of the *status quo*. Assam, however, would welcome the merger, if possible, of Cooch-Behar, Manipur and Tripura, and closer connection with the administration of the North-East Frontier Agency, which is now constitutionally part of Assam. The hill districts have pressed the case for the formation of a hill state. This demand, reiterated at the Tura (Garo Hills) Conference of tribal leaders in October, 1954, contemplates the unification of all the hill districts mentioned in Part A of the table appended to the Sixth Schedule to the Constitution, including also the Naga Hills district. The Naga National Council seeks independence from Assam and India and to remain aloof from the proposed hill state. As a compromise between these extreme positions, but for entirely different reasons, the formation of a Kamatapur State consisting of Goalpara, Garo Hills, Cooch Behar, Darjeeling and Jalpaiguri, or of a Purbachal State consisting of the area round Cachar has also been suggested.

The Hill State

682. We first deal with the demand for the creation of a hill state. This demand, it may be noted, is of comparatively recent origin. When the Sub-Committee of the Constituent Assembly on the North-East Frontier (Assam) Tribal and Excluded Areas, popularly known as the Bardoloi Committee, reported in July, 1947, the Naga demand for independence, as the Committee noted, was not supported by moderate elements. The other proposals made to the Committee ranged from a quasi-independent status to cultural autonomy for the individual districts. The scheme for a hill state had already been put forward and discussed in certain quarters, but had not yet taken any concrete shape. The Sub-Committee's report whose proposals are substantially incorporated into the Constitution rejected these various alternatives either directly or by implication. This report, it may be of interest to note, was supported by the tribal representative.

683. In the period of about eight years that has passed since the Bardoloi Committee reported, there has been an attempt on the part of certain elements in the hill districts to reopen this entire problem. The proposals which have been made for replacing the existing arrangements have, however, been various and conflicting.

684. It is of paramount importance to establish a stable administration in the north-east based on the goodwill of the tribal people, and it is clear that such an administration will have to be primarily concerned with the well-being of the tribes. We have, therefore, examined the proposal for a hill state with great care and sympathy and with particular regard to these objectives.

685. The problem in the hill areas at this stage is at least as much psychological as political. There is no denying the fact that the demand for a hill state partly reflects the separatist pull of the extremist elements. Other factors, however, appear to have lent support to the demand and these are:

(i) suspicion and distrust of the people of the plains by the tribal people of this area;

(ii) the diversity of races and cultures and the different levels of social, educational and political development in the different areas of this region which have prevented the tribal people from coming up to the level of the people in the plains;

(iii) lack of communications in these areas which has made it difficult for the various tribes to come in close contact with the rest of India; and

(iv) the economic backwardness of the region.

It has also been alleged that the Government of Assam has not been as sympathetic and helpful to the tribal people as it should have been.

686. The problem is, in a substantial measure, an inheritance from the pre-independence days. The extremist demands of the present time reflect what has sometimes been labelled the "national park" approach. This was fundamentally the British policy and there were attempts to demarcate the tribal zones and to isolate them, as far as possible, from external influences, preventing, in particular, immigration from elsewhere into the scheduled areas. This went to the extent of stopping Indian officers from entering these areas. The "inner line" regulation in the pre-independence period, although it was ostensibly intended to discourage unnecessary interference with

and the economic exploitation of the tribal people was administered rigorously so as to exclude all contact between them and the inhabitants of the plains districts.

687. The demand for a separate tribal State is partly a hang-over of this policy. With the departure of the British, however, conditions have changed radically in the sense that there is now a growing awareness amongst the tribal people of their political rights as full and equal citizens of the Indian Union, which they did not have, and, indeed, under the conditions which prevailed, could not well have had before Independence.

688. It is clear that, in these changed conditions, it is neither necessary nor desirable to confer on the tribes any immunity from external contacts to such an extent as to hamper their development. Legislation in order to prevent the rapid transfer and alienation of land and efforts to discourage money-lenders and to ease the transition from one level of economic development to another are, of course, necessary. But this policy cannot obviously be so administered as to freeze existing economic and cultural patterns and to inhibit healthy growth.

689. The results of the "inner line" regulation policy, as administered by the British, illustrate the dangers of deliberate and complete segregation. That policy, however, in point of fact, was not enforced so much against Europeans and Christians as against the other Indian communities. The broad effect of throwing the tribal areas open to some but not to all external influences during the period of the British occupation has been to divide the tribal people themselves, and to create, as a result of British and missionary influences, a new class, which has so far remained quite distinct from the general population either in the hills or in the plains. The creation of a new hill state will, in our opinion, accentuate these distinctions. It will, therefore, prove, in the long run, against the interests of the scheduled tribes.

690. During the initial phase of the changeover after 1947 the hill districts may not have received adequate attention. We do not, however, propose to examine the allegations of indifference to the needs of the hill districts, because the whole of Assam is, in a sense, backward. Assam, moreover, has had to face the consequences of Partition, so that the genuine grievances of the hill districts, such as the loss of Pakistan markets for the Garo and Mizo (Lushai) hills districts, or the inadequacy of rail or road communications, have

been the inevitable results of the disruption of Assam's economy rather than the consequences of any policies pursued by the Assam Government.

691. Some of the causes for misunderstanding have also been removed recently, as the implications of the various development and welfare schemes have come to be somewhat better appreciated. It seems to us that there has been, of late, a sincere attempt to bring into existence the machinery of District Councils, which is contained in the Sixth Schedule to the Constitution, and to initiate welfare and development programmes with assistance from the Central Government, provided for in the second proviso to Article 275 (1) of the Constitution.

692. The Government of Assam has tried to provide temporary relief by arranging for the subsidised sale of food, the air-lift of essential commodities and the building of essential roads. Important schemes for reclamation, like the Rongkhong and Nambhor reclamation schemes, pilot projects for *jhum* control and proposals for extending railway lines have also been under consideration. A major amendment to the Assam Land and Revenue Regulation brought into force some years ago permits the creation of tribal belts where normally no non-tribal can acquire land. It is also possible that irrigation-cum-flood control projects on the Dihang and the Barak, proposals for the establishments of some industries in the Garo hills and schemes for the diversification of agriculture in the hills may be undertaken in the future.

693. It is naturally not possible at this stage to forecast the details of the development plans proposed for the hill areas. For our purpose, however, we take note of the important fact that, individually or together, the hill districts will not be able to command, even with such aid as may be granted by the Government of India, the resources in money, material or man-power needed to implement these development programmes.

694. Separation will add to the cost of administration, and the co-ordination of policies and programmes between the State of Assam and the hill areas on the one hand and between the hill districts themselves on the other will become more difficult. The scheme for a hill state, it must be noted, also contemplates that the capital of Assam and of the proposed hill state will be common, and that many institutions, apart from the Governor and the High Court, will be shared—an arrangement which will involve, in practice, a great deal of inconvenience and even conflict.

695. The impression which we have formed as a result of our tour of the area is that a substantial body of public opinion, even in the tribal areas of Assam, has not, by any means, been converted to the view that a new hill state should be formed.

696. Generally speaking, the United Mikir and North Cachar Hills and the Mizo (Lushai) Hills are not in favour of a separate hill state and the district council in the Lushai Hills and the Karbi-a-Durbar (Mikir Hills National Council) are in favour of the *status quo*. The agitation in favour of a hill state is, therefore, confined virtually to the Garo and the Khasi and Jaintia Hills. Owing to their geographical position, these two districts have necessarily a closer association with the adjoining plains districts than the rest of the hill or tribal areas; even in these two districts, therefore, an influential section of opinion views with disfavour the formation of a separate hill state.

697. Taking all these factors into consideration, we have come to the conclusion that the formation of a hill state in this region is neither feasible nor in the interests of the tribal people themselves. The hill districts, therefore, should continue to form part of Assam and no major changes should be made in their present constitutional pattern.

Autonomous bodies

698. A question which figured prominently during the course of our enquiry concerning this region was the working of the district and regional autonomous bodies which were created under the Sixth Schedule to the Constitution. The consensus of opinion seems to be that the scheme is not working satisfactorily. However, as regards the lines on which the schemes of autonomy should be improved, we came across two diametrically opposite views.

699. One section of opinion representing the tribal interests desires as great a measure of autonomy as possible. This section complains of lack of sympathy from the administration, inadequacy of financial resources, interference from above, neglect of the tribal areas by the government, imposition of the Assamese language and culture, and the opening of tribal lands to the settlers from the plains. A private member's bill which is now before Parliament, to amend the Sixth Schedule in certain respects with a view to providing much greater power and autonomy to these bodies, broadly reflects this point of view.

700. On the other hand, there have been complaints to the effect that the experiment of delegating power and authority to the district councils has so far not been quite successful. It has been represented to us that the administration of these councils has tended to be bureaucratic; that the powers delegated to these bodies in respect of primary education have been used only for the benefit of certain classes; and that the system of judicial administration, which the councils have evolved has been unnecessarily expensive and not suited to the special needs of the tribal population. The Assam Government has complained that, while it has surrendered revenue in favour of these councils, the functions which, under the Sixth Schedule, have been allocated to these bodies have not yet been taken over by them, with the result that the local government is saddled with an unnecessarily heavy burden of expenditure. Even in regard to projects which are in the general interest, like the Umtru hydro-electric scheme in the Khasi and Jaintia Hills, there have been difficulties and misunderstandings, largely because of the unhelpful attitude of the district council.

701. We do not propose to examine the merits of the two contending views. All that we would say would be that no proposal for the amendment of the Sixth Schedule, which would have the effect of encouraging disruptive tendencies, should be entertained. The Schedule is intended, by and large, to secure to the tribal population of Assam a simple form of government and a simple procedure for the settlement of disputes consistent with their present state of development and to moderate the impact of outside influences on their lives. Subject to this observation, we would recommend that the question of the working of the Sixth Schedule be examined comprehensively by a body specially constituted for this purpose. Paragraph 14 of the Sixth Schedule empowers the Governor to appoint such a body. This body should, in our opinion, consist of persons of adequate standing from outside the State, who have sympathy with the tribal people and understand their problems. The question should be examined with due regard to the promotion of the best interests of these people and the need for checking disruptive tendencies and securing good administration.

Commissioner for the Hill Districts

702. In the meantime, it seems necessary that some measures should be taken to ensure proper liaison between the Government of Assam and the autonomous district councils and to facilitate the formulation and implementation of schemes for the development of these areas. It is clear to us that a great deal of misunderstanding

is now due to a lack of adequate contact between the Assam Government and the district councils as regards both ordinary administration and development work. We were surprised to note that no use was being made at present of the district officers by the district councils and that no provision had been made in the Sixth Schedule for the maintenance of any contact between them. An important step in the direction of providing better liaison, in our opinion, will be the appointment of a Commissioner to be in charge of the administration and development of all the hill districts. We envisage that the Commissioner would act as the Governor's agent for the various purposes laid down in the Sixth Schedule; and that he with the assistance of the district officers would help the district councils in their various day-to-day problems so as to remove difficulties speedily. He may be assisted by a development board consisting among others of representatives of the different district councils. This should help to focus attention on the economic needs of this area and promote rapid development.

703. The natural resources which are available in the hill districts and the possibility of promoting schemes, which may increase the opportunities for gainful employment and the revenue now accruing from these areas, can be more fully investigated as a result of the constitution of the board. The scope for development, so far as we have been able to judge, is, by no means, negligible. The Umtru hydro-electric project in the Khasi and Jaintia hills, for example, has recently been sanctioned, but the power potential of the Umling river is believed to be much greater, and the second phase of this project and a thermal station at Cherrapunji are now under consideration. In the neighbouring Garo hills, there is believed to be some scope for the development of the coal and cement industries, and the proposal to construct railway lines in this district has been investigated more than once in the recent past, and even engineering surveys were completed some time back.

704. The extension of the north-eastern railway system, so as to cover the two western hill districts, namely, the Garo and the Khasi and Jaintia hills, and the extreme southern district, namely, the Mizo (Lushai) hills, may also have to be investigated. With the extension of communications in the future the development of cottage industries and the progressive replacement of *jhuming* by well-managed forests or fields and plantations growing marketable crops, the economy of the hills can be more completely integrated with that of the plains.

Purbachal

705. The proposal for the formation of a Purbachal State, like the demand for the creation of a hill State, is not new. It was examined by the Congress organisation in 1948 but was not pursued; and in one of the forms in which it has now been revived, the Purbachal scheme provides for the constitution of Cachar, Tripura, the Mizo (Lushai) Hills, the Naga Hills, Manipur and the NEFA into a new state; it, therefore, reproduces to some extent the proposal for the separation of the hill districts from the Assam (Brahmaputra) valley.

706. Some of our objections to the proposal to create a hill state are, therefore, applicable to this case. Moreover, the organisation sponsoring this demand, namely, the Cachar States Reorganisation Committee, itself recognises that this new State will be financially in deficit for quite some time to come. The proposed Purbachal State, under any of the schemes that have been suggested, will have an international boundary on three sides. It is clear that it will have neither the resources nor the stability to provide for the security of the Indian border in this part of the country. It is also obvious that substantial minorities speaking languages other than Bengali will be found in it, with the result that it will provide no real solution of the existing difficulties.

707. The genesis of the Purbachal demand is that since the major part of Sylhet was cut off from India at the time of Partition, the Bengalis in Assam, who used to feel that culturally and even geographically they belonged to Bengal, have found themselves somewhat isolated in what they may now be disposed to regard as an uncongenial environment. It has been represented to us that the activities of the Assam Jatiya Mahasabha and the policies of the local government have not only not reconciled the Bengalis in this part of Assam, but have had quite the opposite result. The Bengali-speaking people have cited for instance the fact that the number of government primary schools in Goalpara district with Bengali as the medium of instruction has fallen from 252 in 1947-48 to 1 at the present time.

708. These complaints in so far as there is some *prima facie* justification for them deserve to be carefully examined. It is difficult for us to believe that the arrangements which have been made at present adequately meet the needs of the Bengali-speaking population in this district, and in particular the problem of primary education in this area should receive early attention. But the creation

of a new State, which may well mean only that one set of problems is exchanged for another, is not in our opinion an appropriate remedy for the grievances of the minorities, if any.

Kamatapur

709. On the grounds which we have already discussed we are also unable to entertain the demand for the creation of a Kamatapur State north-west of Purbachal consisting of Goalpara, Garo Hills, Jalpaiguri, Cooch-Behar and Darjeeling.

Tripura

710. Tripura is a Part C State with a population of 639,029. The predominant language in this State is Bengali, which is spoken by about 59 per cent. of the population. The capital, namely, Agartala, is connected by air with Calcutta, but the State is contiguous to Assam, and while Agartala is equally well-connected by air with Gauhati and Silchar, an important road from Agartala to Churaibari in Assam is now under construction. It will be easy to extend this link and to connect Agartala with Shillong, by means of a road passing through Silchar and Jowai. We recommend that high priority should be accorded to the construction or improvement of these links.

711. As a small Part C State, Tripura cannot obviously stand by itself. The West Bengal Government, moreover, has not claimed this area; and its merger in Assam, in our opinion, can be supported among other reasons on the ground that it will be desirable to bring the entire border between India and Pakistan in this region under one single control, namely, that of the Assam Government.

712. Such a merger will also make it possible to co-ordinate development in Cachar and the contiguous area of Tripura. The Bengali-speaking population after the merger will be a little more than one-fifth of the total population of the State. It should not be difficult for the Assam Government to allay the apprehensions of the Bengali-speaking people by treating this area, which requires development, as a separate administrative division under a commissioner. The special position of Bengali in this division should be recognised for official and educational purposes.

713. If safeguards on these lines are provided the merger of Tripura in Assam will achieve for its people the fulfilment of their aspirations for representative government at the state-level without prejudicing their linguistic and cultural interests. Suitable safeguards can and should also be provided for the tribal people in the proposed administrative division.

The North-East Frontier Agency

714. We have now to deal with the suggestion that the North-East Frontier Agency should be more fully integrated with Assam. Constitutionally, the North-East Frontier Agency is part of Assam, but it presents special features of its own. In the whole area of about 35,000 sq. miles the population has been estimated at only eight lakhs. It is a difficult mountainous country extremely deficient in communications. The work of any administration which is in charge of this area, will, therefore, have to be of a special kind for quite some time to come.

715. In recognition of this fact, the governance of this area has been entrusted for the time being to the President acting through the Governor of Assam, and a separate cadre for the superior posts recruited on an all-India basis, has been created. Central expenditure in this area has been increased very considerably during the last few years, and it is now widely recognised that an efficient and progressive administration is being gradually built up. In these circumstances, the suggestion made by the Assam Government for the early integration of this frontier area is not feasible and the existing arrangements regarding the North-East Frontier Agency should continue.

The Naga Hills District

716. The Naga Hills district presents another special problem. Owing to the activities of the extremist elements, the law and order situation in this area has been unstable in recent years. The Nagas boycotted the elections to the autonomous bodies, with the result that the area has had to be administered directly by the Assam Government.

717. It has been represented to us that the law and order problem in the Naga Hills district is the same as in the Tuensang area of the N.E.F.A., and that unless the entire area is brought under the authority the situation cannot be effectively dealt with. However, it has been stated on behalf of the Assam Government that the Naga Hills district has been relatively quiet during the last two or three years and that there are indications of the people of the area abjuring violence in favour of peaceful methods. After taking the relevant factors into account we have come to the conclusion that it would not be desirable to suggest any change in regard to the Naga Hills district at the present juncture.

The New State of Assam

718. The results of these recommendations may now be summarised. The proposed new State of Assam will include all the areas now constituting the existing State as well as Tripura and will have an area and population of about 89,040 square miles and 9·7 millions respectively.

719. The linguistic complexion of the existing State establishes very clearly its composite character, in spite of the very interesting post-1931 spread of Assamese according to the census figures. It is not surprising that the rapid increase in the past two decades in the number of persons speaking Assamese has been disputed; and the veracity of the 1951 Census figures has been questioned in certain quarters. We have not deemed it necessary to enter into this controversy, but we would like to draw attention to the fact that in spite of this rapid increase the Assamese-speaking population still constitutes only about 55 per cent. of the population of the State.

720. Racially, linguistically and culturally, even the tribes which are described compendiously under a single name, for example, the Nagas, are in reality different each from the other. In spite of a certain tendency towards 'Assamisation', about which the minorities in Assam have complained, the heterogeneous character of Assam has so far been substantially preserved, and our proposals merely recognise this fact.

721. The new State which we propose will have important problems to tackle. This area has been subject to periodical floods, against which protection will have to be sought in part by building irrigation or flood protection works not considered so far; and flood control has to be handled as a regional problem. The road and rail system in the north-east of India is moreover admittedly unsatisfactory in relation to the growing needs of this area including Manipur. Although the position has improved partially since the restoration of rail travel through Pakistan, a well planned programme for the development of communications is clearly necessary. The economy of this region, which depends overwhelmingly on a few industries, also needs a balanced expansion.

722. The task of economic development can be undertaken and substantial cultural autonomy can be enjoyed by the various linguistic and racial groups only if two conditions are fulfilled, namely, that the state of Assam is compact, rich and resourceful, and that

there exists within this State, mutual tolerance and goodwill. Particularist and, if we may say so, chauvinistic trends are bound to retard the progress of the state. They should, therefore, be discouraged in every way. We hope that the recommendations which we have made will be considered in this spirit.

CHAPTER XVII

Manipur

723. The State of Assam, with the boundaries which have been suggested in the preceding Chapter, will not include the existing State of Manipur. This is because we recommend that Manipur should for the present continue to be centrally-administered. We shall explain briefly our reasons for making this recommendation.

724. Manipur is a Part C State, situated on India's eastern border, with a population of about 0·6 million. A unit such as this cannot be considered administratively viable. Consistently, therefore, with the principles discussed in Part II and Chapter I of this part of the report, the merger of Manipur in the adjoining State should be the natural course, the more so when the other Part C State with a comparable population in this region, namely, Tripura, is proposed to be merged in Assam. There are, however, some features peculiar to this unit, which render it desirable that its separate existence should be maintained for the time being.

725. We may first state the main arguments which have been advanced in favour of the continued existence of this unit. Manipur, it is claimed, is a border State; and, as in the case of the North-East Frontier Agency, which is a neighbouring area, security considerations are, or must be, paramount. Manipur, it has also been claimed, has been independent for centuries and its connection with the neighbouring States—and indeed with India itself—is very recent. There is, even today, no railway which links the State with the rest of India. The State is now receiving substantial financial aid from the Centre. Its economic development will be retarded if it is merged either in Assam or in West Bengal or in the hill districts.

726. The racial and linguistic composition of the State is somewhat peculiar. The Meitheis or Manipuris, constituting about 65 per cent. of the population of the State, are the major linguistic group and are to be found mostly in the valley. There has been some settlement by Mizos from the south, by Hmars, Nagas and other tribes and even some immigration from Assam and from Bengal. But the linguistic and cultural individuality of the valley, it is claimed, has remained largely unaffected.

727. Manipuris have accordingly developed a special social and cultural life of their own. This consciousness of a distinct linguistic and cultural individuality accounts for the opposition within the State to suggestions that Manipur should become part of Assam or of a Purbachal State created round Cachar or of a hill state extending from the Mizo (Lushai Hills) district in the south to the North-East Frontier Agency in the north.

728. The validity of some of these arguments may be questioned; and some of them may be plausibly cited in favour of the separate existence of Tripura also. The essential difference, however, between Manipur and Tripura is that the Bengali-speaking people in the neighbouring district, namely, Cachar, already constitute seventy-seven per cent. of the population of the district; and the merger of Tripura in the State would, therefore, be natural to some extent. This important consideration does not apply to Manipur which has no particular linguistic affinity with Assam.

729. Another important consideration we have to bear in mind is that Assam has fairly difficult political and economic problems of its own to solve. Besides, apart from the autonomous hills districts, the administration of the State will have to look after another border unit, namely, Tripura. In these circumstances, it may not be desirable to impose on Assam the additional burden of administering the important border area of Manipur.

730. The only serious alternative to merger in Assam is to create a new State consisting of Manipur and the neighbouring areas like Lushai Hills, Tripura and Cachar. We have already referred to the opposition of the people to this proposal. But the proposal itself is impracticable owing to lack of communications, a variety of languages, difficulties regarding administrative and technical personnel and inadequacy of financial resources.

731. On a careful consideration of the implications of the various possible alternatives, we have come to the conclusion that Manipur should continue to be a centrally-administered territory for the time being.

732. While we make this recommendation, it is quite clear to us that Manipur cannot maintain its separate existence for long and that the ultimate solution should be its merger in the adjoining State of Assam. It is equally clear to us that, so long as it continues as a separate administrative unit, the administrative structure of

Manipur should conform to the pattern we have indicated in Chapter I of this part. We wish to repeat that, if a unit such as Manipur wishes to have representative government at the state level, it must be prepared to join a larger unit. It cannot insist on a separate existence, and demand, at the same time, substantial central aid not only for its economic development but also for the maintenance of expensive representative institutions and uneconomic administrative agencies.

CHAPTER XVIII

ORISSA

733. The last of the territorial units in respect of which proposals for reorganisation have to be considered is Orissa. The province of Orissa was created in 1936 in terms of the Government of India (Constitution of Orissa) Order, but an elaborate enquiry which covered in particular the question of its boundaries preceded this Order and was spread over a period of about thirty years, that is to say, from 1903, when the circular which dealt with the regrouping of provinces was first addressed to the provincial governments, right up to the time when the Order in Council was issued.

734. The question was also considered by three important committees in very considerable detail; the Philip-Duff Committee reported in 1924, the Attlee Committee, which was constituted by the Simon Commission, about six years later, and the O'Donnell Committee in 1932. The reports of these committees formed the subject-matter of prolonged and detailed correspondence between the Government of India and the Secretary of State, in the course of which every important argument was considered and reconsidered from all points of view.

735. Orissa, in short, was carved out of the neighbouring areas, after a review of its boundaries which was more elaborate than was possible in the case of any other State. This has considerably simplified the task of the re-determination of the boundaries of the Orissa State.

736. The major claims made on Orissa are as follows:

(i) the three northern districts of Mayurbhanj, Sundargarh and Keonjhar have been claimed by Bihar on the ground that the people of these areas desire to be associated with Chota Nagpur; and

(ii) the Andhra State has claimed the whole of the Koraput district, the Parlakimedi estate and the Parlakimedi Maliahs of the Ganjam district, and a portion of the Chatarpur and Berhampur taluks of Ganjam constituting a coastal belt in this district extending from the present Andhra boundary up to the Rushikulya river.

737. The principal claims made for or on behalf of Orissa on the other hand are:

(i) a coastal belt and agency tracts consisting of predominantly Oriya and aboriginal areas in Srikakulam district right up to the Vamsadhara river;

(ii) the Phuljhar and Bindra-Nawagarh ex-zamindari areas of the Raipur district, a portion of ex-zamindari areas of Chandrapur now in the Bilaspur district and a portion of the Bastar district;

(iii) the Singhbhum district of Bihar, particularly Seraikella and Kharsawan; and

(iv) a portion in south-west Midnapore district of West Bengal.

738. In Chapter XIV of this part we have already dealt with the Bihar Government's claims on Orissa as also the Orissa claim to Singhbhum or to Seraikella and Kharsawan. We deal here with the other claims.

739. The Andhra claim to Koraput rests on a number of arguments, the most important and relevant of which at the present time is that the trading affiliations of the district with Parvatipuram and the rest of Srikakulam district as well as with Vishakapatnam district are fairly close. The basis of the demand for the other territories which have been claimed is mainly linguistic, Parlakimedi estate and Berhampur town in particular being claimed as outlying Telugu pockets in Orissa.

740. Koraput, however, is a district in which the Oriya majority is absolute; and since Kondh and Paraja in addition are spoken by a little less than one quarter of the population, there is no case for regrading it as an Andhra area. The trading affiliations of this district which have been mentioned are not also such as to justify the disturbance of the existing position. The preponderance of tribes in this district is considerable; and some of the arguments advanced by Andhra, for example, that riots or *fithuries* in the tribal area can be much better dealt with by a government which controls Vishakapatnam, are no longer valid. There is, therefore, no case in our opinion for the transfer of Koraput to Andhra.

741. The Parlakimedi pocket was considered together with the Parlakimedi hill areas at the time that this portion was transferred to Orissa; and although the main ground for this transfer was that

the preference of the Raja of Parlakimedi for Orissa deserved to be considered with sympathy, the transfer was also justified on linguistic grounds. The Berhampur tract was likewise established at that time to be clearly within the area of Oriya influence. There is little reason to upset these decisions now.

742. In the entire district of Ganjam of which these two claimed areas form part, Oriya is the predominant language and Telugu is spoken only by about 15 per cent. of the people. It is quite unnecessary in these circumstances to detach an important coastal belt from the rest of the district.

743. While there is no case in view of what has been said so far for subtracting any territory from Orissa, there is also no case for adding any territory to it.

744. The Telugu majority in Srikakulam district from which portions have been claimed for Orissa is as high as 89 per cent. This majority is likewise pronounced even in the Ichapuram, Sompeta and Tekkali taluks. There is no reason for disturbing these areas or the tribal areas of the west.

745. In the case of the Phuljhar and Bindra-Nawagarh areas of the Raipur district, the O'Donnell Committee found overwhelming public support for their retention in the present Madhya Pradesh. These areas form part of a district in which Hindi is the predominant language and even Chattisgarhi is more important than Oriya. According to the latest Census, the Oriya-speaking population is not in a majority even in Mahasamund, and no other convincing reasons have been advanced in favour of the claim. We see no reason, therefore, to reopen the decision of the O'Donnell Committee regarding this area.

746. These arguments are applicable more or less with the same force also in the case of the Chandrapur claim.

747. We have already dealt with the claims on Bastar in Chapter IX of this part dealing with the new Madhya Pradesh.

748. The area in south-west Midnapore which Orissa has claimed belongs culturally to West Bengal and there has been a progressive increase in Bengali influence. The Oriya population in the claimed areas is negligible at the present time. The Orissa case rests in part on the claim that the historical association of these areas with the

ancient Orissa kingdoms should be respected. The argument is debatable and in accordance with the principles set out in Chapter VIII of Part II cannot be accepted. Moreover, the association in this case is not quite clearly established.

749. This disposes of all the claims by or on Orissa. The area and population of the existing State of Orissa accordingly remain unaffected.

CHAPTER XIX

THE REORGANISED UNITS

750. We have now completed our examination of the various demands for the redemarcation of State territories and the major issues of policy which have arisen in connection with the reorganisation of States. It will be seen that our recommendations do not cover certain areas. We shall briefly explain our reasons for excluding these areas from our enquiry.

751. The Resolution appointing this Commission does not contain any specific reference to the State of Jammu and Kashmir. For obvious reasons, however, we have assumed that we are not expected to deal with the boundaries of this State.

752. We have considered some suggestions regarding the Andaman and Nicobar Islands and we have had the benefit of hearing the views of the Member of Parliament representing this area. No major change in the existing arrangements regarding the administration of these Islands has, however, been proposed, and there does not appear to be any case for disturbing the *status quo*.

753. The territories other than the Andaman and Nicobar Islands, which have been or may be brought under central administration, like Pondicherry, have obviously to be administered under flexible and transitional arrangements for the present. Generally speaking, there may be an interval before they become *de jure* part of India, and the special position and needs of each area may have to be considered. We do not think that it is either necessary or desirable at this stage to fetter the discretion which is vested in the Government of India in terms of Article 243 of the Constitution in respect of the administration of these territories.

754. Before we conclude this part of our report, we should like to say a few words about the picture of the component units of the Indian Union as it emerges from our recommendations. For the sake of convenience, we indicate below the names of the prospective units, as well as their area and population:

STATES

	Area (In sq. miles)	Population (In millions)
Madras	50,170	30·0
Kerala	14,980	13·6
Karnataka†	72,730	19·0

	Area (In sq. miles)	Population (In millions)
Hyderabad	45,300	11·3
Andhra†	64,950	20·9
Bombay	151,360	40·2
Vidarbha	36,880	7·6
Madhya Pradesh	171,200	26·1
Rajasthan	132,300	16·0
Punjab	58,140	17·2
Uttar Pradesh	113,410	63·2
Bihar†	66,520	38·5
West Bengal†	34,590	26·5
Assam	89,040	9·7
Orissa	60,140	14·6
Jammu and Kashmir	92,780	4·4

† Figures in these cases are approximate.

TERRITORIES

Delhi	578	1,744,072*
Manipur	8,628	577,635*
Andamans and Nicobars	3,215	30,971*

*Actual numbers.

755. We may briefly indicate the principal changes which our recommendations will bring about in the existing set-up. One result of the scheme of reorganisation proposed by us will be the elimination of the existing distinctions between the Part A and the Part B States and the disappearance of the Part C States. The second result will be a substantial reduction in the number of States. Thus, as against twenty-seven existing States, there will be only sixteen States. These do not include the two centrally-administered areas, namely, Delhi and Manipur, which now rank as Part C States.

756. This completes what we have to say about territorial changes. It is now necessary to pass to a consideration of the administrative implications of the redistribution of State territories on the lines proposed.

PART IV
ADMINISTRATIVE AND ALLIED MATTERS
CHAPTER I

SAFEGUARDS FOR LINGUISTIC GROUPS

757. An important question connected with the reorganisation of States is that of providing safeguards for linguistic groups which are in a minority in different states. The problem of such groups exists in unilingual states and not merely in composite States. In a way, the problem is a cause as well as an effect of the movement for linguistic units. On the one hand, it is argued that multilingual States arrest the cultural growth of linguistic minorities and retard their political and economic advancement, and, on the other hand, it is contended that it is implicit in the very formative principle of a linguistic State that in such a State linguistic minorities must be reduced to the status of inferior citizens.

758. The scheme of redistribution of State territories which we have recommended will result in many cases in bringing together people speaking a common language. To that extent, it will reduce the number of linguistic minorities. It is, however, quite evident that even if the linguistic principle were applied very rigidly, the problem of linguistic minorities will, by no means, be solved. This is because there are obvious limitations to the realisation of unilinguism at the state level, the limiting factors being the following:

(i) not all the language groups are so placed that they can be grouped into separate states;

(ii) there are a large number of bilingual belts between different linguistic zones; and

(iii) there exist areas with a mixed population even within unilingual areas.

Besides, the Constitution guarantees freedom of movement to all citizens of India. The present picture of the linguistic composition of various administrative units of India, therefore, can, by no means, be regarded as static.

759. It is true that often the complaints about the plight of minorities in composite states or bilingual areas are greatly exaggerated. In fact, we have noticed a tendency to whip up a kind of 'persecution complex' amongst minority language groups to secure their support for certain demands. This, however, does not mean that such groups have nowhere been discriminated against. By way of illustration we

may refer to the enforcement, in a number of States, of domiciliary qualifications and language tests for recruitment to services, which undoubtedly cause hardship to minorities. The problem of linguistic minorities, therefore, is not unreal.

Foreign practice

760. The problem of linguistic minorities in the States of the Indian Union, as compared to the problem of minorities in other countries, is, we must recognise, a limited one. The arrangements for safeguarding the interests of linguistic minorities in other countries were adopted against their own particular backgrounds. We must be careful, therefore, in applying such precedents to our own problems.

761. In other countries, it may be of interest to note, the following expedients have been tried, singly or in combination, to protect the interests of the minorities:

(i) constitution of administrative units on the basis of homogeneous nationalities, realised to a great extent in Switzerland, the U.S.S.R. and Yugoslavia;

(ii) recognition of more than one language as official languages, tried mainly in Switzerland, Canada and South Africa;

(iii) minority representation in the cabinet, tried in Switzerland and Canada;

(iv) guaranteeing to the minorities an effective voice in legislation concerning them, *e.g.*, the Scottish Standing Committee of the House of Commons;

(v) appointment of special ministers to look after the interests of minorities, as, for example, the Secretary of State for Scotland in the British cabinet;

(vi) fundamental rights for protection of minority interests, as in the constitutions of the U.S.S.R., Yugoslavia, Switzerland, Canada and Palestine, and in the pre-1939 constitutions of Poland and Czechoslovakia; and

(vii) assumption of special responsibility by the federal government in respect of minority rights in constituent units, as in Canada.

Provisions of the Indian Constitution

762. The Indian Constitution embodies the bulk of the rights which are generally guaranteed to minorities, within the framework of the fundamental rights of Indian citizens in general. With the exception of Article 335, which provides for special consideration being given to scheduled castes and scheduled tribes in the matter of

appointments to services, the special and transitory provisions contained in Articles 336 and 337 for the Anglo-Indian community, and the directive principle contained in Article 46 for the promotion of educational and economic interests of scheduled castes, scheduled tribes and other weaker sections, the only provisions in the Constitution which have been particularly devised to safeguard the interests of minorities are those contained in Articles 29, 30 and 347.

763. Of these, Article 29 provides that any section of citizens having a distinct language, script or culture shall have the right to conserve the same. It also prohibits discrimination in the matter of admission to educational institutions maintained or aided by the State.

764. Article 30 provides that "all minorities, whether based on religion or language, shall have the right to establish and administer educational institutions of their choice". It also provides that, in giving aid to educational institutions, the State shall not discriminate against the institutions managed by such minorities.

765. Article 347 enables the President to direct, in appropriate cases, the use of minority languages in the administration.

766. If the relevant provisions of the Indian Constitution are compared with the corresponding provisions of some of the European constitutions, it will be found that the substance of fundamental rights usually guaranteed to minorities in other countries is provided for under our Constitution, except for the right to receive instruction in the mother-tongue in state or municipal schools at the primary stage.

Principles which should govern safeguards for linguistic minorities

767. During the course of our enquiry, the question of reinforcing the existing system of safeguards for minorities figured prominently. It was strongly urged before us that the safeguards for minorities embodied in the Constitution have proved inadequate and ineffective against the cultural oppression of linguistic minorities and their economic exploitation. Whatever the merits of this assertion, we have to take into consideration the fact that large sections of public opinion, both among the proponents and the opponents of linguistic states, favour the strengthening of the existing constitutional guarantees to linguistic minorities.

768. We realise that overemphasis on the rights of minorities and too many special safeguards for them would tend to keep the minority-consciousness alive and might thereby hamper the growth of a common nationhood. We, are, therefore not in favour of setting up too

elaborate a system of guarantees to the minorities which would, in our opinion, complicate rather than solve the problem. At the same time, we are impressed by the need of according to the linguistic minorities sufficient opportunity for development so that they may not suffer from a sense of neglect or discrimination.

769. Before we make our specific recommendations on the subject, we wish to indicate the broad principles and objectives which have governed our approach to the problem. These are:

(i) as the problem of linguistic minorities is common to unilingual as well as polyglot areas, the measures to be adopted should be such as can be applied to linguistic as well as composite States;

(ii) while minorities are entitled to reasonable safeguards to protect their educational, cultural and other interests, it has to be borne in mind that such safeguards should not so operate as to perpetuate separatism or to impede the processes of natural assimilation;

(iii) the system of guarantees to minorities should not be such as to lend itself to misuse by parties interested in promoting a sense of disloyalty to the State; and

(iv) it should be clearly understood that a state in which a particular language group constitutes the majority cannot be considered to be the custodian of the interests of all people speaking that language, even when they are residents of other States.

Disabilities of linguistic minorities and suggested safeguards

770. Following the principles we have set out in the preceding paragraphs, we do not think that a number of suggestions which were made to us are feasible or will be in the interests of linguistic minorities themselves. Thus, for instance, the question of their representation in the State cabinets cannot be governed by any rule but must depend on the circumstances of each case.

771. So far as allegations of discriminatory treatment in the field of commerce, trade and industry are concerned, there are adequate provisions in the Constitution to deal with such discrimination. To the extent that a State Government acts in disregard of these provisions, no system of guarantees other than the right to move a court of law will be of any use. We hope, however, that good sense will prevail, that non-discrimination will be the rule, and that it will not be necessary for the minorities to have recourse to legal remedies.

772. The problem of fair distribution of development expenditure is not confined only to areas in which linguistic minorities are found. We have elsewhere made recommendations for the appointment of a permanent body, of adequate standing, to ensure that development expenditure is as far as possible equitably distributed over the various areas which need attention.

The right to instruction in the mother-tongue

773. The more important aspects of the problem, however, are the right of linguistic minorities to instruction in their mother-tongues, the use of minority languages in the administration, and the representation of the minorities in the State services. The language of instruction in educational institutions and the language of the administration are matters that touch, in practice, many vital aspects of the life of every individual. They, therefore, constitute what we regard as the core of the problem of linguistic minorities.

774. We first deal with the question of the right of minorities to instruction in the mother-tongue. The Indian Constitution guarantees to the minorities the right to private schools but does not specifically recognise the right to instruction in the mother-tongues in public schools. It seems to us that linguistic minorities do not have the resources required to establish and maintain their own educational institutions particularly in rural areas. In such cases, therefore, a positive duty should be cast on the State to provide for facilities to the minorities for education in the mother-tongue at the primary school stage.

775. It may be recalled that the right of each language group to have education in the mother-tongue in public schools at the primary school stage has been recognised by the Congress Working Committee in its resolutions adopted in August, 1949, and May, 1953. The right has also been recognised in principle by the State Governments as well as the Government of India. This is clear from the resolution adopted at the Provincial Education Ministers' Conference held in August, 1949, which has been approved by the Government of India, and now serves as a guide to the State Governments in making arrangements for the education of their school-going children whose mother-tongue is different from the regional language. This resolution states:

> "The medium of instruction and examination in the junior basic stage must be the mother-tongue of the child and, where the mother-tongue is different from the regional or

State language, arrangements must be made for instruction in the mother-tongue by appointing at least one teacher, provided there are not less than 40 pupils speaking the language in the whole school or 10 such pupils in a class. The mother-tongue will be the language declared by the parent or guardian to be the mother-tongue. The regional or State language, where it is different from the mother-tongue, should be introduced not earlier than Class III and not later than the end of the junior basic stage. In order to facilitate the switching-over to the regional language as medium in the secondary stage, children should be given the option of answering questions in their mother-tongue, for the first two years after the junior basic stage."

776. From the data supplied to this Commission by the State Governments it appears that most of the States are endeavouring to implement this resolution, though it is difficult to say to what extent it is being carried out both in the letter and in the spirit. The resolution is only recommendatory; the States are, therefore, not following a uniform policy. After carefully examining the background of the question, the reasons why the suggestion for making suitable provision in the Constitution on the subject did not find favour with the Constituent Assembly, and the views expressed before us, we have come to the conclusion that the right of the minorities to have education in the mother-tongue at the primary stage, subject to a sufficient number of students being available, should be placed on a more stable footing than is the position at present. We, therefore, recommend that constitutional recognition should be given to this right and that the Central Government should acquire power to issue appropriate directives for the enforcement of this right on the lines of the provisions contained in Article 347 of the Constitution.

777. So far as secondary education is concerned, the policy of the Government of India, as embodied in the Resolution of the Central Advisory Board of Education adopted in 1949, has been that regional languages should be introduced at the secondary stage, with provision for instruction in the mother-tongue even at this stage if the number of pupils in the area is sufficient to justify establishment of separate schools, or for instruction in the same school if one-third of the pupils in the school ask for it. We are doubtful if this deals with the problem adequately. It is, of course, clear that, so far as secondary education is concerned, it will have to be treated differently from the education at the primary stage. We, therefore, do not recommend

the extension of the principle of the constitutional recognition of the right to have instruction in mother-tongue to secondary education. At the same time, we feel that the Government of India should, in consultation with State Governments, lay down a clear policy and also take more effective steps to implement it.

The use of minority languages for official purposes

778. The next question to be considered is the use of the minority languages for official purposes. Article 347 of the Constitution, as we have already stated, empowers the President to provide for the use of a minority language also in the administration of a State. We understand that so far no order has been issued under this Article and it has been left more or less to the States concerned to regulate the use of the minority languages for administrative purposes.

779. From the information furnished to us it appears that the States of Uttar Pradesh, Bihar, Madhya Bharat, Madhya Pradesh, Rajasthan, Ajmer and Saurashtra have adopted legislation under Article 345, recognising the respective regional language or languages as the official language or languages in the States concerned. In other States, English continues to be the official language. Some States have recognised more than one official language. Thus, in Madhya Pradesh, both Hindi and Marathi are the official languages at all levels. The Punjab and PEPSU have demarcated two distinct zones—a Punjabi-speaking zone and a Hindi-speaking zone. In Bombay and Hyderabad, official business at district and taluk levels is conducted in the languages of these units.

780. In Hyderabad, PEPSU, Rajasthan, Travancore-Cochin and Madhya Bharat, the regional language or languages have been recognised for use in the High Court. In other States, English continues to be the language of the High Court.

781. As regards the lower courts, there is no State, with the exception of Assam, in which English is used exclusively in the lower courts. In most States, where English is used in the High Court, the subordinate courts use both English and the regional languages, the general practice being that judgments are written in English and other work is done in the regional languages. Several States have permitted the use of the minority languages in subordinate courts. Bihar, Bombay, Andhra, Madras, Orissa, Hyderabad, Travancore-Cochin and West Bengal have allowed the use of two, or even three, languages in certain areas.

782. The present position, therefore, is that, while it is generally agreed that minority languages should receive due recognition in bilingual areas, a clear policy has not so far been laid down for regulating the use of the minority languages in the administration.

783. We do not desire to make any recommendation about the details of the policy to be followed in prescribing the use of minority languages for official purposes. However, we are inclined to the view that a State should be treated as unilingual only where one language group constitutes about seventy per cent or more of its entire population. Where there is a substantial minority constituting thirty per cent. or so of the population, the State should be recognised as 'bilingual' for administrative purposes.

784. The same principle might hold good at the district level; that is to say, if seventy per cent. or more of the total population of a district is constituted by a group which is a minority in the State, the language of the minority group, and not the State language, should be the official language in that district. It will also be of advantage if, in bilingual districts, municipal areas, or other smaller units such as taluks, where there are minorities constituting fifteen to twenty per cent of the population, documents which are used by the people at large, such as government notices, electoral rolls, ration cards, etc., are printed in both the languages. It should also be permissible to file documents in the courts etc. in the minority language. Likewise, where the candidates seeking election to any local bodies are required to have a working knowledge of a language, the knowledge of a language of such minor language groups should be given recognition.

785. These suggestions are for the consideration of the Government of India. What we wish to emphasise is that the Government of India should adopt, in consultation with the State Governments, a clear code to govern the use of different languages at different levels of State administrations and that effective steps should be taken to ensure that this code is followed.

Discriminatory treatment in the matter of recruitment to services

786. Recruitment to the services is a prolific source of discontent amongst linguistic minorities. The main complaint is that a number of States confine entry to their services to permanent residents of the State, 'permanent residents' being defined in varying ways. These domicile tests, it is contended, have been so devised as to exclude the minority groups from the services.

737. The residence required under these rules varies from three years in certain cases to fifteen years. These rules are, strictly speaking, in contravention of Article 16(1) of the Constitution. They have apparently been allowed to continue in terms of Article 35(b) pending a general review of the position.

788. This review, we understand, has now been undertaken. Legislation is likely to be promoted in Parliament in order to regulate the extent to which it would be permissible for a State to depart in future from the principle of non-discrimination as between citizen and citizen, as laid down in Article 16(1). We strongly recommend that the contemplated legislation should be taken up early, and that, if any departure from the principle of non-discrimination is to be authorised at all, it should be such as to cause minimum hardship.

789. One form which discrimination against language groups takes, it has been stated, is the tendency in certain States to make their services a preserve for the predominant language group by prescribing a high test of proficiency in the regional language or by making this language the medium in the various competitive tests. At present, higher competitive examinations are conducted in most States in English. Some States, however, have allowed an option to offer one or more of the regional languages. In a number of States there is also a compulsory paper in the regional language. For lower examinations one of the regional languages is the medium and also a compulsory subject. Most States insist on a departmental examination of proficiency in the regional language or the local dialect for candidates whose mother-tongue is other than the regional language.

790. That all public servants should be conversant with the official language or languages of the State admits of no dispute. The point for consideration, however, is whether candidates belonging to one language group should have an initial advantage over those belonging to the other language groups. We feel the present practice in certain States tilts the scales in favour of the dominant language group, and consider it both practicable and desirable that, for services known as the 'State services', apart from the main language of the State, the candidates should have the option to elect, as the medium of examination, the Union language—English or Hindi—or the language of a minority constituting about fifteen to twenty per cent. or more of the population of the State. A test of proficiency in the State language should be held, in that event, after selection and before the end of the period of probation. In the case of subordinate services, however, the State language could continue to be the medium of examination.

791. So far as promotions or disciplinary and other matters connected with services are concerned, no conceivable safeguards can ensure justice, should those in power choose to fill important posts on grounds other than those of administrative purity, efficiency and fairness. It is desirable, however, to constitute State Public Service Commissions in such a manner as to ensure that these bodies are not affected by particularist trends. This objective can be achieved to some extent by constituting, so far as possible, one Public Service Commission for more than one State. Under the Constitution, appointments to Public Service Commissions serving more than one State are made by the President. We recommend that this principle be extended even to Public Service Commissions serving only single States. This arrangement, we are sure, will give these bodies a higher stature and more independence.

Agency for enforcing safeguards

792. We now come to the question of devising a suitable agency to enforce the rights of the linguistic minorities. It follows from what we have stated earlier that the Centre should not only be responsible for prescribing policies governing certain important matters, such as the education of minority groups and the use of minority languages for official purposes, but also for due observance of such policies.

793. One suggestion that has been made to us is the creation of a Central Ministry for Minority Affairs. Since the Centre's responsibility, under the scheme we have in view, will be confined to the enforcement of safeguards in the educational field and to making arrangements for the use of the minority languages in the administration, a separate Central Ministry will not be justified.

794. Another proposal which has been put forward in certain memoranda received by us is that a Statutory Commission for Minority Affairs should be appointed. This Commission, it has been suggested, should be a non-political quasi-judicial, advisory body. The most important argument in favour of such an arrangement would be that it would instil confidence into the minorities. On the other hand, it will have a serious disadvantage in that the existence of a tribunal before which State Governments could be impugned might lead to vexatious claims and counter-claims and might encourage the minorities to look constantly beyond the borders of the State for the redress of their grievances, real or imaginary. There is a large area of administration in which the minorities will have to

depend on the goodwill of the dominant language group. Any effort, therefore, to enforce "strict justice" to linguistic minorities might lead to the worsening of the relations between the State Governments and the minority groups. We, therefore, do not regard this as a satisfactory solution of the problem.

795. Under the Government of India Act of 1935, the responsibility for protecting the interests of minorities was cast on the provincial Governors. Public opinion in India, however, viewed the special powers of Governors and the provisions for the protection of minority interests as convenient instruments of the policy of "balance and counterpoise" by which the then rulers of India sought to perpetuate their power. When the Constitution was framed, the position of the Governor was examined against this background; and there was a considerable body of opinion against the grant of special powers to a nominated Governor. The Constitution has, therefore, recognised the Governor as a purely constitutional head, without any discretionary functions.

796. In the course of the debate on the Andhra Bill, it was suggested that the Governors of multilingual States might be vested with special powers to protect the interests of the minorities. But the proposal did not find favour with Parliament.

797. Against this background, we hesitate to revive the suggestion for vesting special powers in the Governors to ensure that the minorities are not discriminated against. There are, however, clear advantages in utilising the services of the Governor for supervising the implementation of the policies of the Central Government in regard to linguistic minorities. With his detached outlook and knowledge of the requirements of administration, the Governor would be better suited for this task than a judicial or quasi-judicial Commission. The arrangement would also not involve extra expenditure.

798. We have carefully examined the objections to such an arrangement. It is understandable that the Governor should not exercise discretionary functions in the state field. There is no reason, however, why the Governor should not function as an agent of the Central Government in regard to a matter which is of national concern. There is nothing anti-democratic about such an arrangement, because the Central Government will be responsible to the Union Parliament for functions performed by the Governor as its agent. It will amount only to supervision by the larger democracy over the smaller democracies in respect of matters of national concern.

799. To the extent that the Governor acts in accordance with the Instrument of Instructions issued to him, his role as an agent of the Centre need not bring him into conflict with his cabinet. However, with a view to minimising the possibility of any such conflict, it may be provided that, when the Governor finds the State Government acting in disregard of the Central Government's policies, he should, in the first instance, advise the State Government to take the measures necessary for the implementation of such policies; if the State Government disagreed with him, he should have the right to refer the matter to the Central Government, along with his advice and the views of the State Government. The decision of the Central Government should be issued as a directive from the President.

800. The arrangement which we have suggested will involve no constitutional amendment. It will have the clear advantage of entrusting the task of advising the Central as well as State Governments to a person who is on the spot and is in a position to weigh the relative needs and interests of the linguistic minorities as well as of the administration.

801. Before we conclude, we wish to emphasise that no guarantees can secure a minority against every kind of discriminatory policy of a State Government. Governmental activity at State level affects virtually every sphere of a person's life and a democratic government must reflect the moral and political standards of the people. Therefore, if the dominant group is hostile to the minorities, the lot of minorities is bound to become unenviable. There can be no substitute for a sense of fairplay on the part of the majority and a corresponding obligation on the part of the minorities to fit themselves in as elements vital to the integrated and ordered progress of the State.

CHAPTER II

The Integration of Services

802. In Chapter I of Part II of this report we have made a brief reference to the unsettling effects of the reorganisation of States. In this Chapter and in the next we proceed to examine the administrative implications of reorganisation and to suggest certain measures which may have to be taken in order to curtail the period of transition.

803. The most urgent problems, perhaps, which the reorganised States will have to tackle will be those connected with the integration of the personnel drawn from various areas into the administrative cadres of the new States and the rationalisation of the administrative structure. We have deemed it necessary to deal with this matter at some length, because the reorganisation of the States is likely to be undertaken at a time when the burden thrown on the administrative services will be very great.

804. The constitution of this Commission has led to a number of claims and counter-claims, and has created a degree of emotional unrest, resulting in the deterioration of the law and order situation in certain areas. For some time to come the responsibilities of governments and the services in the disputed areas may, therefore, be particularly heavy. The general elections are also due to be held shortly; and the second five-year plan may be well under way by the time the proposed reorganisation takes effect. The cumulative strain which all this will impose on the administrative services may be expected to be so considerable that the greatest importance must be attached to the maintenance of the morale of the services and to measures which are necessary to ensure that administrative efficiency is not impaired.

805. In recent years problems more or less similar to those with which the new administrations will be faced have had to be handled in connection with the integration of the princely states and also in connection with the formation of Andhra. We have already referred to the fact that the integration of the services in the Part B and Part C States has proved to be much more difficult than was anticipated. This process has had to be spread over very nearly six or seven

years, and even now in some cases it has not been completed. The lack of any clear criteria for the gradation of the service personnel inherited from the integrated States, the free exercise of the rights of appeal against decisions taken by competent authority, and the failure on the part of the State Governments either to finalise the decisions taken or to accord to the problem the priority which it deserved seem to explain this delay. Whatever the reasons, the uncertainty which prevailed in the initial years after the formation of the present Part B and Part C States has been such as to affect service morale and to impair efficiency.

806. The separation of Andhra was relatively simple, considered merely from the administrative point of view. But even in this case we understand that the allocation of the personnel belonging to the all-India and other services to the new unit had at certain stages to be negotiated between the two areas of the composite Madras State. This negotiation proved, in the event, to be not too difficult. It is not clear, however, whether in the absence of special arrangements a detailed division of the existing administrative cadre and the personnel will prove to be equally easy in the case of the States which will have to be broken up.

807. This is not a matter in respect of which a policy of drift, or what amounts virtually to that, can be considered satisfactory. The Government of India, no less than the State Governments concerned, will have to give to this question very high priority.

808. The reconstitution of the sanctioned state cadres will have to be taken in hand as soon as the new units are set up. This should not involve any difficulty except in so far as common services or posts which cannot be clearly related to any particular area are concerned. Even in these cases, it should normally be possible to arrive at decisions by agreement.

809. Against the posts thus determined, the allotment of personnel may be made primarily on the basis of the option of the employees. This option should be respected as far as possible, but it must be consistent with the public interest, which will require a division which on the one hand will be satisfactory to the services as a whole and on the other hand will be fair to the new States themselves.

810. The integration of services which will follow the determination of the cadres and the allotment of personnel should be based on definite principles which should, as far as possible, be of uniform application throughout India. Some of the principles which seem

prima facie to be suitable are that seniority among the officers in the State of origin *inter se* should not be disturbed, and that the existing scales of pay and conditions of service should not be varied to the disadvantage of those who are now in employment, and should be continued until such time as uniform pay scales, not less advantageous than those enjoyed by them in the parent State, are evolved. It is also of the greatest importance that the body constituted to integrate the service personnel of the different States should be such as to inspire confidence and that only one appeal from a decision regarding integration should be permitted.

811. It is not necessary at this stage to enter into any greater detail. The procedure which was adopted in the case of Andhra was to constitute two committees composed of the members of the services themselves, representing the separating areas of composite Madras; and these committees did most of the work in the first instance. *Prima facie,* this procedure seems to be suitable.

812. The Government of India are directly concerned with the reallocation to the prospective States of the personnel of the all-India services and normally the Governments of the new States should be responsible for the division and reconstitution of the rest of the services. We wish, however, to draw the attention of the governments concerned to one important aspect of the problem with which they will be called upon to deal. An eminent public man pointedly drew our attention to the fact that the existing smaller units which may be integrated with the larger States should not be treated as annexed territories, and that government servants belonging to these smaller units should be treated fairly and even generously. We realise the importance of this question and hope that the reorganisation of the administrative machinery in the States will be effected in such a manner that no section or group may be left with a sense of grievance.

813. After the scheme for reorganisation has been given effect to, it may be necessary for some of the new administrations to review the number and territorial extent of the existing districts and Commissioners' charges, with particular reference to the rationalisation of the administrative structure. However, this problem is not one of very great urgency, and the review may be taken in hand when the initial phase of reorganisation is over.

CHAPTER III

FINANCIAL AND OTHER ADMINISTRATIVE MEASURES.

814. The integration of services and the constitution of the administrative structure will not be the only problems arising out of the reorganisation of States. In this Chapter we deal with other important questions which will also have to be considered in implementing the scheme of reorganisation which we have proposed.

Finance Commission

815. In terms of Article 280 of the Constitution the second Finance Commission is now due to be appointed. Assuming that the recommendations of the second Finance Commission take effect from 1st April, 1957, an announcement regarding the setting up of this Commission cannot perhaps be delayed for any length of time. It will be an obvious advantage if decisions on the reorganisation proposals are taken before the Commission commences its enquiry. Otherwise another such body may have to go into the question of the financial needs of the newly-created units.

Second Five-Year Plan

816. The existing States are expected to be prepared to take up and implement from 1st April, 1956, the second five-year plan which is likely to be finalised by that date. We have referred already to the fact that there may be some dislocation during the initial period of this plan. However, if decisions regarding reorganisation are taken and implemented without avoidable delay, the difficulties arising out of reorganisation would be faced and overcome in the early years of the next plan period.

817. The new units may be expected to deal with their problems with a due sense of urgency and awareness of the need for cutting short the period of transition to the extent practicable. But we should like to mention the more important points deserving the attention of the Government of India and the prospective States.

Financial aid to new units

818. It would be necessary to provide for some help to the newly-constituted units during the period of transition when the administrative and financial implications of reorganisation are being considered. It has been the normal practice for the Government of

India in the past, whenever new States have been created or when accommodation is needed for any other reason, to grant ways and means advances to the States which may require them in order to help them to tide over their difficulties. We presume that such assistance will be available also in the initial years after reorganisation.

819. It has been suggested that revenue gap grants-in-aid to the new units, as in the case of the existing Part C States, may likewise be paid in the initial years; and that the Centre should assume, in effect, the residual responsibility for supporting the revenue budgets of the States until such time as other arrangements can be made. It is doubtful, however, whether it will be possible or desirable for the Centre to undertake a blanket commitment on these lines which is bound to be indefinite, in preference to more normal and orthodox arrangements.

820. Pending a comprehensive review, we would suggest that grants-in-aid on revenue or capital accounts as well as long-term loans should be available to the new States as nearly as may be on the existing basis. The Government of India might refix the existing statutory and development grants and long-term loans (including amounts promised but not disbursed to the States) with reference to:

(i) the principles, if any, on which the grants have been recommended or sanctioned; or

(ii) failing any definite principle, the population of the reorganised units as compared to the existing States; and

(iii) the purposes for which long-term loans have been granted.

821. This modification of the existing pattern of grants and loans to meet the needs of the new situation may be reviewed in the light of the recommendations of the next Finance Commission. However, the need for such action immediately after, or even in advance of, the reconstitution of the new States is clear.

822. It is also necessary here to refer to one minor complication. According to Article 278 of the Constitution, revenue gap grants-in-aid are paid to three of the existing Part B States, in accordance with the agreements entered into between the Government of India and the States concerned at the time of the federal financial integration, as amended thereafter from time to time. In the set-up contemplated after reorganisation, some areas now included in these Part B

States will be integrated with other States. The construction of Article 278 and the interpretation of the agreements arrived at in terms of that Article may in that event cause some difficulty. Having regard to the needs of the new States and to various other considerations, it would, however, be fair to regard the payments under Article 278 as outright grants and to apportion them population-wise among the new States until such time as the position is reviewed by the Finance Commission.

823. In the case of the Part C States, the acceptance of our recommendations will necessitate an amendment of Article 264(b) of the Constitution. The legislation or rules under the authority of which a prescribed percentage of the divisible pools of income-tax and central excise attributable to the Part C States is now retained with the Centre will, likewise, need a consequential change. Pending a detailed review, appropriate portions of the divisible pools which are now retained with the Centre may be distributed among the new units where necessary in the ratio of the population.

Division of assets and liabilities

824. As soon as the budgetary position and prospects of the new units have been clarified, arrangements for the division of the assets and liabilities will have to be taken in hand. This question can be considered in two parts, namely, the general principles on which the assets and liabilities are to be divided, and the mechanics of this division.

825. The general principles on which assets and liabilities will have to be divided may now be said to have crystallised sufficiently in the light of such experience as the governments have had. Generally speaking, a fair basis of division will be that where the assets exceed the liabilities—

(i) the movable assets of a State which is being divided should be distributed by agreement as equitably as possible, the most satisfactory basis being the ratio of the population;

(ii) each area which is being separated should take over the liabilities corresponding to the book values of the immovable assets which are located in the area and the movable assets which are claimed;

and where the liabilities exceed the assets—

(i) the movable assets should be distributed as equitably as possible, and

(ii) each area which is being separated from a composite State should take over liabilities corresponding to the book values of the immovable assets which are located in that area and such movable assets as it is entitled to claim, and

(iii) the balance of the liabilities should be divided as equitably as possible, the most satisfactory basis being the population ratio.

The Government of India will no doubt be able to formulate general principles on these or other lines.

826. We are aware that in practice special problems may also have to be considered. We, however, feel that the distribution of assets and liabilities should be governed by some general principles which as far as practicable should be uniformly enforced.

827. On one point, it may be necessary to make an exception to the general rule and to consider some special arrangements. In the case of the present Part C States, the accounts of which were merged into those of the Centre, the scheme of reorganisation which is contemplated will necessitate a complete separation of their balances from those of the Centre. In these cases, it would be a laborious process if consolidated-fund and public account balances, attributable to those areas were to be worked out in the light of the actual transactions. It will be convenient, therefore, if the financial settlements in the case of Part C States are not elaborate, but are based on a broad review of the position as it exists today and the needs of these areas.

828. The principles on which assets and liabilities are divided will presumably be stated in appropriate parliamentary legislation. But these principles will have to be applied to the facts of each case in the initial years after reorganisation and this will create a considerable volume of accounts work.

829. The difficulties involved in this process should not be underestimated. Normally, it takes a number of years for a complete and satisfactory division to be effected. The importance of the problem is not, of course, very great, for a notional division has been found to be workable for most purposes. Nevertheless, prolonged periods during which the division of assets and liabilities remains only notional must be regarded as unsatisfactory; and we would suggest the creation, if possible, of some special machinery for expediting the final settlements.

Inter-state agreements

830. We have stressed elsewhere the need for adequate arrangements being made for ensuring the orderly progress of the major irrigation and power projects which have already been taken up before or under the first five-year plan. A number of inter-state agreements regarding the allocation of water rights have been concluded or finalised recently. On the reorganisation of States, some of these agreements may require to be changed. In the case of the Krishna and the Godavari and the Bhakra-Nangal projects, for example, the State Governments concerned have now arrived at partial or complete agreements as a result of which planning has become easier. Similar agreements have been reached, or are likely to be reached, regarding the allocation of the cost and benefits of the Bhakra project and the utilisation of the Periyar waters for the production of power. In other cases, as in the Cauvery basin in the South, there are subsisting awards or agreements which go back many years. If no agreements are devised to adapt them to the needs of the newly-constituted States quickly some degree of confusion is likely to be caused. Provision for such adaptation may have to be made in the legislation to be enacted under Articles 3 and 4, either by specifying the rights and obligations of the prospective States or by empowering the Central Government to make the necessary adaptation in consultation with the State Governments concerned.

Legislation regarding river valleys and water disputes

831. In the course of our enquiry we came across a number of cases in which claims were preferred for the transfer of particular areas on the ground that control over the catchment area of a river or over the dam site or the benefit area was necessary. We have not attached too much importance to these suggestions, for the reason partly that legislation which has already been introduced in Parliament makes specific provision for the regulation and development of inter-state rivers.

832. The general scheme of the River Boards Bill, which was introduced in Parliament in May, 1955, is that advisory River Boards, charged with the formulation of plans for the development of inter-State rivers or river valleys, will be set up under the aegis of the Centre (finance will be provided by the Government of India). Schemes prepared by these advisory bodies are intended to be placed before the governments concerned, who may modify, reject or approve these schemes. Approved schemes will be regarded as final. If there are any difficulties or disagreements regarding these schemes,

a concerned government may raise this matter, in which case the dispute will be decided by a single arbitrator.

833. The Water Disputes Bill, 1955, also introduced in Parliament in May, 1955, contemplates that on a request from a State Government, the Centre will constitute an *ad hoc* water disputes tribunal in each case involving a water dispute. An important provision in this Bill is the prohibition of a seigniorage, or rate, or fee in respect of the use of the waters of an inter-State river.

834. As we have already pointed out in Chapter V of Part II, these two bills taken together do not perhaps clothe the Central Government with all the powers which it may need. Nevertheless, the clarification of the position in respect of inter-State rivers which is proposed is, we think, timely, and even overdue. We should recommend that the contemplated legislation should be passed and brought into force as early as possible.

Regional grievances

835. Reference has been made elsewhere in this report to the grievances of particular areas on the ground of arrested economic development. We have tried to examine these grievances, and while it has been difficult to strike a balance-sheet of the gains and losses of the various areas, so far as we have been able to judge, these complaints are, generally speaking, exaggerated.

836. The feeling that some areas have been or will be neglected, is, however, one which, whether it is rational or not, has to be taken into consideration as an existing fact. If it is at all possible, it will be desirable, therefore, to devise such arrangements in future that no State or area will have any ground for complaint.

837. Some attempts have been made in the past, mainly as a result of non-official efforts, to provide adequate assurances of non-discrimination and equal treatment along these lines. The Sri Baug Pact of 1937 in the case of Andhra, and the Akola Pact of 1947 and the Nagpur Pact of 1953 in the case of Maharashtra may be cited as examples. These pacts represent an attempt to spread as equitably as possible the benefits and advantages which may be derived from the location of important offices or institutions of the State Government and from the expenditure of the State Governments in general.

838. We have carefully examined the question whether it will be possible to suggest certain broad lines of action to the reorganised

States. Apart, however, from other difficulties, an attempt to prescribe in advance the direction in which expenditure will be incurred to meet regional or local demands seems to us to be bad in principle; and we would be reluctant to depart from the salutary principle that a Government should not be tied to commitments which it may not be able to fulfil and which may not later on reflect the needs of the times.

Special Development Boards

839. Consistently with this view, the only special arrangement for areas which are now economically undeveloped, which seems to us to be suitable, is that development boards may be constituted in these areas, wherever conditions justify such an expedient, in order that the needs of these areas may be properly studied and schemes adequate to meet them formulated. Advisory planning bodies, we understand, have been constituted in most States. Our suggestion in effect only extends this principle.

840. We have already referred in Chapter I of Part III to the possibility of a provision being made in the Constitution authorising the Centre to exercise supervisory powers in relation to the development of certain economically undeveloped areas during a period, say of ten years. This provision is only intended by way of caution. These areas will, we think, be reassured, if supervisory authority for a short period is thus retained by the Government of India.

Body to look into economic grievances of areas

841. Apart from the special needs of specific under-developed areas, there is one important aspect of the distribution of development expenditure which, in our opinion, calls for serious consideration. During the course of our investigations we found that most of the demands for constituting new States were based primarily on alleged unfair and unequal distribution of development expenditure. These complaints, it may be stated, are not confined, and cannot in the nature of things be confined to multi-lingual States, but exist also in unilingual States. As we have stated earlier, the conclusion we have reached is that, by and large, these complaints are greatly exaggerated. However, considering that such complaints and counter-complaints have proved to be a prolific source of internal discord in various States, we consider it necessary that a permanent body consisting of persons, who would inspire public confidence, should be appointed for the purpose of looking into the economic grievances

of different areas. The proposed body should serve a two-fold purpose. It should help on the one hand to remove wrong impressions, and on the other to redress the legitimate grievances of the various areas. It will be an advantage if this body includes some members of the Planning Commission and reports its findings to the National Development Council. We feel that such an arrangement will go a long way towards eliminating friction and distrust arising out of the feeling that certain areas are getting special or undue consideration at the expense of others.

Industrial location plan

842. Another important question is the equitable distribution of Central Government expenditure. Responsibility in respect of many development schemes has now passed to the Central Government, and the country is on the eve of rapid industrialisation. In these circumstances, the consideration of an industrial location plan may be of value at this stage, as it will ensure that Central Government expenditure is, as far as possible, spread uniformly all over the country.

843. This question of the location of industries has already been agitated by some States in connection with the proposed establishment of the steel and fertiliser factories which are being planned by the Government of India; and as the public sector grows in importance, claims and counter-claims by various States for a share of the Central Government's attention are likely to increase. These claims cannot, however, be dealt with satisfactorily, unless the framework of an industrial location plan, to which they can be related, is available.

844. It is not necessary at this stage to anticipate the difficulties of formulating a national policy in regard to the location of industry; and it would be premature to discuss the details of such a policy. We would recommend, however, that the entire question should be examined, so that the reorganised units might be assured or reassured that subject to the availability of natural resources and the requirements of the different industries, there would be an equitable distribution of Central Government expenditure, particularly of that part of the expenditure which will be incurred on the industrial plan.

Conclusion

845. The suggestions contained in this Chapter relate to matters which will have to be considered by the Government of India in the light of the decisions which may be taken on our report and the

manner in which they are implemented. Our purpose in discussing these questions has been mainly to invite the attention of the Government of India to the difficulties of the transition and to urge that the greatest importance should be attached to mitigating the effects of the dislocation and uncertainty which must follow any scheme of reorganisation.

CHAPTER IV

THE UNITY OF INDIA

846. We have now come to the end of our appointed task. The problem of reorganisation of States has aroused such passions and the claims which have been made are so many and so conflicting that the background against which this whole problem has to be dealt with may quite often be obscured or even forgotten. In order that the recommendations which we have made may be viewed in proper perspective, we should like to emphasise two basic facts. Firstly, the States, whether they are reorganised or not, are and will continue to be integral parts of a Union which is far and away the more real political entity and the basis of our nationhood. Secondly, the Constitution of India recognises only one citizenship, a common citizenship or the entire Indian people, with equal rights and opportunities hroughout the Union.

847. It may seem that we have merely stated what should be)bvious to all. It is, however, patent that, if the implications of these important facts had been fully appreciated and generally accepted, the question of territorial redistribution would not have developed into a major national problem of disquieting proportions. It has been most distressing to us to witness, during the course of our enquiry, a kind of border warfare in certain areas in which old comrades-in-arms in the battle for freedom have been pitted against one another in acrimonious controversy, showing little appreciation of the fact that the States are but the limbs of the same body politic and that territorial readjustments between them should not assume the form of disputes between alien powers. Deliberate efforts to whip up popular frenzy by an appeal to parochial and communal sentiment; threats of large-scale migration; assertions such as that, if a certain language group is not allowed to have an administrative unit of its own, its moral, material and even physical extinction would follow as an inevitable consequence; and finally incidents such as those in Goalpara, Parlakimedi, Ludhiana and Amritsar; all point to an acute lack of perspective and balance.

848. A great deal of this heat and controversy may prove to be a passing phase. Nevertheless, it would be unwise not to take note of these disruptive trends. One view, which is strongly held by certain sections of public opinion, is that only a unitary form of government

and division of the country into purely administrative units can provide the corrective to the separatist tendencies. We feel, however, that in the existing circumstances this approach would be somewhat unrealistic. Other methods have, therefore, to be found to keep centrifugal forces under check.

849. Unfortunately, the manner in which certain administrations have conducted their affairs has itself partly contributed to the growth of this parochial sentiment. We have referred earlier to the domicile rules which are in force in certain States, governing eligibility to State services. The desire of the local people for the State services being manned mainly by "the sons of the soil" is understandable, but only up to a point. When such devices as domicile rules operate to make the public services an exclusive preserve of the majority language group of the State, this is bound to cause discontent among the other groups, apart from impeding the free flow of talent and impairing administrative efficiency.

850. We were greatly concerned to observe that in one State for instance, domicile rules were applied not only to determine eligibility for appointment to the public services but also to regulate the awards of contracts and rights in respect of fisheries, ferries, toll-bridges, forests and excise shops. The conditions to be satisfied for acquiring a domicile in this State are also generally such as to deserve some notice. These conditions are: (a) ownership of a homestead in the State; (b) residence in such a homestead for ten years; (c) a clear intention to live in the State till death; and (d) renunciation of the old domicile, which is to be established by such circumstantial evidence as whether the applicant has landed property or other interests in his native place, or whether he pays frequent visits to that place.

851. Such stipulations, in our opinion, are not only inconsistent with Articles 15, 16 and 19 of the Constitution but go against the very conception of an Indian citizenship. We do not feel called upon to pronounce on the purely legal aspects of these restrictions, but we have no doubt whatsoever that their total effect is the exact opposite of what was intended by the Constitution.

852. In Chapter I of this Part we have already recommended that the domicile rules in force in certain States should be replaced by appropriate Parliamentary legislation as contemplated in Article 35(a)(i) of the Constitution.

853. It has, however, been alleged before us that certain State governments have imposed restrictions, in practice though not in

theory, on the acquisition of property by outsiders. It is obvious that, if such administrative malpractices exist, they should be immediately discarded. Otherwise, the concept of a common Indian citizenship would have no meaning.

854. There are certain other measures which, if adopted, will, we hope, help in correcting particularist trends and also in securing greater inter-State co-ordination for the efficient implementation of all-India policies.

855. Our first proposal is that, as far as possible, about fifty per cent of the new entrants in any cadre of an existing All-India Service should be from outside the State concerned. We understand that several State governments have already accepted the proposition that one entrant every year in the Indian Administrative Service should be taken from outside the State. We are given to understand that this amounts approximately to only one-third of the total annual allotment of personnel to the Indian Administrative Service. Besides, the principle, in the form in which it has been accepted, does not take into account the fact that twenty-five per cent of the vacancies in the Indian Administrative Service are filled by promotion. We would, therefore, recommend that, in order that the fifty per cent target might be achieved, the computation should be made after deducting the number of posts in any State to be filled by promotion; and these principles should apply to all the All-India Services. It would also be necessary to ensure that the proportion of members of the All-India Services recruited from outside the State is not reduced in practice by such devices as the deputation of officers to the Centre.

856. We also consider that, apart from the Indian Administrative Service and the Indian Police Service, some more All-India Services should now be constituted. The question of reconstituting all-India cadres for certain technical departments and particularly the suggestion that the Indian Service of Engineers should be revived, has, we understand, been under the consideration of the Union Ministries concerned for some time. The Central and State Governments have to work in very close co-operation in executing important development projects, which necessitates that technical personnel should be recruited and trained on a common basis and that they should have uniform standards of efficiency and the feeling of belonging to common and important cadres.

857. We recommend, therefore, that the following Services, namely, the Indian Service of Engineers, the Indian Forest Service, and the Indian Medical and Health Service should now be constituted.

858. The *raison d'etre* of creating All-India Services, individually or in groups, is that officers, on whom the brunt of the responsibility for administration will inevitably fall, may develop a wide and all-India outlook. This advantage will become illusory, however, if members of the All-India Services remain too long either in the service of any particular department or on deputation to the Central Government. In so far as the present All-India Services are concerned, the Centre is already aware of the problem, and transfers to and from the States are intended to be arranged regularly. It is doubtful whether, in practice, it has been easy to give effect to what the Central Government has already accepted in principle. But we think that, in the set-up which we recommend, regular transfers to and from the Centre will be even more important.

859. Another point which we would emphasise is that the training of probationers to the All-India and Central Services should be such that they should have a good introduction to the essentials of Indian geography, history, religions, customs and manners. We realise that, even if the period of training were extended, it would not be possible to impart detailed instruction in these subjects. What is desired, however, is that the probationers, when they complete their training should have an all-India outlook and should cease to consider themselves as Andhras, Tamilians, Marathas or Bengalis etc. The present emphasis on regional languages in the Universities will inevitably lead to the growth of a parochial attitude, which can only be corrected by a system of training which emphasises the all-India point of view. We understand that it has been recently agreed that a detailed knowledge of the five-year plan should form part of the curriculum of studies for the new entrants to the Indian Administrative Service. We suggest that, in addition, basic and essential knowledge of Indian history, geography, religions, customs and manners be included in the curriculum of studies for new entrants to the All-India and Central Services.

860. There is another suggestion which we wish to make about the training of the members of the All-India and Central Services. The progressive adoption of Hindi for the official purposes of the Union will, no doubt, be an important factor towards national unity. But it is of very considerable importance that languages other than Hindi should also figure much more prominently in the training programme of the All-India and Central Services than is now the case. In a recent statement of the policy of the Government of India, regarding the medium in which competitive examinations for the All-India Services are to be conducted in future, there is a refer-

ence to a proposal that candidates from the Hindi-speaking areas should be asked to pass a qualifying examination in one Indian language other than Hindi. The details of the Government of India's policy will have to be settled in due course. We only wish to suggest that the principle might be extended to the Central Services also and to add that the arrangements proposed are essential in order to ensure the transfer of service personnel from one State to another. The Indian language other than Hindi should preferably be a South Indian language.

861. Guided by the consideration that the principal organs of State should be so constituted as to inspire confidence and to help in arresting parochial trends, we would also recommend that at least one-third of the number of Judges in a High Court should consist of persons who are recruited from outside that State. In making appointments to a High Court bench, professional standing and ability must obviously be the over-riding considerations. But the suggestion we have made will extend the field of choice and will have the advantage of regulating the staffing of the higher judiciary as far as possible on the same principles as in the case of the Civil Service.

862. As we have already observed, the progressive adoption of Hindi for the official purposes of the Union should operate as a unifying factor. A common national language, however, to be a really integrating force should have a wider range. English, though a foreign language, has helped to bring the people of different regions in India closer to each other firstly because it has been the official language both at the central and at the provincial levels, and secondly because it has been the medium of instruction for higher education throughout the country: It has, therefore, provided a common vehicle for higher thought as well as for administrative activity and has helped to maintain common standards at the higher educational institutions.

863. Hindi is to replace English to a limited extent. At the national level Hindi will replace English, but in the States it is to be succeeded to a large extent by the regional languages. The Official Language Commission, recently appointed by the Government of India, will, no doubt, consider fully the manner in which the constitutional provision about the adoption of Hindi as the official language is to be enforced. It is, however, quite obvious that replacement of English bv Hindi should be so phased that there may

be no vacuum from the point of view of social and political intercourse between different parts of the country and that standards of higher education in the country do not suffer.

864. Any possible decline in the standards of education must be viewed with grave concern, because with her progressive advance in the political, social, economic and technical fields, India will require men of high calibre, and the training of such men must depend on our educational system.

865. A wide field of choice for higher education and migration from universities and other institutions for higher education has been possible in this country, not only because English has so far been the medium of instruction in these institutions, but also because the standards of teaching and research have been, generally speaking, comparable. Some of these institutions are contemplating the adoption of the regional languages as the media of instruction. If English in any of these institutions is replaced prematurely, and if facilities are not provided for acquiring necessary proficiency in that language in the interests of higher research, standards of higher education are bound to suffer.

866. It has to be remembered that English is an important international language and that a knowledge of it makes available to Indian students the results of advanced studies and higher research in other progressive countries. As the Secondary Education Commission has pointed out, provision has been made in many foreign countries for acquiring a knowledge of English or other foreign languages. In the U.S.S.R., for example, a foreign language is compulsory subject in the Soviet middle and secondary schools. Suitable measures will, therefore, have to be adopted to encourage the study of English and other foreign languages at our important educational institutions, even after the adoption of the regional languages as the media of instruction.

867. We fully realise the importance of the study of Hindi and the regional languages, but we feel that for the present the use of English in higher technical studies does not come into conflict with the growth of these languages.

868. From the point of view of national unity, it is also of great importance that there should be closer understanding between the north and the south. All institutions and establishments which help to bring about such an understanding should receive particular encouragement from the Government of India. The Osmania University in Hyderabad is one of such institutions. We suggest

that this University may be placed under the Central Government. The medium of instruction at this University should be Hindi; and if standards of instruction at this institution are maintained at a high level, this would attract students from the adjoining areas and be of advantage to the South.

869. We also consider it necessary that another central university should be established further south with emphasis on Hindi and that in the principal North Indian universities there should be faculties for the study of South Indian languages and cultures.

870. The proposals which we have made in the preceding paragraphs are intended to bring about greater administrative integrity and to provide against any particularist trends being promoted within the administration itself or in the country at large. Important as these measures are, it is obvious that they are by themselves not adequate to give a deeper content to Indian nationalism. National unity can develop into a positive and living force capable of holding the nation together against the disruptive and narrower loyalties only if there is a real moral and mental integration of the people. Fortunately, forces making for such integration are already at work. What is necessary is that nothing should be done to impede their freeplay. We should like to say something on this subject before we conclude.

871. India is now on the eve of vast economic and social changes. These changes must affect every institution and will call for a constant review of our traditional methods of thought and ways of life.

872. One of the important developments in recent times has, for example, been the country's conversion to the ideal of social, political and economic equality. We do not mean to minimise the difficulties in the way of realising this ideal of equality, to which the country is now committed. Nevertheless, it is a great advance that the comparatively backward sections of the community are now in the picture. An important source of tension within the body politic is, therefore, being progressively removed.

873. Internal migration on a scale which renders unrealistic any attempt to regard the linguistic situation in any area as static is another major factor which has now to be taken into account. Economic opportunity and the rapid development of communications have contributed, in recent years, to this general increase in mobility within the Indian Union. Even age-old conceptions regarding personal laws, including in particular the law of succession to property in Hindu society which used to be regarded as unalterable,

are now in the process of being changed, to suit the needs and requirements of a modern and developing society. With the vast increase in industrialisation that is now being planned under the auspices of the Centre, it is also inevitable that migration within the country will increase even further. More and more cities or pockets, which are Indian rather than provincial in character, are, in consequence, bound to come into existence all over the country.

874. The consequences of economic planning to which the country is now committed are very great. When resources are mobilised and investment is undertaken at the national rather than at the regional or State level, the States will inevitably get more and more integrated in a joint endeavour for the economic advancement of the nation as a whole.

875. In formulating our proposals for reorganisation, we have naturally been most anxious to discover and to respect the greatest common measure of agreement between the various ponits of view. But we have also taken note of the operation of the dynamic forces to which reference has been made in the preceding paragraphs. We, therefore, wish to emphasise that considered in its proper perspective, the reorganisation of the States can only be regarded as providing the necessary adjustments to remove tensions and to enable the Union to function more effectively.

876. It is the Union of India that is the basis of our nationality. It is in that Union that our hopes for the future are centred. The States are but the limbs of the Union, and while we recognise that the limbs must be healthy and strong and any element of weakness in them should be eradicated, it is the strength and the stability of the Union and its capacity to develop and evolve that should be the governing consideration of all changes in the country.

877. Regionalism has a legitimate place in a country as large as India, but unless its limitations are recognised, and the supremacy of the Union not merely in the political but also in the economic thinking of the country is fully accepted, it will be a source of weakness to us as a nation. If this is generally realised, we have no doubt that the issues arising out of the reorganisation of the States will not be allowed to assume the proportions of major political controversies.

878. Free India is now on the move. What has already been achieved can be viewed with a measure of legitimate pride. The manner in which the very difficult problem of princely India was solved in the anxious and bewildering circumstances following the

Partition will, by itself, be a standing testimony to the political wisdom and strength of the Indian people and their firm determination to eradicate artificial barriers and cramping loyalties.

879. We conclude in the hope that the scheme of reorganisation which we have proposed will be viewed against this background and that men of goodwill will co-operate with those charged with the onerous responsibility of reconciling competitive claims and of balancing regional sentiments with national interests in giving effect to the decisions which might be taken, in an atmosphere of tolerance and understanding.

S. FAZL ALI,*
Chairman.

H. N. KUNZRU,
Member.

K. M. PANIKKAR,**
Member.

P. C. CHAUDHURI,
Secretary.

NEW DELHI,
Dated 30th September, 1955.

*It should be mentioned that, owing to my long connection with Bihar, I have refrained from taking any part in investigating and deciding the territorial disputes between:

(1) Bihar and West Bengal; and

(2) Bihar and Orissa.

Further, whatever is to be found in this report in regard to Himachal Pradesh is subject to my separate note on that area which has been appended to this report.

S. FAZL ALI.

**Subject to my note on Uttar Pradesh.

K. M. PANIKKAR.

Note on Himachal Pradesh

I regret that I am unable to subscribe to the recommendations which my esteemed colleagues propose to make about Himachal Pradesh. In my judgment, this State should continue as a separate unit and should be under the direct control of the Central Government.

2. The opinion which I have expressed is not very different from the opinion which appears to have been formed by the States Ministry of the Government of India shortly after the State of Himachal Pradesh came into existence. This is clear from certain letters issued on behalf of the Ministry defining the objective it had in view in regard to the future of this State and from a note prepared after Sardar Patel's death incorporating his views in regard to the Part C States. This note shows that while Sardar Patel contemplated the ultimate merger of the majority of the Part C States in the neighbouring areas, his intention was to continue Himachal Pradesh under "Central guardianship and tutelage" as "any merger with the Punjab was bound to be locally unpopular".

3. It is true that we are not bound by the opinion of the States Ministry, but I think that we should not completely disregard it. In any event, as a result of my own independent investigation, I have, for reasons which I am about to state, come to the conclusion that it will not be wise to merge Himachal Pradesh in the Punjab.

4. I am convinced that there is a great deal of uneasiness among the people of Himachal Pradesh over the question of its being merged in the Punjab and that this feeling is both genuine and widespread. As I have already mentioned, shortly after the creation of Himachal Pradesh it was sensed by Sardar Patel that the proposal to merge it in the Punjab would be locally unpopular. Further, it appears that early in 1950 there was a proposal that the jurisdiction of the East Punjab High Court should be extended to Himachal, but no action was taken in regard to this suggestion because it seems to have been recognised that "the sentiment of the hill people was opposed to the extension of the authority of any of the administrative organs of the East Punjab to Himachal". It would thus be seen that long before the Commission came into existence it was known that any attempt to merge Himachal Pradesh in the Punjab would cause

considerable dissatisfaction in the area. That the attitude of the people has not changed since, is apparent from the fact that with the exception of two small groups, all the political parties—the Congress, the Praja Socialists and the Communists—as also the great majority of the persons who appeared before the Commission have strongly opposed the merger proposal.

5. What seems to account for the great anxiety of the people of Himachal Pradesh not to be associated with the Punjab is their deep-seated distrust of the men of the plains. It is just possible that this feeling of distrust is to some extent a legacy of the pre-Independence princely regime which employed a large number of retired officers from the Punjab who, for some reason or other, were not able to win the confidence of the local people. It may also be partly due to advantage being taken, in the past, of the ignorance and poverty of the people of Himachal Pradesh by persons from outside the State. However that may be, it seems to me that the forcing of a permanent arrangement, such as is envisaged in the merger proposal, on an unwilling and unequal party will be extremely unpopular and will not provide the mutual good-will and co-operation so necessary for the successful functioning of democracy.

6. The extremely backward and exploited people of this State have, since their emancipation from feudal regime, gained a keen awareness of their new status and opportunity. It is highly important that no step is taken which may damp their new-found enthusiasm and eagerness to progress and to catch up with the more advanced sections of the Indian population. From this point of view, placing them in a position of subordination—which merger will amount to at this stage—would, in my opinion, instead of contributing to their progress, greatly retard it. Obviously, the voice of this hill area in the common legislature would be an extremely feeble voice and the sheer weight of numbers would drown even this voice.

7. It seems to me that in the interests of the Punjab itself it is desirable that the two areas should be kept separate. A somewhat disturbing feature of the political life of the Punjab today is the existence of certain differences—based on grievances, real or imaginary—among its three well marked regions. To bring another region with a distinctiveness, individuality and problems of its own into the picture will only complicate matters and add considerably to the difficulties of the Government of the Punjab. Punjab will have to face a new minority problem, as the people of Himachal

Pradesh feel that they have not much in common with the people of the Punjab.

8. A weighty argument in favour of merger is that there will be saving on expenditure by providing for a common legislature, a common High Court, a common Head of the State and a common administrative set-up. But administrative economy by itself will be of little value, if sufficient attention is not paid to the much more important consideration of administrative convenience and efficiency. A common legislature will not adequately meet this requirement because, as I have already stated, the influence of the members of Himachal Pradesh will be hardly felt in the legislature wherein representation is based on numbers. The system of judicial administration now in force in Himachal Pradesh, under which the Judicial Commissioner visits every district, seems to me admirably to suit the requirements of her people who need cheap and expeditious justice. The expensive and time-consuming formalities involved in taking the appeals to the Punjab High Court, which is not so easily accessible, will rob the hillmen of the advantage which they enjoy today. Nor will a common head of the State serve the purpose adequately, because what is needed in the hills is the intimate and personal touch of the head of the State with the common man. Having regard to these disadvantages consequent on merger, the saving that will be effected will not be of much significance. The extra cost that a separate administration under the Central Government might entail will be amply compensated by the advantages of a sympathetic and intensive administration.

9. I am also greatly impressed by an important argument presented in one of the memoranda submitted to us, which is quoted below:

> "The Punjab has two very great problems to solve (1) the communal problem and (2) the law and order problem. The deteriorating relations between the Hindus and Sikhs in the Punjab have caused concern not only to the Punjab Government but to the Government of India......The disease runs very gravely (even) in the services......Himachal Pradesh, fortunately, is spared all this malady; for it is a State predominantly of the Hindus and no communal problem whatsoever exists here. Even the language problem, which has baffled the administrators in Punjab is non-existent in Himachal Pradesh. People speak Pahari, the more educated being influenced by chaste Hindi. Hindi alone is taught in

schools and other institutions. Thus the State is not troubled at all by the complicated communal and language problems of the Punjab....Any merger of the two would completely upset the present social order in the hills and is bound to result in a very strong reaction from the people."

10. The advocates of the amalgamation of Himachal Pradesh with the Punjab lay some emphasis on the economic links between the two areas, and they particularly refer to the advantages to be derived from the orderly implementation of the Bhakra project. I am, however, unable to see how this fact by itself should lead inevitably to the inference that the two areas must be integrated. Apart from certain other over-riding considerations favouring retention of Himachal Pradesh as a separate unit, attention may be drawn to paragraph 186 of the report wherein we have stated:

> "India's development plan may increasingly take the shape of a centrally-directed effort to locate and implement projects which are intended to give the highest return within the shortest periods, the benefits accruing to the country as a whole and not merely to any particular areas or regions in it."

With the Centre controlling and administering Himachal Pradesh, I do not visualise any difficulty whatsoever in the way of the orderly implementation of plans regarded vital for the development of the plains. On the other hand, I should think that a Central administration in Himachal would, instead of interfering with, help the task of preserving the catchment area of the Sutlej and the Beas and of undertaking the necessary soil conservation measures. The amalgamation of the two States may understandably be advantageous to the Punjab in certain respects; but it is somewhat doubtful whether Himachal Pradesh would be substantially benefited by it or, at any rate, the benefit which will accrue will be such as to out-weigh the undesirable consequences of a forced amalgamation. As for the argument that the Punjab needs the transfer of some area of Himachal Pradesh in connection with the Bhakra project, I would leave the matter to the Central Government which might take a decision after fully considering the report of the Hejmadi Committee and the feelings of the local people. On my part, I refrain from making any suggestion in respect of this question as we had no occasion to hear the parties concerned.

11. One of the arguments against small units is that for manning their services they do not usually attract or retain talent, since they have few opportunities and rewards to offer. There is also a tendency in such small units for the Government to undertake detailed and direct administration, and thereby deprive the services of their initiative, drive and sense of responsibility. These considerations will not, as far as I can see, have much force in the case of Himachal Pradesh. As a centrally-administered unit, its administrative personnel would be drawn from the All-India Services who will not have to work under the suggested handicaps and can be expected to place national interests above parochial interests and bring to bear on their administrative work the perspective and breadth of outlook so necessary for a successful administration.

12. Himachal Pradesh is a backward area on the development of which considerable outlay is obviously called for, at least for some time. It is extremely doubtful if the Punjab can shoulder the burden and develop the area in as rapid a manner as would seem desirable in this strategic northern border state. In any case, it being admitted on all hands that the Centre would have to spend large sums of money on the development of the area for some time to come, even if it were merged in the Punjab, I do not see why in these circumstances the area should not be under the direct control of the Centre. We have a special responsibility in keeping the people of the border areas like Chini and Pangi and also those of the rest of the Himachal Pradesh contented and happy and in guarding against any feeling being created in them that they are not so well looked after as the people across the border. With this special responsibility and with the imperative need for guarding the frontier exposed to infiltration, the national interests will, in my opinion, be best served by the Centre directly controlling the area. In my opinion, having recourse to such palliatives as the appointment of a Minister belonging to Himachal Pradesh in the Punjab Cabinet and the setting up of a Special Development Board will neither satisfy the people of Himachal Pradesh nor meet their needs. The appointment of a local person as Minister has not given satisfaction in other areas, the complaint being that since his selection rests with the Chief Minister the Minister concerned is sometimes apt to overlook the true interests of the region in his anxiety to maintain good relations with the rest of the Cabinet. The Development Board, however carefully constituted, will after all be a poor substitute for direct Central administration which will exclusively devote itself to the rapid progress of this region.

13. The Commission has been told that after some years Central aid would not be necessary. It may be that this is too optimistic a view, but, however that may be, it appears to me that any expenditure that may be incurred by the Central Government in developing this backward area and bringing the people living in it to the level of the more advanced sections to be found in the rest of the country will be fully justified in so far as it will serve the larger interests of the country.

14. Himachal Pradesh is a typical instance where the arguments in favour of small units outlined in paragraph 212 of this report can be applied with advantage. As a separate unit, it may be able to provide an intensive programme of social welfare measures which would not be possible if it is merged in the Punjab. In so far as the need for such a programme is pressing in this backward area, the case of Himachal Pradesh for separate existence need hardly be emphasized.

15. In paragraph 285 of this report it has been recommended that wherever the vital, strategic and other considerations are involved, the areas have to be administered by the Centre. I believe that Himachal Pradesh is one of such areas and, therefore, I would strongly recommend its being treated as a centrally-administered territory.

S. FAZL ALI.

NEW DELHI,
Dated 30th September 1955.

Note on Uttar Pradesh

The position of Uttar Pradesh in the Union of India is something which no one interested in the reorganisation of the States of India can legitimately overlook. It contains over 63 million people or over one-sixth of the population of India. It is divided into 51 districts, and the average population in each district is over 1.2 millions. An army of officials (nearly 260,000) is required to administer it. The uniqueness of this position will become apparent when it is remembered that the next largest State in India, Bihar, has only a population of 40 millions (or less than two-thirds of Uttar Pradesh), while most of the other States have less than 30 millions. In population *the Uttar Pradesh is nearly equal to Andhra, Telangana, Karnataka and Kerala* put together, larger than the combined population of the Punjab, Rajasthan and the new Madhya Pradesh (including Mahakosal, Vindhya Pradesh, Madhya Bharat and Bhopal). The imbalance created by the existence of a State of this size in a federation seems to me to be fairly obvious.

2. I consider it essential for the successful working of a federation that the units should be fairly evenly balanced. Too great a disparity is likely to create not only suspicion and resentment but generate forces likely to undermine the federal structure itself and thereby be a danger to the unity of the country. This is clearly recognised everywhere. In most federal constitutions, though wide variations exist in respect of the population and resources of the unit, care is taken to limit the influence and authority of the larger States. Thus in the United States of America, for example, though the States are of varying population and resources and the State of New York has many times the population, say of Nevada, the constitution provides for equal representation of every state in the Senate. In the Soviet Union also, in which Great Russia has a larger population than most other units of the Federation taken together, representation in the House of Nationalities is weighted against her so that the other units of the Federation may not be dominated by the larger unit. In the Bismarckian Reich again, though Prussia had a dominant position from the point of view of population, she was given less representation in the *Reichsrat* or the house representing the states than she was entitled to (less than one-third) and the permanent presidency of that body was vested in Bavaria, clearly demonstrating that even here—where there was a concentration of

political, military and economic power in one state—it was considered necessary, in the interests of the union, to give weightage to the smaller units and also to reduce Prussia to the position of a minority in the *Reichsrat,* States Council, which enjoyed greater powers than the *Reichstag* or the House of the People.

3. Unfortunately, the Indian Constitution contains no such provision to diminish the disparity or to counteract the dominant influence of one unit, let alone to secure the equality of the States. In both Houses of Parliament representation is, broadly speaking, on the basis of population. Thus in the Lok Sabha, Uttar Pradesh has 86 members (out of 499) and in the Rajya Sabha it has 31 (out of 216).

4. If one were realistic and took into consideration the manner in which governments functioned all over the world, it would be easy to see that this preponderant influence which would accrue to a very large unit could be abused, and would in any case be resented by all the other constitutent units. Modern governments are controlled, to a greater or lesser extent, by party machines, within which the voting power of a numerically strong group goes a very long way. It is also undeniable that there is a natural tendency for the representatives of a state to form or to be brought together into such a powerful political bloc. The real issue, therefore, is whether it is desirable to place any unit in a position to exercise an unduly large measure of political influence.

5. The consequence of the present imbalance, caused by the denial of the federal principle of equality of units, has been to create feelings of distrust and resentment in all the States outside Uttar Pradesh. Not only in the southern States but also in the Punjab, Bengal and elsewhere the view was generally expressed before the Commission that the present structure of government led to the dominance of Uttar Pradesh in all-India matters. The existence of this feeling will hardly be denied by anyone. That it will be a danger to our unity, if such feelings are allowed to exist and remedies are not sought and found now, will also not be denied. Since the normal constitutional device for equalising grave disparities between the units in a federation, that is the provision of equal or at least heavily weighted representation in the house representing the federal principle, is not now possible in our case, and even if it were possible, would not now be a satisfactory solution, in view of the dominant position of the House of the People, the only remedy open to us is to reconstitute the overgrown state in such a manner as to lessen the differences—in short to partition the state. This seems to me an obvious proposition.

6. The objections which have been advanced against this proposal may now be considered.

7. One of the commonest arguments advanced before us by leaders in Uttar Pradesh was that the existence of a large, powerful and well-organised state in the Gangetic Valley was a guarantee for India's unity; that such a state would be able to correct the disruptive tendencies of other states, and to ensure the ordered progress of India. The same idea has been put to us in many other forms such as that Uttar Pradesh is the "back bone of India", the centre from which all other states derive their ideas and their culture, etc. It is not necessary to examine these claims seriously for nothing is more certain to undermine our growing sense of unity than this claim of suzerainty or paramountcy by one state over others.

8. A second argument which has been advanced is that the Uttar Pradesh is a homogeneous and integrated state and that to partition it would be to ruin its economy and to create discontent. In this connection the agitation that followed the partition of Bengal has been pointed out to us as a warning. The process of administrative unification of this area started only in 1775 when Asaf-ud-daula made over to the English East India Company some territory in the south-eastern portion of the State as it is constituted today. The doab between the Ganga and the Yamuna was acquired by the British from Sadat Ali, Nawab of Oudh, only in 1801, and Kumaon and Garhwal were annexed in 1816 after the Anglo-Gurkha war. The territory north of the Yamuna was ceded by the Mahrattas between 1803 and 1805, after the Second Mahratta War. Oudh, of course, was annexed very late (by Lord Dalhousie in 1856). For all practical purposes, therefore, the existing State of Uttar Pradesh has had a continuous history of less than a hundred years. The argument that it is a well-knit area which cannot be broken up without undesirable consequences is not, in these circumstances, impressive.

9. On the other hand, there is plenty of evidence that nothing has happened during these hundred years to alter the basic fact that this area has but little unity. There is or can be very little in common between the still nomadic inhabitants of the Garhwal and Kumaon Himalayas or of the hilly area of Bundelkhand on the one hand and the inhabitants of the fertile Gangetic Valley on the other. Even within the plains, the Khadar and Bungar (dry) areas in the Meerut division are quite different from the fertile valley of the Ganga which has been further enriched by the Ganga Canal. Not unnaturally, the problems of these areas also differ; and

an administration which has so large a population to look after is not necessarily in the best position to attend to the particular regional problems of these areas.

10. The example of Bengal quoted as a warning does not bear examination. Bengal was a historic unity, and besides, its partition was frankly for the purpose of creating a Muslim majority unit in East Bengal. The partition of Bengal was thus not merely an injustice to the Bengali people but an attempt to favour one community at the expense of another. The present proposal is based on purely political and administrative grounds and does not cause injustice to any one.

11. Thirdly, it has been contended that the size of the Uttar Pradesh contributes to economy in administration. In its memorandum submitted to this Commission, the Uttar Pradesh Government has stated that the percentage of expenditure on civil administration in Uttar Pradesh is lower than in many other Part A States; and from this, the conclusion has been drawn that the existing State of Uttar Pradesh is in a position to save considerably on overheads. I find it somewhat difficult to accept this argument. There are several States in India where the percentage of expenditure on administrative services is less than in the Uttar Pradesh, as the following figures from Appendix IX of the Report of the Finance Commission, 1952, will indicate:

STATES	1950-51	1951-52	1952-53
Assam	*19.6*	20.4	*16.7*
Bihar	30.0	*26.4*	25.4
Bombay	*25.7*	*26.6*	*24.2*
Madhya Pradesh	28.9	27.7	*23.1*
Madras	*27.6*	27.9	25.6
Orissa	*24.6*	27.9	26.3
Punjab	31.2	30.6	29.9
Uttar Pradesh	28.4	27.0	24.6
West Bengal	*25.3*	27.7	25.5
Hyderabad	*26.1*	*26.0*	*20.0*
Madhya Bharat	*24.1*	*26.6*	*23.1*
Mysore	*12.9*	*15.0*	*13.1*
Pepsu	28.6	32.3	28.0
Rajasthan	29.6	29.8	28.5
Saurashtra	34.6	31.4	31.0
Travancore-Cochin	*12.0*	*12.3*	*11.4*

(Percentage figures which are lower than that of the Uttar Pradesh have been italicised). Even more revealing is the *per capita* expenditure on general administration. In 1950-51, this was 0·8 for Uttar Pradesh. For Assam, Bihar, Mysore and Travancore-Cochin, the figure was less, while it was the same for Madhya Pradesh, Orissa, West Bengal and Hyderabad. In 1951-52, again, the *per capita* expenditure on general administration was less in Bihar, Hyderabad and Travancore-Cochin. In 1952-53, it was less in Assam, Bihar, Madhya Pradesh, Orissa, Hyderabad, Mysore and Travancore-Cochin.

12. Moreover, the test of economical and efficient administration is obviously whether a State is or has been in a position to increase the expenditure on nation-building services. It does not appear that the Uttar Pradesh can claim any particular advantage or achievements in this matter. Again I give certain figures from Appendix IX of the Finance Commission's Report. The *per capita* expenditure on social services in Uttar Pradesh in 1950-51 was Rs. 2.4, against Rs. 3.1 for Assam, Rs. 6.0 for Bombay, Rs. 3.3 for Madras, Rs. 3.1 for Punjab, Rs. 3.6 for West Bengal, Rs. 3.2 for Hyderabad, Rs. 3.9 for Madhya Bharat, Rs. 6.9 for Mysore, Rs. 3.4 for Pepsu, Rs. 5.2 for Saurashtra and Rs. 4.2 for Travancore-Cochin. The *per capita* expenditure on social services in Uttar Pradesh for 1950-51 was the same as for the undeveloped State of Rajasthan, *viz.*, Rs. 2.4. In 1951-52, only in Bihar and Orissa was the *per capita* expenditure on social services less than in Uttar Pradesh. As against Rs. 2.4 for Uttar Pradesh, the figure was as high as Rs. 5.7 in both Bombay and Mysore. Even in Rajasthan the figure was Rs. 2.8. In 1952-53, the tale was repeated and only in Bihar and Orissa was *per capita* expenditure on social service less than in Uttar Pradesh. As against Rs. 2.7 for Uttar Pradesh, Mysore had a figure of Rs. 6.8 and Bombay Rs. 6.0. The same story is revealed in the matter of education. In all the years from 1950-51 to 1952-53, only Bihar and Orissa have spent less per head on education than Uttar Pradesh; all other States have spent more. As against Rs. 1.1 in 1950-51 for Uttar Pradesh, Bombay spent Rs. 3.5.; in 1951-52, Bombay spent Rs. 3.4, as against Rs. 1.2 for Uttar Pradesh; in 1952-53, Bombay spent Rs. 3.6, Mysore Rs. 3.7, Travancore-Cochin Rs. 3.6 and Saurashtra Rs. 3.0, as against Rs. 1.3 for Uttar Pradesh. These figures are revealing enough.

13. Further, I find no evidence to justify the claim that the Uttar Pradesh Government because of the size of the State has been a particularly efficient one. Uttar Pradesh has the lowest literacy of all the Part A States in India including Orissa and even some of the Part B and C States. The following figures from the Census Report of 1951 show how bad the position is:

STATE	*PERCENTAGE*
Andhra	15·0
Assam	18·1
Bihar	12·2
Bombay	24·6
Madras	21·8
Madhya Pradesh . .	13·5
Orissa	15·8
Punjab	16·1
Uttar Pradesh . . .	10·8
West Bengal . . .	24·5
Mysore	20·3
Saurashtra . . .	18·5
Travancore-Cochin . .	46·4
Ajmer	20·1
Coorg	27.2
Delhi	38·4
Kutch	17·1
Manipur	11·4
Tripura	15·5

(vide Census Paper No. 5, 1954)

14. Even the report on education in the States of the Indian Union which gives slightly different figures does not alter the fact that Uttar Pradesh is now probably the most backward Part A State in the matter of education. Nor could the State claim that in the matter of medical services, road transportation and maintenance of law and order it is in a better position than Bombay or the Southern Indian States.

15. The argument put forward by some of the M.L.As. from the western districts in their memorandum submitted to us clearly show that the claim of homogeneity and the desire of the different areas of the Uttar Pradesh to remain together have, to say the least, been over-stated. The points they have raised deserve consideration and indicate that in some parts of the State at least there is a feeling of serious dissatisfaction. I have no desire to go into the merits of the complaints made by them and the arguments they have advanced in favour of the separation of the western districts beyond saying that they provide evidence of the existence of a considerable body of opinion desiring, on administrative and economic grounds, the creation of a separate state in Western Uttar Pradesh. It has been

argued that these demands are of recent origin and therefore do not deserve serious consideration. The agitation for separation may not be of old standing but then it has to be remembered that substantial economic and social development by the State has been taken up only recently and economic rivalries have, therefore, only recently come to the forefront.

16. Lastly, it has been held that even accepting that the present imbalance created by the disproportionate size of Uttar Pradesh is something which requires consideration, there is no case for a partition of the state as the imbalance is not due to anything Uttar Pradesh itself has done, but is the result of other states having been partitioned. It is argued, that when Bengal, Madras and the Punjab existed as unpartitioned states, there was no great disparity between the major units and if as a result of the creation of Pakistan the Punjab and Bengal were partitioned and if further the Andhras and the Tamils could not live together and had therefore to separate, these provide no justification for reducing the size of Uttar Pradesh. Granted that the present predominance of Uttar Pradesh is due to the division of Bengal and the partition of Madras for neither of which Uttar Pradesh is in any way to blame. But the essential point to consider is that a new situation has thereby been created which affects the political structure of India and generates forces likely to affect its unity and stability. In such circumstances, it is in my opinion irrelevant to consider whether Uttar Pradesh had any responsibility in bringing about the present situation. The plain fact is that the present situation has to be faced in the general interests of India, especially from the point of view of eliminating those developments and trends which create suspicion and resentment in other States situated further away from the capital.

17. If a partition of Uttar Pradesh would cause hardship to any considerable section of people of the residual State, or generally create political instability, then the opposition to it could have been understood. No such arguments have been advanced. In fact even after a partition of the kind suggested below, Uttar Pradesh will still have a population of over 40 millions and will continue to be the biggest unit in India. It would have the major industrial area of Kanpur, and would include the cities of Allahabad, Lucknow and Banaras. The State would still have a larger population than Bihar and Bombay (as we have proposed it to be reconstituted), and the present situation would be greatly remedied.

18. From the point of view of the interests of the people of Uttar Pradesh, the partition would involve no hardship. The districts of Dehra Dun, Naini Tal and Pilibhit would be left in residuary Uttar Pradesh, which would thus have control over the headworks of the Sarda Canal system. The river and canal waters would have to be shared between the new State and the residuary Uttar Pradesh. This should not cause any difficulties, as such sharing is the normal feature in India. The various parts of residuary Uttar Pradesh, including Kumaon Division, would also be physically contiguous. Indeed, the partition would be greatly to the advantage of the people of Uttar Pradesh, as the present unmanageable size of this State, as I have pointed out earlier, stands in the way of efficient administration.

19. We are today at a critical stage of our political evolution. The problem of the reorganisation of the States touches the very root of our political structure. We are proposing now a rationalisation of the units which constitute the federation and it is our hope that the states constituted as we have proposed will provide a sound and strong foundation for our unity. If on this occasion when the whole problem of the states' structure in relation to the Centre is being seriously considered, we omit to rectify what I consider to be the major and basic weakness of the Indian Constitution—the extraordinary disparity between one unit and the rest—then in my opinion we will only be strengthening the forces of disunity by making it practically impossible to tackle this problem at any later stage. I am convinced that the decision the Government of India takes about Uttar Pradesh will determine the course of our evolution the sanctity, the strength and the faith of the people in our Constitution, which should be the palladium of our rights and the source of our political unity. It is my deep conviction that if at this time when the whole issue is before the country, this unnatural feature of our Constitution is not set aright, the faith of the people in the Constitution—which consciously or otherwise provides for the predominance of one area—will be weakened. It is solely out of this feeling that I have ventured to place my views on record.

The proposal

1. My proposal is that a new State should be created consisting of the Meerut, Agra, Rohilkhand and Jhansi Divisions of Uttar Pradesh (*minus* Dehra Dun district of Meerut Division and Pilibhit district of Rohilkhand Division), the district of Datia from Vindhya Pradesh and the four districts of Bhind, Morena, Gird (Gwalior) and Shivpuri from Madhya Bharat.

2. The total area of this State would be 51,346 sq. miles, and the total population, according to the 1951 Census, will be 24,365,931.

3. The area of residuary Uttar Pradesh would be 74,998 sq. miles, and the population 41,182,075, according to the 1951 Census.

4. The new State might have Agra as its capital and might be called the "State of Agra". Agra will be conveniently situated from the point of view of communications. The State thus constituted would be manageable in size and population, and will generally speaking be homogeneous with resources sufficient to carry out its development programmes.

5. The current revenue of the districts included in the proposed Agra State was of the order of Rs. 27-28 crores, with a surplus of Rs. 1 to 1·5 crores, during the period of three years ending March, 1953. The current revenue of residuary Uttar Pradesh was of the order of Rs. 35·5 crores during the same period, with a deficit of Rs. 3·75 to 4 crores. The size of the revenue budget has increased, for various reasons, in the case of both the units since March, 1953. But there is no reason to anticipate that Western Uttar Pradesh will have to face financial embarrassment. Equally, Eastern Uttar Pradesh will be able to make up its initial deficit by reviewing some of its taxation measures. The new Finance Commission will, no doubt, take all factors into account and try to minimise the deficit of residuary Uttar Pradesh.

K. M. PANIKKAR.

NEW DELHI,
Dated 30th September 1955.

SUMMARY OF CONCLUSIONS AND RECOMMENDATIONS.

I. States of the Indian Union.

The present structure of the States of the Indian Union has been largely determined by the accidents and circumstances attending the expansion of British rule in India. (Paragraph 14).

2. The formation of British Indian provinces in the eighteenth and nineteenth centuries was governed by considerations of administrative convenience and economy and reasons of military strategy and security. With the emergence of nationalism towards the end of the nineteenth century the policy of balance and counterpoise began to override purely administrative considerations in making territorial changes. (Paragraphs 15 to 27).

3. At the time of their integration the former princely states were in different stages of development. Some transitional expedients had, therefore, to be adopted to fit these units into the constitutional structure of India which added to the disparities already existing between British Indian provinces. These disparities led to the classification of the States of the Indian Union into three categories, namely, Part A, Part B and Part C States. (Paragraphs 28 to 40).

4. No State of the Indian Union represents a pre-existing sovereign unit. A special feature of the Indian Constitution is that it empowers Parliament to admit or establish new States, to increase or diminish the area of an existing State or to alter its boundaries. (Paragraphs 41 to 43).

II. Rationale of Reorganisation

5. The British gave only qualified support to the linguistic principle in making territorial adjustments between administrative units. (Paragraphs 46 to 50).

6. The Indian National Congress accepted in 1920 linguistic redistribution of provinces as a political objective. During recent years, however, there has been a growing recognition of the need to balance the linguistic principle with other factors such as national unity, administrative, economic and other considerations. (Paragraphs 51 to 66).

7. Andhra was formed by the separation of the Telugu-speaking districts of Madras but in determining the boundaries of even this State factors like cultural affinity, administrative convenience and economic well-being were considered along with language. (Paragraphs 68 to 71).

III. Time for Reorganisation.

8. The problem of the reorganisation of States is urgent as with large-scale planning the country has to think in terms of enduring political units. The integration of States has removed the main hurdle in the way of rationalisation of the existing units. Further deferment of a general reorganisation will cause dissatisfaction and disappointment. (Paragraphs 72 to 91).

IV. Factors bearing on Reorganisation

9. In proposing any changes in the existing structure, due consideration should be given to the unsettling consequences of reorganisation. The changes proposed should be such as would compensate, in terms of the welfare of the people, for the administrative dislocation and the heavy burden on the administrative and financial resources of the country which they entail. (Paragraphs 92 to 106).

10. In the interests of national unity, it is necessary that the administrative and political structure of the country should be based on the primacy of the nation. (Paragraphs 107 to 112).

11. The administrative set-up in strategic areas should be determined primarily by considerations of national security. When border areas are not under the direct control of the Centre, it would be safer to have relatively large and resourceful States. (Paragraphs 113 to 116).

12. It is neither possible nor desirable to reorganise States on the basis of a single test of either language or culture; a balanced approach, which takes all relevant factors into account, is necessary. (Paragraphs 117 to 169).

13. Financial viability has an important bearing on reorganisation proposals, but it has to be considered along with other relevant factors. (Paragraphs 170 to 184).

14. Some degree of dislocation in the working of the next plan is likely to be caused by any scheme of reorganisation; this dislocation, however, should be considered along with the possible advantages of reorganisation. Steps should also be taken to minimise the unsettling effects of reorganisation. (Paragraphs 185 to 196).

15. The States cannot be so reorganised as to conform to economic regions. Nor can the principle of economic self-sufficiency within an administrative unit be regarded as a clear criterion. Consistently with these principles it would be desirable to avoid as far as possible wide disparities in resources between the various States. (Paragraphs 197 to 210).

16. The units should be large enough to ensure administrative efficiency and the co-ordination of economic development and welfare activities. (Paragraphs 211 to 220).

17. The wishes of the people should be regarded as an important factor bearing on reorganisation but they have to be considered along with other relevant factors. (Paragraphs 221 to 228).

18. The facts of the existing situation are more important than the previous historical associations of different areas. Undue importance cannot be attached, therefore, to historical arguments. (Paragraphs 229 to 231).

19. Geographical contiguity of the units is important from the point of view of administrative convenience. Other geographical factors have to be regarded as secondary. (Paragraphs 232 and 233).

20. No proposals for reorganisation should be determined by a single test. Conclusions have to be reached after taking into consideration the totality of circumstances in each case. (Paragraph 235).

V. Basic pattern of the component units

21. The existing constitutional disparity between the different constituent units of the Indian Union should disappear as a necessary consequence of reorganisation. (Paragraphs 236 to 239).

22. Part B States can be equated with Part A States by omitting Article 371 of the Constitution and by abolishing the institution of the Rajpramukh. (Paragraphs 240 to 245).

23. The existing Part C States which provide no adequate recompense for all the constitutional, administrative and financial problems which they pose should, to the extent practicable, be merged in the adjoining larger States. (Paragraphs 246 to 268).

24. In respect of three of the Part C States, namely, Himachal Pradesh, Kutch and Tripura, the Central Government should retain

supervisory power for a specified period to maintain their present pace of development. (Paragraphs 269 to 275).

25. Such of the existing Part C States as cannot be merged in the adjoining areas for security and other imperative considerations should be administered by the Centre as "territories". (Paragraphs 276 to 284).

26. The component units of the Indian Union should thus consist of two categories:

(a) "States" forming primary federating units of the Indian Union; and

(b) "territories" which are centrally-administered. (Paragraphs 285 to 287).

VI. Proposals for Reorganisation

27. According to the scheme of reorganisation which is dealt with in Chapters II to XIX of Part III of this report, there should be sixteen constituent units, to be called States, and three administered territories. The proposals regarding these units are summarised below.

STATES

28. 1. *Madras.*—This State should include the existing territories subject to the following adjustments, namely,

(i) the five taluks of Agastheeswaram, Thovala, Kalkulam, Vilavancode and Shencotta, now forming part of Travancore-Cochin, should be transferred to the State of Madras, and

(ii) the districts of Malabar and South Kanara and the Kollegal Taluk of the Coimbatore district should be detached from Madras. (Paragraphs 289 to 301).

2. *Kerala.*—The State of Kerala should be formed, which should consist of the following areas:

(a) the State of Travancore-Cochin *minus* the five taluks proposed to be transferred to Madras;

(b) the Malabar district (including Fort Cochin and the Laccadive Islands), the Kasaragod Taluk of the South Kanara district and the Amindive Islands. (Paragraphs 302 to 318).

3. *Karnataka.*—The State of Karnataka should be created consisting of the following areas:—

(a) the present State of Mysore, excluding the Siruguppa taluk, the Bellary taluk, the Hospet taluk and a small portion of the Mallapuram sub-taluk of the Bellary district;

(b) the four Kannada-speaking districts of Bombay, namely, Dharwar, Bijapur, North Kanara and Belgaum, (except the Chandgad taluk of Belgaum district);

(c) the districts of Raichur and Gulbarga from Hyderabad;

(d) the South Kanara district of Madras *minus* the Kasaragod taluk;

(e) the Kollegal taluk of the Coimbatore district of Madras; and

(f) Coorg. (Paragraphs 319 to 358).

4. *Hyderabad.*—Apart from the districts of Raichur and Gulbarga, the Marathwada districts should also be detached from the Hyderabad State. The residuary State which should continue to be known as Hyderabad should consist of the Telugu-speaking districts of the present State of Hyderabad, namely, Mahbubnagar, Nalgonda, Warangal (including Khammam), Karimnagar, Adilabad, Nizamabad, Hyderabad and Medak, along with Bidar district, and the Munagala enclave in the Nalgonda district belonging to the Krishna district of Andhra.

The residuary State of Hyderabad might unite with Andhra after the general elections likely to be held in or about 1961, if by a two-thirds majority the legislature of the Hyderabad State expresses itself in favour of such unification.

The future of the remaining areas of Hyderabad, consisting of the districts known as Marathwada, is dealt with later on under Bombay. (Paragraphs 359 to 393).

5. *Andhra.*—The Andhra State should for the time being continue as it is, subject to certain minor adjustments which are mentioned below.

The taluks of Siruguppa, Bellary and Hospet and a portion of the Mallapuram sub-taluk of the Bellary district should be transferred to Andhra.

The Munagala enclave of the Krishna district, as has already been stated, should be transferred to Hyderabad.

There should be no change in the present position regarding Madras City and its future should be regarded as finally settlsë. (Paragraphs 394 to 401).

6. *Bombay.*—The State of Bombay should be reconstituted so as to include the existing Bombay State *minus* the Abu Road taluk of the Banaskantha district and the Kannada-speaking districts of Dharwar, Bijapur, North Kanara and Belgaum (excluding the Chandgad taluk), *plus* the following areas:

(a) the Marathi-speaking districts of Hyderabad, namely, Osmanabad, Bhir, Aurangabad, Parbhani and Nanded;

(b) Saurashtra; and

(c) Kutch. (Paragraphs 402 to 439).

7. *Vidarbha.*—A new State to be known as Vidarbha should be created, consisting of the following Marathi-speaking districts of Madhya Pradesh, namely, Buldana, Akola, Amravati, Yeotmal, Wardha, Nagpur, Bhandara and Chanda. (Paragraphs 440 to 457).

8. *Madhya Pradesh.*—After the separation of Vidarbha, a new State, which may be known as Madhya Pradesh, should be created consisting of:

(i) the 14 districts of the residuary Madhya Pradesh;

(ii) the whole of Bhopal and the whole of Vindhya Pradesh;

(iii) Madhya Bharat except the Sunel enclave of the Mandsaur district; and

(iv) the Sironj sub-division of the Kotah district of Rajasthan. (Paragraphs 458 to 493).

9. *Rajasthan.*—After the proposed merger of Sironj in the new Madhya Pradesh State, Rajasthan should continue in its present form subject to the addition of territories mentioned below:

(i) Ajmer, and

(ii) the Abu Road taluk of the Banaskantha district of Bombay, the Sunel enclave of the Mandsaur district of Madhya Bharat and the Loharu sub-tehsil of the Hissar district of the Punjab. (Paragraphs 494 to 513).

10. *The Punjab.*—There is no case for dividing the present Punjab State. PEPSU and the Himachal Pradesh should, however, be merged in the Punjab. (Paragraphs 514 to 579).*

The Loharu sub-tehsil of the Hissar district, as already stated, should be transferred to Rajasthan. (Paragraph 506).

Apart from the safeguards referred to in paragraph 24 of this summary, Himachal Pradesh should be represented in the Punjab cabinet by at least one member. (Paragraph 564).

---

* Subject to Chairman's note on Himachal Pradesh.

11. *Uttar Pradesh.*—There is no case for dividing the Uttar Pradesh, and this State should continue in its existing form. (Paragraphs 595 to 614).*

12. *Bihar.*—It does not seem to be either necessary or desirable to create a Jharkhand State in south Bihar; the special needs of this area should, however, be recognised.

Seraikella and Kharsawan should continue to be part of Bihar.

Some adjustments in two eastern districts belonging to Bihar are indicated under West Bengal. (Paragraphs 615 to 630).**

13. *West Bengal.*—A portion of the Purnea district east of the river Mahananda and the Purulia sub-district of the Manbhum district *minus* the Chas thana should be transferred from Bihar to West Bengal. (Paragraphs 631 to 676).**

Subject to the recommendations summarised in the immediately preceding paragraph, no boundary adjustments seem to be called for in order to satisfy claims and counter-claims in respect of the border areas of Bihar, West Bengal, Assam and Orissa.

14. *Assam.*—Assam should continue as it is subject to the changes mentioned below.

The demand for the creation of a hill State in Assam is impracticable and there is also no reason, having regard to the peculiar features and circumstances of Assam, why a separate hill State should be created; special attention should, however, be paid to the development of the hill districts and an enquiry into the working of the autonomous bodies created under the Sixth Schedule to the Constitution should be undertaken.

Tripura should be merged in Assam.

The present arrangements with regard to the North East Frontier Agency should continue. (Paragraphs 677 to 722).

15. *Orissa.*—No changes are called for in the boundaries of Orissa which were fixed in 1936 after prolonged and detailed examination. (Paragraphs 733 to 749).**

16. *Jammu and Kashmir.*—No recommendations are made in regard to Jammu and Kashmir. (Paragraph 751).

TERRITORIES.

29. The units or areas which have not been dealt with so far will be directly administered by the Centre and will be known as territories.

---

* Subject to Shri K. M. Panikkar's note on Uttar Pradesh.

** Chairman has not associated himself with investigating and deciding the territorial ispures to which Bihar is a party.

1. *Delhi.*—Delhi should be constituted into such a centrally-administered territory; the question of creating a municipal Corporation with substantial powers should be considered. (Paragraphs 580 to 594).

2. *Manipur.*—Manipur should be a centrally-administered territory for the time being. The ultimate merger of this State in Assam should be kept in view. (Paragraphs 723 to 732).

3. *Andaman and Nicobar Islands.*—The *status quo* in the Andaman and Nicobar Islands should continue. (Paragraph 753).

30. The arrangements in regard to areas which have been or may be brought under Central administration in future, either before or after becoming *de jure* part of the territory of India, must be flexible, until the position is finally clarified. (Paragraph 753).

VII. Safeguards for linguistic groups

31. Constitutional recognition should be given to the right of linguistic minorities to have instruction in their mother-tongues at the primary school stage subject to a sufficient number of students being available. The Central Government should acquire power to enforce this right on the lines of the provisions contained in Article 347 of the Constitution. (Paragraphs 757 to 776).

32. The Government of India should adopt, in consultation with the State Governments, a clear code to govern the use of different languages at different levels of State administrations and take steps, under Article 347, to ensure that this code is followed. (Paragraphs 778 to 785).

33. The domicile tests in force in certain States operate to the disadvantage of minority groups. The Government of India should, therefore, undertake legislation under Article 16(3) of the Constitution in order to simplify and liberalise the requirements as to residence. (Paragraphs 786 to 788).

34. In examinations regulating entry into the public services of the states, a candidate should have the option to elect as the medium, apart from the main language of the State, the Union language, namely, English or Hindi, or the language of a minority constituting about fifteen to twenty per cent or more of the population of the State. (Paragraphs 789 and 790).

35. As far as possible, Public Service Commissions should be constituted to serve more than one State. (Paragraph 791).

36. Appointments to Public Service Commissions serving even single states should be made by President as in the case of appointments to joint Public Service Commissions. (Paragraph 791).

37. The services of the Governors should be utilised for enforcing the safeguards for linguistic minorities. (Paragraphs 792 to 800).

VIII. Administrative and other matters

38. The reconstitution of the sanctioned state cadres and the integration of services should be accorded very high priority, and must be decided on the basis of certain general principles, due regard being paid to the options of the employees, the need for a mixed element in the services, *inter se* seniority in the State of origin, etc., and also the needs of the new States. (Paragraphs 802 to 810).

39. The body constituted to integrate the service personnel of different States should be one that inspires confidence, and only one appeal against decisions regarding integration should be permitted. (Paragraph 810).

40. After the scheme of reorganisation has been given effect to, it may be necessary for some of the new administrations to review the number and territorial extent of the existing districts as well as Commissioners' charges and the rationalisation of the administrative structure. (Paragraph 813).

41. Decisions on the reorganisation proposals should, if possible, be taken before the next Finance Commission commences its enquiries. (Paragraph 815).

42. It may be necessary to grant ways and means advances to newly-constituted units in order to help them to tide over temporary difficulties. (Paragraph 818).

43. Pending a comprehensive review, grants-in-aid on revenue or capital account as well as long-term loans should be made available to the new units as nearly as possible on the existing basis. The Government of India should refix the existing statutory and development grants and long-term loans with reference to the principles on which such grants or loans have been sanctioned. (Paragraphs 819 to 821).

44. Payments under Article 278 of the Constitution may be continued and apportioned population-wise among new units until such time as the position is reviewed by the Finance Commission. (Paragraph 822).

45. Pending the amendment of Article 264(b) of the Constitution, appropriate portions of the divisible pools pertaining to the Part C States, which are now retained by the Centre, may be distributed among the new units, where necessary, in proportion to their population. (Paragraph 823).

46. Assets and liabilities should be divided on the basis of principles which should as far as practicable be of general application. (Paragraphs 824 to 826).

47. Financial settlements in the case of Part C States need not be elaborate, but may be based on a review of the position as it exists today and the needs of these areas. (Paragraph 827).

48. The question of setting up some special machinery to expedite the final settlements regarding assets and liabilities should be considered. (Paragraphs 828 and 829).

49. It will be necessary to adapt current inter-state agreements regarding water rights, etc., with due regard to the broad basis on which they may have been drawn up, and this question should be taken up as soon as possible after decisions regarding reorganisation have been reached. (Paragraph 830).

50. The creation of special development boards for certain areas which are under-developed should be considered. (Paragraph 839).

51. A permanent body, in which members of the Planning Commission may be included, should be set up in order to examine the grievances, if any, on the score of the alleged neglect of certain areas. (Paragraph 841).

52. The Government of India should consider the question of formulating an industrial location policy for the whole of India, in order to ensure the equitable distribution of development expenditure. (Paragraphs 842 to 844).

53. As a general rule, fifty per cent. of the new entrants in the All-India Services should be from outside the State concerned, this computation being made after deducting the number of posts in any State which are to be filled by promotion. (Paragraph 855).

54. Certain All-India Services, namely, the Indian Service of Engineers, the Indian Forest Service and the Indian Medical and Health Service should be constituted. (Paragraphs 856 and 857).

55. Regular transfers to and from the Centre and the States in respect of personnel belonging to the All-India Services should, as far as possible, be arranged. (Paragraph 858).

56. The curriculum of studies for the new entrants to the All-India and Central Services should include such basic and essential subjects as Indian history, geography, religions, customs and manners. (Paragraph 859).

57. In formulating a policy regarding the recognition of Hindi in competitive examinations for the All-India and other services, the need for encouraging the study of other Indian languages, and particularly of the South Indian languages, should be kept in view. (Paragraph 860).

58. At least one-third of the number of Judges in the High Court of a State should consist of persons who are recruited from outside that State. (Paragraph 861).

59. For some time to come, English should continue to occupy an important place in our universities and institutions of higher learning even after the adoption of Hindi and the regional languages for official and educational purposes. (Paragraphs 862 to 867).

60. The Osmania University should be placed under the Central Government and the medium of instruction in this university should be Hindi. One more central university should be established further South and arrangements should be made for the study of South Indian languages in the north. (Paragraphs 868 and 869).

61. Reorganisation has a legitimate place in this country, but its limitations must be recognised. If the supremacy of the Union not merely in the political but also in the economic thinking of the country is fully realised, the issues arising out of the reorganisation of States should not assume the proportions of major political controversies. (Paragraphs 871 to 879).

APPENDIX A

MINISTRY OF HOME AFFAIRS

RESOLUTION

New Delhi, the 29th December 1953

No. 53/69/53-Public.—The Government of India have been giving careful consideration to the problem of the States which are constituent units of the Indian Union. These States, as they exist today, are largely the result of historical processes and the spread and consolidation of the British Power in India. On the attainment of Independence, India was partitioned and the independent State of Pakistan was created. A process of merger and integration took place in regard to what were then called the "Indian States". This integration of the old Indian States, which was brought about within a very short-period, was an event of historic significance. The integration, however, was naturally based to a large extent on the old pattern which existed before independence.

2. The pattern of States in the Union is thus the result of historical accident and circumstances. Their mere existence for a hundred years or more developed political, administrative and cultural associations within and between them.

3. The greater development of political consciousness among the people and the growing importance of the great regional languages led gradually to demands for the formation of certain States on a linguistic basis. Each such separate problem was however closely inter-related with other problems, and any formation of a new state necessarily affected a number of other States. It thus became increasingly difficult to consider any such problem in isolation.

4. The language and culture of an area have an undoubted importance as they represent a pattern of living which is common in that area. In considering a reorganisation of States, however, there are other important factors which have also to be borne in mind. The first essential consideration is the preservation and strengthening of the unity and security of India. Financial, economic and administrative considerations are almost equally important, not only from the point of view of each State, but for the whole nation. India has embarked upon a great ordered plan for her economic, cultural and moral progress. Changes which interfere with the successful prosecution of such a national plan would be harmful to the national interest.

5. The Government of India have come to the conclusion that the whole question of the reorganisation of the States of the Indian Union should be carefully examined, objectively and dispassionately, so that the welfare of the people of each constituent unit, as well as of the nation as a whole, is promoted. The Government have accordingly decided to appoint a Commission to conduct such an examination.

6. The Commission will consist of Shri Saiyid Fazl Ali, at present Governor of Orissa, Shri Hriday Nath Kunzru, Member of the Council of States, and Shri Kavalam Madhava Panikkar, at present Ambassador of India in Egypt, of whom Shri Saiyid Fazl Ali shall be the Chairman of the Commission.

7. The Commission will investigate the conditions of the problem, the historical background, the existing situation and the bearing of all important and relevant factors thereon. They will be free to consider any proposal relating to such reorganisation. The Government expect that the Commission would, in the first instance, not go into the details, but make recommendations in regard to the broad principles which should govern the solution of this problem and, if they so choose, the broad lines on which particular States should be reorganised, and submit interim reports for the consideration of Government.

8. The Commission will be at liberty to devise their own procedure for their work, for collecting information and for ascertaining public opinion. The Commission will ordinarily hold their sittings in private.

9. The Commission will have a Secretary and such staff and advisers as may be considered necessary.

10. The Commission will make their recommendations to the Government as soon as may be practicable, and not later than the 30th June, 1955.

A. V. PAI,
Secretary.

APPENDIX B

PRESS NOTE

STATES REORGANISATION COMMISSION

The States Reorganisation Commission, after giving due consideration to the procedure that would be most suitable for the expeditious execution of the task entrusted to them, have decided to dispense with a questionnaire. They invite members of the public as well as public associations interested in the problems of the reorganisation of States to put their views and suggestions before the Commission by submitting written memoranda on matters on which they feel they can assist them. The Commission expect that wherever any concrete suggestions are made they will be supported by historical and statistical data and, if any proposal regarding the formation of any new State or States is made, it will, if possible, be accompanied by one or more maps, as the case may be.

It may be recalled that the Government of India Resolution, dated 29th December 1953, in pursuance of which the Commission has been appointed, has referred to certain factors which are to be kept in view in the reorganisation of States in these words:—

> "The language and culture of an area have an undoubted importance as they represent a pattern of living which is common in that area. In considering a reorganisation of States, however, there are other important factors which have also to be borne in mind. The first essential consideration is the preservation and strengthening of the unity and security of India. Financial, economic and administrative considerations are almost equally important, not only from the point of view of each State, but for the whole nation. India has embarked upon a great ordered plan for her economic, cultural and moral progress. Changes which interfere with the successful prosecution of such a national plan would be harmful to the national interest".

The Commission hope that due regard will be paid to these factors in the preparation of memoranda.

The Commission look forward to full and whole-hearted cooperation from the public in discharging their heavy responsibility and hope that they will respond to this invitation which is being extended to them through the Press.

The Commission will appreciate if six copies of each memorandum are forwarded to:—

The Secretary,

States Reorganisation Commission,

New Delhi,

so as to reach him not later than 24th April 1954.

STATES REORGANISATION COMMISSION.

New Delhi, February 23, 1954.